Ultimate Kotlin Multiplatform for App Development

Build High-Performance Android, iOS and Web Apps Using Kotlin Multiplatform, Ktor, Koin, and Modern UI Frameworks

Gowtham Shanmugaraj Ganesan

www.orangeava.com

First Published: December 2025

Published By: Orange Education Pvt Ltd, AVA®

Address: 9, Daryaganj, Delhi, 110002, India

275 New North Road Islington Suite 1314 London,
N1 7AA, United Kingdom

ISBN (PBK): 978-93-49888-30-2
ISBN (E-BOOK): 978-93-49888-90-6

Scan the QR code to explore our entire catalogue

www.orangeava.com

Dedicated To

To My Beloved Wife, **Priya Rameshkumar***, Whose Love, Strength, and Unwavering Encouragement Gave Me the Courage to Step into Writing– A Journey I Might Never Have Started Without Her. Her Belief in Me Turned My Hesitation into Determination, and Her Support Made Every Late Night and Challenge Worthwhile. This Book is as Much Hers as it is Mine.*

To My Dear Daughter, **Yaazhini Gowtham Shanmugaraj***, Who Reminds Me Every Day of Curiosity, Wonder, and the Joy of Learning. Her Smile is the Inspiration behind My Perseverance.*

With Heartfelt Gratitude to My Parents, K.S. Ganesan and T. Nagarathinam, and with the Blessings from my Grandparents, V. Thiyagarajan and V. Saraswathi, Whose Values Continue to Light My Way, and Shape who I am Today.

About the Author

Gowtham Shanmugaraj Ganesan is a versatile full-stack developer with over 14 years of experience building secure, scalable, and high-performance applications across backend and mobile platforms. With a strong foundation in Java and Spring Boot, he has delivered robust server-side systems supported by RESTful APIs, OAuth 2.0-based security, Hibernate/JPA, asynchronous messaging, and performance-optimized architectures.

Complementing his backend expertise, Gowtham is a seasoned Android engineer skilled in Kotlin, Java, Jetpack Compose, and Kotlin Multiplatform (KMP). His work with KMP focuses on creating shared codebases across Android, iOS, Web, and Desktop, enabling teams to ship consistent, modular, and maintainable applications.

Gowtham's commitment to professional excellence is reflected in his Oracle Certified Java Programmer (OCJP) credential and Android Developer Nanodegree. His toolkit spans modern frameworks and libraries including Ktor, Koin, kotlinx. serialization, SQLDelight, JUnit, Mockito, and WireMock. He is equally passionate about testing, CI/CD automation, and DevOps workflows that ensure reliable software delivery.

Beyond engineering, Gowtham is dedicated to teaching, mentoring, and knowledge sharing. His book, *Ultimate Kotlin Multiplatform for App Development*, distills complex concepts into practical guidance, empowering developers to confidently adopt multiplatform strategies. He actively contributes to open-source projects and shares experiments on GitHub (@gowthamraj07), collaborating with the global developer community.

At the heart of his journey is his family where his wife, Priya, encourages him to explore writing, while his daughter, Yaazhini inspires his curiosity with her sense of wonder.

About the Technical Reviewer

Imran Solanki has over 13 years of experience in building robust and scalable software solutions across multiple domains, including telecommunications, health tech, IoT, logistics, and finance. His journey began with low-level systems programming, where he worked on Windows driver development and ported FLAC encoding to wireless speaker systems. Since then, he has transitioned through diverse roles–mobile application developer, back-end engineer, and technical consultant-always with a strong focus on impact, performance, and quality.

Imran has contributed to projects for leading global organizations such as Avaya and Cisco, developed video surveillance and WebRTC applications, and helped modernize platforms for digital pharmacies and investment firms. He has architected and developed backend systems using Java, Kotlin, Ruby on Rails, and .NET Core, and is fluent in cloud infrastructure and DevOps tooling. Kotlin has been a consistent part of his toolkit–from the early days of Android development to building payment gateway systems and exploring Kotlin Multiplatform to share code across web, mobile, and backend platforms.

A strong believer in sharing knowledge, Imran has taught university-level computer science subjects and led hands-on training sessions in Kotlin, Java, Python, Unix OS, and system programming. His dedication to community learning has extended to speaking at events such as Google AI Camp and contributing to prominent open-source Go libraries including urfave/cli and go-fuego.

Currently working as a Senior Consultant, Imran thrives in building technically sound systems and leading focused engineering teams. He enjoys collaborating with cross-functional stakeholders to deliver solutions that balance technical rigor with business goals.

Acknowledgments

This book would not have been possible without the unwavering support of my wife, Priya, whose constant motivation gave me the confidence to turn an idea into reality. I extend my thanks to my daughter, Yaazhini, who unknowingly inspires me with her innocence and endless curiosity–I dedicate each page of this book to her future of learning and discovery.

I owe a special debt of gratitude to **Mr. Imran Solanki**, who served as the technical reviewer. His meticulous feedback, sharp eye for detail, and thoughtful suggestions greatly enhanced the quality and accuracy of this work.

I also extend my heartfelt thanks to **Mr. Sumit Rawat**, project coordinator at Orange Education Pvt. Ltd., whose guidance, encouragement, and coordination throughout the publishing process ensured that this manuscript reached its best form.

I am deeply grateful to all my colleagues, mentors, and peers in the developer community, whose discussions and encouragement shaped my understanding of Kotlin Multiplatform.

I also wish to acknowledge the JetBrains and Kotlin teams for creating and nurturing such an innovative ecosystem, and the growing developer community whose contributions and libraries make Kotlin Multiplatform thrive.

Finally, I am thankful to the entire publishing team at **Orange Education Pvt. Ltd.** for their patience and professionalism in helping me bring this book to life!

Preface

Kotlin Multiplatform is reshaping how developers build applications by enabling shared business logic across Android, iOS, Web, and beyond, while preserving the flexibility of platform-specific user interfaces. This book, ***Ultimate Kotlin Multiplatform for App Development***, has been designed as a practical guide covering Kotlin fundamentals, diving deep into multiplatform architecture, and equipping you with the tools to deliver production-ready apps.

The content is structured to take you from the very basics of Kotlin Programming to advanced Multiplatform Development and Deployment strategies. The following is a roadmap of what each chapter covers.

Chapter 1: Introduction to Kotlin

This chapter introduces Kotlin as a modern, concise, and safe programming language. You will learn its history, evolution, and key features such as null safety and interoperability with Java. The chapter concludes with setting up your development environment, and writing your first Kotlin program.

Chapter 2: Basics of Kotlin Programming

Here, we explore the building blocks of Kotlin. You will learn the variables, data types, control flow, functions, null safety, and collections. With practical examples, this chapter ensures that you can confidently write the simple and effective Kotlin programs.

Chapter 3: Advanced Kotlin Programming

This chapter deepens your knowledge with advanced object-oriented programming, functional programming techniques, co-routines, and concurrency. You will also study Kotlin's advanced type system and error handling, preparing you to write scalable and maintainable codes.

Chapter 4: Understanding Kotlin Multiplatform

We introduce Kotlin Multiplatform concepts such as shared code vs. platform-specific code, the expect/actual mechanism, supported platforms, and project architecture. You will also learn the benefits and challenges of adopting a multiplatform strategy.

Chapter 5: Building a Multiplatform Project

This chapter provides a hands-on walkthrough for creating your first multiplatform project. From configuring IDEs and Gradle to structuring shared and platform-specific code, you will learn the best practices, while building a fully functional sample application.

Chapter 6: Utilizing Multiplatform Libraries and Tools

We explore essential libraries and tools such as **Ktor** for networking, **Koin** for dependency injection, **kotlinx.serialization** for data handling, **SQLDelight** for database management, and **Multiplatform Settings** for preferences. You shall also learn about Jetpack Compose Multiplatform and the Kotlin Multiplatform Mobile (KMM) plugin.

Chapter 7: Android Development with Kotlin Multiplatform

This chapter shows how to integrate the shared codes into Android apps. Using Jetpack Compose, you can build modern UIs, while reusing business logic and ensuring faster development cycles, without compromising on native experience.

Chapter 8: iOS Development with Kotlin Multiplatform

You will set up iOS integration with Xcode, call into shared business logic from Swift, and build SwiftUI interfaces. The chapter also covers Cocoapods integration, frameworks, and testing your multiplatform app on simulators and devices.

Chapter 9: Web Development with Kotlin Multiplatform

Here, we extend multiplatform development to the web using Kotlin/JS and Kotlin/React. You will also learn how to create responsive web apps that reuse shared logic, while building browser-ready UIs.

Chapter 10: Testing and Debugging Multiplatform Code

You will learn unit testing, integration testing, and platform-specific testing. This chapter also covers debugging techniques and tools, ensuring that your shared and native code works reliably across platforms.

Chapter 11: Continuous Integration and Deployment

This chapter introduces automation pipelines for multiplatform apps. You will also configure GitHub Actions and other CI/CD tools to build, test, and deploy Android, iOS, and web apps consistently and efficiently.

Chapter 12: Performance Optimization

We shall discuss profiling, memory management, and optimization techniques to ensure smooth performance across devices. You will also learn to spot bottlenecks, and apply improvements in multiplatform projects.

Chapter 13: Best Practices for Multiplatform Development

This chapter compiles guidelines on project structure, modularization, dependency management, documentation, and security. These best practices help to ensure that your projects remain clean, scalable, and maintainable.

Chapter 14: Case Studies and Future Trends

The final chapter explores real-world multiplatform projects, industry best practices, and upcoming trends. You will also gain insights into how leading teams are adopting Kotlin Multiplatform, and where the ecosystem is headed for.

Thus, by the end of the book, you will have traveled from the fundamentals of Kotlin Programming to Advanced Multiplatform Strategies. More importantly, you will be ready to confidently architect and deliver robust applications across Android, iOS, Web, and beyond- all powered by a single codebase.

Get a Free eBook

We hope you are enjoying your recently purchased book! Your feedback is incredibly valuable to us, and to all other readers looking for great books.

If you found this book helpful or enjoyable, we would truly appreciate it, if you could take a moment to leave a short review with a 5 star rating on Amazon. It helps us grow, and lets other readers discover our books.

As a thank you, we would love to send you a free digital copy of this book, and a **30%** discount code on your next cart value on our official websites:

www.orangeava.com

www.orangeava.in (For Indian Subcontinent)

☑ **Here's how:**

Leave a review for the book on Amazon.

Take a screenshot of your review, and send an email to **info@orangeava.com** (it can be just the confirmation screen).

Once, we receive your screenshot, we will send you the digital file, within 24 hours.

Thank you so much for your support – it means a lot to us!

Downloading the code bundles and colored images

Please follow the links or scan the QR codes to download the ***Code Bundles and Images*** of the book:

https://github.com/ava-orange-education/Ultimate-Kotlin-Multiplatform-for-App-Development-

The code bundles and images of the book are also hosted on ***https://rebrand.ly/0b7763***

In case there's an update to the code, it will be updated on the existing GitHub repository.

Errata

We take immense pride in our work at **Orange Education Pvt Ltd,** and follow best practices to ensure the accuracy of our content to provide an indulging reading experience to our subscribers. Our readers are our mirrors, and we use their inputs to reflect and improve upon human errors, if any, that may have occurred during the publishing processes involved. To let us maintain the quality and help us reach out to any readers who might be having difficulties due to any unforeseen errors, please write to us at :

errata@orangeava.com

Your support, suggestions, and feedback are highly appreciated.

DID YOU KNOW

Did you know that Orange Education Pvt Ltd offers eBook versions of every book published, with PDF and ePub files available? You can upgrade to the eBook version at **www.orangeava.com** and as a print book customer, you are entitled to a discount on the eBook copy. Get in touch with us at: **info@orangeava.com** for more details.

At **www.orangeava.com**, you can also read a collection of free technical articles, sign up for a range of free newsletters, and receive exclusive discounts and offers on Print Books and eBooks.

PIRACY

If you come across any illegal copies of our works in any form on the internet, we would be grateful if you would provide us with the location address or website name. Please contact us at **info@orangeava.com** with a link to the material.

ARE YOU INTERESTED IN AUTHORING WITH US?

If there is a topic that you have expertise in, and you are interested in either writing or contributing to a book, please write to us at **business@orangeava.com**. We are on a journey to help developers and tech professionals to gain insights on the present technological advancements and innovations happening across the globe and build a community that believes Knowledge is best acquired by sharing and learning with others. Please reach out to us to learn what our audience demands and how you can be part of this educational reform. We also welcome ideas from tech experts and help them build learning and development content for their domains.

REVIEWS

Please leave a review. Once you have read and used this book, why not leave a review on the site that you purchased it from? Potential readers can then see and use your unbiased opinion to make purchase decisions. We at Orange Education would love to know what you think about our products, and our authors can learn from your feedback. Thank you!

For more information about Orange Education, please visit **www.orangeava.com**.

Table of Contents

CHAPTER 1
Introduction to Kotlin

Introduction

Welcome to the world of Kotlin, a language that has swiftly risen to prominence in the realm of modern app development. As we embark on this journey, this chapter will serve as your gateway, introducing you to the essentials of Kotlin. Hence, whether you are a seasoned developer or a newcomer to programming, understanding Kotlin's foundation will equip you with the knowledge to leverage its full potential.

In this chapter, we will delve into the history and evolution of Kotlin, uncovering the motivations behind its creation, and its rapid adoption in the developer community. We will firstly explore its key features and advantages, and set up your development environment. By the end of this chapter, you will have written your first Kotlin program, and gained insight into why Kotlin is a game-changer in today's tech landscape. So, let us dive in and discover what makes Kotlin so special, and how it can revolutionize your coding experience.

Structure

In this chapter, we will cover the following topics:

- A Brief Overview
- History and Evolution
- Key Features
- Advantages of Using Kotlin
- IDE Setup
    - Installing Kotlin SDK
    - Configuring Your IDE (IntelliJ IDEA, Android Studio)
- Write "`Hello World`"
- Overview of Kotlin's Role in Modern App Development

A Brief Overview of Kotlin

Kotlin is more than just a programming language; it is a developer's delight. Created by JetBrains, the minds behind IntelliJ IDEA, Kotlin was designed to be a modern, expressive, and versatile language that addresses many of the limitations of Java. With its statically typed nature, Kotlin runs on the Java Virtual Machine (JVM), and can also be compiled into JavaScript or native code, offering unparalleled flexibility.

The language is built on three core principles: Simplicity, safety, and interoperability. Kotlin's concise syntax drastically reduces boilerplate code, making your codebase cleaner and easier to maintain. Its null safety feature helps prevent the dreaded null pointer exceptions, a common source of bugs in Java. Perhaps, one of the most compelling aspects of Kotlin is its seamless interoperability with Java, allowing you to mix Kotlin and Java code within the same project effortlessly.

Since Google's announcement in 2017, recognizing Kotlin as a first-class language for Android development, its popularity has soared. Developers appreciate its modern features and ease of use, which translate into faster development times and more robust applications. But Kotlin is not just for Android; its multiplatform capabilities mean you can write code that runs on iOS, Web, and beyond, all from a single codebase.

Thus, as you navigate through this chapter, you will gain a solid understanding of Kotlin's core features, and see firsthand why it has become a favorite among developers. We will cover everything from setting up your development environment to writing your first Kotlin program. By the end, you will not only understand what Kotlin is, and why it is so powerful, but you will also be ready to start coding in Kotlin yourself. So, let us get started on this exciting journey!

History and Evolution of Kotlin

The story of Kotlin begins in 2010, within the halls of JetBrains, a software development company renowned for its powerful IDEs like IntelliJ IDEA. JetBrains' developers, faced with the limitations and verbosity of Java, set out to create a new language that could run on the Java Virtual Machine (JVM), but with enhanced capabilities and more concise syntax. Thus, Kotlin was born.

Kotlin was named after Kotlin Island, near St. Petersburg, Russia, where JetBrains' headquarters are located. The language was publicly unveiled in 2011, and from the outset, it promised to address many of the pain points experienced by Java developers. JetBrains aimed to create a language that was modern, expressive, and most importantly, one that could seamlessly interoperate with Java.

The first official stable release of Kotlin, version 1.0, arrived in February 2016. This milestone marked Kotlin's entry into the mainstream developer community. Developers were quick to appreciate Kotlin's clear syntax, null safety features, and interoperability with the existing Java code. Therefore, Kotlin was designed to be intuitive for developers familiar with Java, making the transition smooth and appealing.

The real turning point for Kotlin came in 2017 when Google announced at its annual Google I/O conference that Kotlin was now an officially supported language for Android development. This endorsement was a game-changer. Suddenly, Kotlin was thrust into the spotlight, with a massive influx of developers, eager to explore this new tool. The Android community, which had long been reliant on Java, embraced Kotlin for its brevity, expressiveness, and modern features.

Since then, Kotlin has continued to evolve at a rapid pace. JetBrains has consistently released updates and new features such as co-routines for asynchronous programming and Kotlin Multiplatform for cross-platform development. In 2018, Kotlin became the fastest-growing language on GitHub, reflecting its widespread adoption and vibrant community.

The evolution of Kotlin did not stop with mobile development. JetBrains' vision for Kotlin extends to various domains including server-side development with frameworks such as Ktor, web development with Kotlin/JS, and even data science with KotlinDL. The language's versatility and adaptability have made it a valuable asset across multiple facets of software development.

Thus, Kotlin's journey from a niche language to a mainstream powerhouse has been remarkable. Its continuous improvement, robust feature set, and strong community support underscore its potential to shape the future of programming. As we proceed through this book, you will see how Kotlin's rich history and thoughtful evolution make it a compelling choice for modern app development. Hence, whether you are building for Android, the web, or any other platform, Kotlin offers the tools and features to create high-quality, maintainable code.

Key Features of Kotlin

Kotlin is packed with salient features that make it a joy to work with, providing both the power and flexibility needed to tackle modern development challenges. Here is an in-depth look at some of the key features that set Kotlin apart:

Concise Syntax

One of the first things you will notice about Kotlin is its concise syntax. Kotlin drastically reduces boilerplate code, making your codebase cleaner and more readable. For example, simple data classes that require multiple lines in Java can be written in just a few lines in Kotlin. This conciseness extends to various aspects of the language, including variable declarations, function definitions, and control structures.

Example:

```
// Equivalent code in Java

public class User {
    private String name;
    private int age;
    public User(String name, int age) {
        this.name = name;
        this.age = age;
    }
    // Getters and setters
}

// A simple class in Kotlin
data class User(val name: String, val age: Int)
```

Null Safety

Kotlin's type system is designed to eliminate the danger of null references, a common source of bugs in many languages, including Java. By default, variables cannot hold a null value, which helps prevent null pointer exceptions. If a variable can hold null, it must be explicitly declared as nullable using the '**?**' symbol.

Example:

```
var nonNullable: String = "Hello"
// nonNullable = null // Compilation error

var nullable: String? = "Hello"
nullable = null // Allowed
```

To safely handle nullable variables, Kotlin provides several operators such as the safe call operator `?.`, the Elvis operator `?:`, and the non-null assertion operator `!!`. (Caution: Beginners often overuse this !! operator.)

Example:

```
val name: String? = null

// Safe call operator
val length: Int? = name?.length // Returns null if name is null

// Elvis operator
val lengthOrZero: Int = name?.length ?: 0 // Returns 0 if name is
null
```

```
// Non-null assertion operator
val forcedLength: Int = name!!.length // Throws NullPointer
Exception if name is null
```

Interoperability with Java

Kotlin was designed to work alongside the existing Java codebases. This makes it easy to incrementally adopt Kotlin in legacy applications or large enterprise projects that rely heavily on Java.

Example:

```
// Kotlin calling Java
val list = ArrayList<String>()
list.add("Hello")
// Java calling Kotlin
KotlinClass kotlinClass = new KotlinClass();
kotlinClass.kotlinFunction();
```

Coroutines

Asynchronous programming can be complex and error-prone, but Kotlin simplifies it with coroutines. Coroutines allow you to write asynchronous code in a sequential style, making it easier to read and maintain. They are lightweight, and can be used for tasks such as network calls, I/O operations, and more, without blocking the main thread.

Example:

```
import kotlinx.coroutines.*
fun main() = runBlocking {
    launch {
        delay(1000L)
        println("World!")
    }
    println("Hello,")
}
```

Extension Functions

Kotlin allows you to extend the functionality of the existing classes without modifying their source code. Extension functions let you add new methods to classes, which can make your code more modular and reusable.

Example:

```
fun String.isPalindrome(): Boolean {
    return this == this.reversed()
```

```
}
fun main() {
    println("refer".isPalindrome()) // Output: true
}
```

These features, among others, make Kotlin a powerful and flexible language for modern development. Its concise syntax reduces the time and effort required to write and maintain code, while its null safety and interoperability with Java provide robust tools to prevent bugs and integrate seamlessly with the existing projects. Co-routines and extension functions further enhance Kotlin's capabilities, making it easier to write efficient, clean, and reusable code.

As you continue to explore Kotlin through this book, you will see how these features can be applied to create high-quality, maintainable applications across various platforms. In fact, Kotlin's modern design and powerful features are why it has become a favorite among developers and a cornerstone of contemporary app development.

Advantages of Using Kotlin

The following are the advantages of using Kotlin:

Increased Productivity

Kotlin is designed to enhance developer productivity through several key features that streamline coding processes, and reduce the efforts required to write and maintain applications. Here is how Kotlin boosts productivity:

Concise Syntax

Kotlin's syntax is more expressive and concise compared to many other languages, including Java. This means developers can achieve the same functionality with fewer lines of code, reducing the time spent writing boilerplate code.

Example:

```
// Kotlin
val items = listOf("laptop", "desktop", "mobile")
for (item in items) {
    println(item)
}

// Java
List<String> items = Arrays.asList("laptop", "desktop", "mobile");
for (String item : items) {
    System.out.println(item);
}
```

Type Inference

Kotlin's type inference reduces the need for explicit type declarations, making code shorter and easier to read without sacrificing type safety.

Example:

```
val number = 29 // Type is inferred as Int
```

Smart Casts

Kotlin automatically casts types when it is safe to do so, reducing the need for explicit casting and making the code cleaner.

Example:

```
fun demo(x: Any) {
    if (x is String) {
        println(x.length) // Smart cast to String
    }
}
```

Reduced Boilerplate Code

Kotlin's features, such as data classes, lambda expressions, and property delegation, help reduce boilerplate code, making development faster and more enjoyable.

Example:

```
// Kotlin data class
data class User(val name: String, val age: Int)
```

By leveraging these features, developers can write code more efficiently, leading to shorter development cycles and quicker iterations. The overall effect is a significant boost in productivity, allowing developers to focus on solving complex problems, rather than getting bogged down by repetitive tasks.

Multiplatform Capabilities

One of Kotlin's standout features is its support for multiplatform development. Kotlin Multiplatform allows developers to write common codes that can be shared across various platforms, including Android, iOS, Web, and backend applications. This capability offers several advantages:

Code Reusability

With Kotlin Multiplatform, you can write common business logic once, and share it across multiple platforms. This reduces code duplication, and ensures consistency across different versions of your applications.

Example:

```
// Shared code
expect fun platformName(): String

fun greet() {
    println("Hello from ${platformName()}")
}
```

Platform-Specific Implementations

While the shared code handles common functionality, Kotlin Multiplatform allows for platform-specific implementations using the expected/actual mechanism. This ensures that platform-specific features and APIs can be utilized, without compromising the shared codebase.

Example:

```
// Android implementation
actual fun platformName(): String {
    return "Android"
}

// iOS implementation
actual fun platformName(): String {
    return "iOS"
}
```

Seamless Integration

Kotlin Multiplatform integrates seamlessly with the existing project structures and tools. Hence, whether you are adding Kotlin Multiplatform to a new project or an existing one, the integration process is smooth and straightforward, minimizing disruptions to your development workflow.

Example:

```
// Gradle setup for multiplatform projects
plugins {
    kotlin("multiplatform") version "1.5.21"
}

kotlin {
    android()
    ios()
```

```
        js {
            browser {
                // configure settings
            }
        }
    }
```

Efficient Maintenance

Maintaining a single codebase for shared logic reduces the efforts required for updates and bug fixes. Changes made to the shared code automatically propagate to all platforms, ensuring consistency and reducing the risk of platform-specific bugs.

Consistent User Experience

By sharing code across platforms, you can ensure a consistent user experience in terms of functionality and behavior. This consistency is crucial for applications that need to provide the same features and performance across different devices and operating systems.

Rapid Prototyping and Development

Kotlin Multiplatform accelerates the development process by allowing developers to quickly prototype and test features across multiple platforms. This rapid iteration cycle is especially valuable for startups and agile teams that need to bring products to market quickly.

Community and Ecosystem

Kotlin Multiplatform is supported by a vibrant community and a growing ecosystem of libraries as well as tools. JetBrains continuously updates and improves Kotlin Multiplatform, and the community contributes libraries and frameworks that simplify cross-platform development.

Example Libraries:

- **Ktor:** A framework for building asynchronous servers and clients.
- **Koin:** A lightweight dependency injection framework.
- **SQLDelight:** A type-safe database library for Kotlin Multiplatform.

By leveraging Kotlin's multiplatform capabilities, developers can significantly streamline their development processes, reduce code redundancy, and deliver consistent, high-quality applications across various platforms. This approach not only saves time and resources but also ensures a seamless user experience, making Kotlin an ideal choice for modern, cross-platform development.

Through these enhanced productivity features and robust multiplatform capabilities, Kotlin empowers developers to build efficient, scalable, and maintainable applications that stand the test of time and technological advancements.

Setting Up the Development Environment

Before diving into Kotlin programming, it is essential to set up your development environment. This section will guide you through the steps to install Kotlin, and configure your Integrated Development Environment (IDE), ensuring that you have everything you need to start coding.

Installing Kotlin

There are several ways to install Kotlin, depending on your preferred setup and platform.

1. **Using the Kotlin Compiler**:
   a. Download the latest version of the Kotlin compiler from the official Kotlin website (https://kotlinlang.org/).
   b. Unzip the downloaded file, and add the bin directory to your system's PATH.
   c. Verify the installation by opening a terminal and running:
   ```
   kotlinc -version
   ```
2. **Using SDKMAN!: SDKMAN!** is a convenient tool for managing multiple versions of software development kits.
   a. Install SDKMAN! by following the instructions on sdkman.io(https://sdkman.io/).
   b. Use SDKMAN! to install Kotlin:
   ```
   sdk install kotlin
   ```
3. **Using Homebrew (macOS)**: Homebrew is a popular package manager for macOS.
   a. Install Homebrew by following the instructions on brew.sh(https://brew.sh/).
   b. Use Homebrew to install Kotlin:
   ```
   brew install kotlin
   ```

Configuring Your IDE (IntelliJ IDEA, Android Studio)

IntelliJ IDEA and Android Studio are the recommended IDEs for Kotlin development, offering robust support and a wide range of features to enhance productivity.

IntelliJ IDEA

IntelliJ IDEA, developed by JetBrains, is a powerful IDE that provides excellent support for Kotlin.

Installing IntelliJ IDEA:

a. Download IntelliJ IDEA from the JetBrains website.

b. Install the downloaded package by following the on-screen instructions.

Setting Up Kotlin in IntelliJ IDEA:

a. Open IntelliJ IDEA and create a new project.

b. Select "`Kotlin`" as the project type.

c. Choose the project SDK (JDK), and configure the project settings.

d. IntelliJ IDEA will automatically set up the project with the necessary Kotlin dependencies.

Example:

```
# Create a new Kotlin file in your project
fun main() {
    println("Hello, Kotlin!")
}
```

Android Studio

Android Studio, based on IntelliJ IDEA, is the official IDE for Android development, and provides excellent Kotlin support.

Installing Android Studio:

a. Download Android Studio from the Android Developers website.

b. Install the downloaded package by following the on-screen instructions.

Setting Up Kotlin in Android Studio:

a. Open Android Studio, and create a new project.

b. Select "`Kotlin`" as the language for the new project.

c. Configure the project settings, such as the project name, package name, and save location.

d. Android Studio will automatically set up the project with the necessary Kotlin dependencies.

Example:

```
# Create a new Kotlin file in your project
fun main() {
    println("Hello, Kotlin!")
}
```

Verifying the Setup: To verify that your environment is correctly set up, create a new Kotlin file and write a simple program.

Example:

```
fun main() {
    println("Hello, Kotlin!")
}
```

Run the program to ensure everything is working correctly. If you see "`Hello, Kotlin!`" printed in the console, your development environment is ready.

Summary

Setting up the development environment for Kotlin is straightforward, whether you use IntelliJ IDEA, Android Studio, or the Kotlin compiler directly. With these tools in place, you are now ready to start writing Kotlin code. The next sections will guide you through writing your first Kotlin program, and exploring Kotlin's role in modern app development.

Writing Your First Kotlin Program

Now that your development environment is set up, it is time to write your first Kotlin program. This section will guide you through creating a simple "`Hello, Kotlin!`" program, which will familiarize you with the basics of Kotlin syntax, and the process of running Kotlin code in your IDE.

Creating a New Kotlin File

1. In IntelliJ IDEA:
    a. Open IntelliJ IDEA, and create a new project (if you have not already).
    b. Right-click on the `src` folder in the Project view and select `New` > `Kotlin File/Class`.
    c. Name the file `Main`, and select `File` as the type.
    d. IntelliJ IDEA will create a new Kotlin file, `Main.kt`, in the `src` folder.

2. In Android Studio:
   a. Open Android Studio and create a new project (if you have not already).
   b. Right-click on the **app/src/main/java** directory in the **Project** view and select **New** > **Kotlin File/Class**.
   c. Name the file Main and select File as the type.
   d. Android Studio will create a new Kotlin file, **Main.kt**, in the specified directory.

Writing the "Hello, Kotlin!" Program

In the newly created **Main.kt** file, write the following code:

```
fun main() {
    println("Hello, Kotlin!")
}
```

This program defines a main function, which is the entry point of the application. The **println** function prints the string "**Hello, Kotlin!**" to the console.

Running the Program

1. **In IntelliJ IDEA**:
   a. To run the program, click the green run icon next to the main function, or right-click the **Main.kt** file and select **Run 'MainKt'**.
   b. IntelliJ IDEA will compile and run the program, displaying the output in the Run window.
2. **In Android Studio**:
   a. To run the program, click the green run icon next to the main function, or right-click the **Main.kt** file and select **Run 'MainKt'**.
   b. Android Studio will compile and run the program, displaying the output in the Run window.

Output:

The console should display:

```
Hello, Kotlin!
```

Detailed Explanation of First Program

Let us break down the "**Hello, Kotlin!**" program to understand its components and syntax in a more detailed manner.

1. **`fun main() { ... }`**: The main function is the entry point of a Kotlin application. It is defined using the fun keyword, followed by the function name main.
2. **`println("Hello, Kotlin!")`**: The **`println`** function is used to print text to the console. It takes a string argument and prints it, followed by a newline character.

Explanation with Example

```
fun main() {
    // This is a comment
    println("Hello, Kotlin!") // Prints "Hello, Kotlin!" to the
console
}
```

3. Comments in Kotlin are marked with **`//`** for single-line comments, and **`/* ... */`** for multi-line comments.
4. The **`println`** function can be replaced with print if you do not want to add a new line after the output.

Input and Output in Kotlin

- For more interactive programs, you can use the **`readLine`** function to read input from the console.

```
fun main() {
    println("Enter your name:")
    val name = readLine()
    println("Hello, $name!")
}
```

- This program prompts the user to enter their name, reads the input using readLine, and prints a personalized greeting.

Common Errors and Troubleshooting

- **Syntax Errors:** Ensure that you follow Kotlin's syntax rules, such as proper use of curly braces **`{}`** for function bodies.
- **Compilation Issues:** If the program does not compile, check for missing dependencies or incorrect project configuration.
- **Runtime Errors:** Ensure that inputs are valid, and that the program handles possible exceptions.

By understanding the components and syntax of this simple program, you are better equipped to write more complex Kotlin applications. This foundational knowledge will be built upon in subsequent chapters, where we will explore more advanced Kotlin features and programming paradigms.

Overview of Kotlin's Role in Modern App Development:

Kotlin has quickly become a favorite among developers for various types of applications, especially in the mobile and server-side domains. This section explores Kotlin's impact, and its widespread adoption in the development community.

Popularity and Adoption

- **Google's Endorsement:** In 2017, Google announced official support for Kotlin as a first-class language for Android development. This endorsement significantly boosted Kotlin's adoption, with many new and existing Android projects being written in Kotlin.
- **Industry Adoption:** Major companies, including Pinterest, Uber, and Trello, have adopted Kotlin for their Android apps, citing benefits like improved developer productivity and code quality.

Key Industries Using Kotlin

- **Mobile Development:** Kotlin is now the preferred language for Android development, thanks to its modern features, enhanced safety, and concise syntax.
- **Server-Side Development:** Kotlin is gaining traction in server-side development with frameworks like Ktor, which provide a modern and efficient way to build server applications.
- **Web Development:** Kotlin/JS allows developers to write the Kotlin code that compiles to JavaScript, enabling the use of Kotlin in web development projects.

Community Support and Resources

- **Vibrant Community:** Kotlin has a robust and active community of developers who contribute to its growth through open-source projects, libraries, and frameworks.
- **Educational Resources:** Numerous tutorials, courses, and documentation are available to help developers learn Kotlin, and stay updated with the latest features and best practices.
- **Conferences and Meetups:** Events like KotlinConf and local Kotlin meetups provide opportunities for developers to learn from experts, network with peers, and share their experiences.

By understanding Kotlin's role in modern app development, you can appreciate its advantages, and see why it has become a go-to language for many developers. This knowledge will serve as a strong foundation as you explore Kotlin's capabilities in more depth throughout this book.

Multiplatform Development

One of Kotlin's most revolutionary aspects is its support for multiplatform development. Kotlin Multiplatform allows you to write common codes that can be shared across multiple platforms, including Android, iOS, web, and desktop applications.

- **Platform-Specific Implementations**: While shared code handles common functionality, Kotlin allows for platform-specific implementations using the expect/actual mechanism.

  Example:

```
// Android implementation
actual fun platformName(): String {
    return "Android"
}

// iOS implementation
actual fun platformName(): String {
    return "iOS"
}
```

- **Code Reusability**: With Kotlin Multiplatform, you can write your business logic once, and share it across different platforms. This reduces duplication, ensures consistency, and simplifies maintenance.

  Example:

```
// Shared code
expect fun platformName(): String
fun greet() {
    println("Hello from ${platformName()}")
}
```

- **Seamless Integration**: Kotlin Multiplatform integrates smoothly with the existing project structures and tools, minimizing disruptions to your workflow. This makes it easier to add multiplatform capabilities to both new and the existing projects.
- **Efficient Maintenance:** Maintaining a single codebase for shared logic reduces the efforts required for updates and bug fixes. Changes made to the shared code propagate to all platforms, ensuring consistency, and reducing platform-specific bugs.

- **Community and Ecosystem**: Kotlin Multiplatform is supported by a vibrant community, and a growing ecosystem of libraries as well as tools, such as Ktor for server-side development, Koin for dependency injection, and SQLDelight for type-safe database access.

Exam Libraries

- **Ktor:** A framework for building asynchronous servers and clients.
- **Koin:** A lightweight dependency injection framework.
- **SQLDelight:** A type-safe database library for Kotlin Multiplatform.

By leveraging Kotlin's multiplatform capabilities, you can streamline your development processes, reduce code redundancy, and deliver consistent, high-quality applications across various platforms. This approach not only saves time and resources but also ensures a seamless user experience, making Kotlin an ideal choice for modern, cross-platform development.

Through these enhanced productivity features and robust multiplatform capabilities, Kotlin empowers developers to build efficient, scalable, and maintainable applications that stand the test of time and technological advancements.

Conclusion

As we conclude Chapter 1, you have taken your first significant steps into the world of Kotlin. From understanding its history and rapid rise in popularity to exploring the key features that make it a modern, powerful language, you now have a solid foundation on which to build. We have discussed how Kotlin's concise syntax, robust safety features, and seamless interoperability with Java have made it a favorite among developers, particularly in the Android ecosystem. You have also seen how Kotlin's support for multiplatform development can streamline your workflow, and increase productivity, allowing you to write code that runs across various platforms with ease.

With your development environment now set up, and your first Kotlin program successfully running, you are ready to dive deeper into the language. The knowledge you have gained in this chapter serves as a launching pad for the more detailed exploration ahead.

As we move into the next chapter, "*Basics of Kotlin Programming*," we will begin to unpack the core elements of Kotlin's syntax and structure. We shall also explore the fundamental building blocks of the language such as variables, data types, and control flow structures, which will be essential as you start to build more complex applications. This next chapter will equip you with the tools and understanding you need to write effective Kotlin code, and set the stage for tackling more advanced programming concepts later on.

Thus, the journey you have embarked on is just the beginning, and with each chapter, you will gain deeper insights as well as practical skills that will make you a proficient Kotlin developer. So, let us move forward into *Chapter 2, Basics of Kotlin Programming*, where we will start mastering the basics of Kotlin programming, laying the groundwork for everything that follows in your Kotlin development journey.

Chapter 2
Basics of Kotlin Programming

Introduction

Welcome to *Chapter 2*, where we begin our deep dive into the fundamental building blocks of Kotlin programming. Now that you have been introduced to Kotlin's history, key features, and the advantages it offers, it is time to roll up your sleeves, and start coding. This chapter is all about getting hands-on with Kotlin, starting from the basics, and gradually building up your knowledge.

In this chapter, we will explore the core elements that form the foundation of any Kotlin program. You will also learn about variables, data types, and how to work with them effectively. We shall cover all the essential concepts such as control flow statements, functions, and null safety, which are crucial for writing robust and efficient Kotlin code. Thus, whether you are new to programming or transitioning from another language, this chapter will equip you with the knowledge and skills you need to write for your first meaningful Kotlin applications.

By the end of this chapter, you will have a solid understanding of Kotlin's syntax and programming paradigms, enabling you to write clean, concise, and effective codes. These basics are not just theoretical–every concept will be illustrated with practical examples and exercises that you can follow. along with. Hence, mastering these basics is essential, as they form the bedrock upon which all your future Kotlin development will be built.

So, let us get started on this exciting journey into the core of Kotlin programming. Whether you are coding for mobile, web, or backend systems, these fundamentals will serve as your toolkit for creating powerful and flexible applications in Kotlin.

Structure

In this chapter, we will cover the following topics:

- Basic Syntax and Structure of Kotlin
- Variable Declaration and Initialization
- Understanding Data Types and Type Inference
- Working with Nullable Types and Null Safety
- Control Flow Statements in Kotlin
- Functions and Return Types in Kotlin
- Exploring Kotlin's String Interpolation
- Utilizing Ranges and Collections in Kotlin
- Handling Exceptions and Errors in Kotlin
- Writing and Running Simple Kotlin Programs

Basic Syntax and Structure of Kotlin

Kotlin is designed to be both expressive and concise, with a syntax that is easy to read and write. This section introduces you to the fundamental aspects of Kotlin's syntax and structure, providing a foundation that will allow you to write clear and efficient codes.

- **Functions (`fun` keyword):** Functions in Kotlin are defined using the `fun` keyword. They encapsulate reusable logic.

  Example: A `greet` function takes a name, and returns a greeting message.

  ```
  fun greet(name: String): String {
      return "Hello, $name!"
  }
  ```
- **Variables and Data Types:** Kotlin has `val` for immutable and `var` for mutable variables. The type system is strong, and supports type inference.
- **Control Flow:**
  - `if-else`: Basic conditional checks.
  - `when`: A powerful switch-like statement for decision-making.
- **Loops:**
  - `for`: Iterates over ranges or collections.
  - `while` **and** `do-while`: Loop based on conditions.

- **Null Safety:** Kotlin aims to eliminate null pointer exceptions with non-nullable types by default. Nullable types are explicitly declared, and tools like the safe call (`?.`) and Elvis operator (`?:`) help manage nullability.
- **String Interpolation:** Embed variables and expressions directly into strings using **$** and **${}** syntax.
- **Collections:** Kotlin offers immutable and mutable collections like lists, sets, and maps, with easy iteration and functional operations such as map, filter, and for each.

Variable Declaration and Initialization

In any programming language, variables are the fundamental units that allow developers to store, manipulate, and retrieve data. In Kotlin, variable declaration and initialization are designed to be both intuitive and flexible, enabling you to write clean, concise, and expressive codes. Understanding how to declare and initialize variables is a crucial skill for any Kotlin developer, as it lays the groundwork for effectively managing data throughout your programs.

Immutable (`val`) vs Mutable (`var`) Variables

One of the first decisions, you will make when declaring a variable in Kotlin is whether it should be immutable or mutable. Kotlin offers two keywords for variable declaration:

- **`val` (Value):** Use `val` when you want to declare an immutable variable, meaning once it is assigned a value, that value cannot be changed. This concept is akin to a constant in other programming languages. Using val promotes safety and predictability in your code because you can trust that the value of a val will remain constant throughout its scope.
- **`var` (Variable):** On the other hand, var is used for mutable variables, where the value can be changed as needed. This flexibility allows you to update the variable's value at any point in your program, which is useful in scenarios where the data might change over time, such as user input, counters, or loop iterators.
- **Why it matters:** Choosing between val and var influences how predictable and maintainable your code is. Favoring val by default makes your code safer, while var should be used intentionally when a change is truly required.

  Example:

```
val immutableName = "Kotlin" // Immutable variable
var mutableAge = 25 // Mutable variable
```

```
// Trying to reassign immutableName will result in a compilation
error:
// immutableName = "Java" // Error: Val cannot be reassigned

// Reassigning mutableAge is allowed:
mutableAge = 26
```

Type Declarations and Type Inference

Kotlin is a statically typed language, which means that every variable has a type that is known at compile-time. However, Kotlin also has a powerful feature called type inference, which allows the compiler to automatically deduce the type of a variable based on the value assigned to it. This reduces the need for explicit type declarations, and makes the code more concise without losing clarity.

Explicit Type Declaration

In some cases, you may want to explicitly declare the type of a variable to enhance readability or to avoid ambiguity. This is particularly useful when the type cannot be immediately inferred from the initial value or when working with more complex data types.

Example:

```
val language: String = "Kotlin" // Explicit type declaration
var version: Double = 1.5 // Explicit type declaration
```

Type Inference

In many situations, you can omit the type declaration, and Kotlin will automatically infer the type based on the value assigned to the variable. This feature not only simplifies the code, but also helps prevent errors by ensuring that the inferred type matches the assigned value.

Example:

```
val greeting = "Hello, Kotlin!" // Type inferred as String
var year = 2023 // Type inferred as Int
```

In the above examples, the compiler infers that greeting is a String, and year is an Int based on the values assigned to them. This type inference mechanism works for both val and var variables.

Late Initialization with `lateinit`

There are situations where you might not be able to initialize a variable immediately, especially when dealing with class properties that depend on external data or resources. Kotlin provides the **lateinit** modifier to handle such cases. The **lateinit** keyword is used with var to indicate that the variable will be initialized later. This modifier can only be applied to non-nullable types, and cannot be used with primitive data types.

Example:

```
class User {
    lateinit var username: String

    fun initializeUser() {
        username = "JohnDoe"
    }

    fun printUsername() {
        if (this::username.isInitialized) {
            println("Username: $username")
        } else {
            println("Username is not initialized")
        }
    }
}

fun main() {
    val user = User()
    user.initializeUser()
    user.printUsername() // Output: Username: JohnDoe
}
```

In this example, the username is declared with **lateinit**, meaning it will be initialized later in the **initializeUser** function. Before accessing it, the code checks if the variable has been initialized using the **this::username.isInitialized** syntax. This approach allows you to delay initialization without resorting to nullable types, thereby maintaining type safety.

Constant Values with const

For values that are constant and known at compile-time, Kotlin offers the **const** modifier. Constants declared with const are evaluated during compilation, making them efficient, and ensuring that they remain unchanged throughout the program's execution. const can only be applied to **val** variables of primitive types or String.

Example:

```
const val PI = 3.14159
const val MAX_USERS = 100
```

```
fun main() {
    println("The value of PI is $PI")
    println("Maximum allowed users: $MAX_USERS")
}
```

Constants like **PI** and **MAX_USERS** are defined at the top level of the file or inside an object (a singleton class), and they can be accessed from anywhere in the program. Using const helps you avoid magic numbers in your code, making it more readable and maintainable.

Nullable Variables

Kotlin is designed with null safety in mind, which is a significant improvement over other languages such as Java where null pointer exceptions are a common issue. By default, variables in Kotlin cannot hold a null value unless explicitly declared as nullable using **?** symbol. This strict handling of nullability reduces the likelihood of runtime errors, and makes your code more robust.

Example:

```
var nullableString: String? = "Kotlin"
nullableString = null // This is allowed

var nonNullableString: String = "Kotlin"
// nonNullableString = null // Error: Null cannot be a value of a
non-null type String
```

To work with nullable variables, Kotlin provides several tools:

- **Safe Call Operator (?.)**: Safely accesses a property or calls a method on an object only, if it is not null.
- **Elvis Operator (?:)**: Provides a default value if the expression to the left of the operator is null.
- **Non-null Assertion (!!)**: Asserts that a nullable variable is not null, throwing a **NullPointerException**, if it is null.

Example:

```
fun getLength(text: String?): Int {
    return text?.length ?: 0 // Returns 0 if text is null
}

fun main() {
    val length = getLength(null)
    println("Length: $length") // Output: Length: 0
}
```

In this example, the safe call operator (**?.**) is used to access the length property of text, and the Elvis operator (`?:`) provides a default value of 0, if text is null. This approach ensures that the code is safe from null pointer exceptions, while providing a clear and concise way to handle nullable types.

Variable Scope and Shadowing

The scope of a variable refers to the region of the code where the variable is accessible. Understanding variable scope is necessary for writing clear and bug-free code. In Kotlin, variables can be declared at different levels:

- **Local Scope:** Variables declared within a function or block are only accessible within that function or block.
- **Global Scope:** Variables declared outside of any function or class can be accessed from anywhere within the file.
- **Class/Member Scope:** Variables declared within a class are accessible within the class and its members.

Example:

```
val globalX = 10 // Global scope

fun printX() {
   val localX = 20 // Local scope
   println("Local X: $localX")
}

fun main() {
   printX()
   println("Global X: $globalX")
}
```

In this example, globalX is accessible from anywhere in the file, while localX is only accessible within the printX function.

Variable Shadowing

Kotlin allows a variable declared in a narrower scope to shadow a variable with the same name in an outer scope. While this can be useful, it is essential to use shadowing judiciously to avoid confusion.

Example:

```
val x = 5 // Global scope

fun printX() {
   val x = 10 // Shadows the global variable
   println("X inside function: $x")
```

```
}

fun main() {
    printX()
    println("X outside function: $x")
}
```

Here, the local variable x inside **printX** shadows the global **x**, making the global **x** inaccessible within the function. This feature should be used with care to maintain code clarity.

Understanding Data Types and Type Inference

Kotlin, as a statically-typed language, ensures that the type of every variable, expression, and function is known at compile-time. This type safety provides a layer of security and reliability in your code, reducing the chances of runtime errors. However, Kotlin's sophisticated type inference system also adds a level of flexibility and conciseness, allowing developers to write less verbose codes without compromising clarity or safety. In this section, we will delve into Kotlin's data types, how they work, and how the compiler infers types, making your coding experience more efficient.

Primitive Data Types

Kotlin has a comprehensive set of primitive data types that cover the basics needed for most of the programming tasks. These include:

- Integers: **Byte**, **Short**, **Int**, **Long**
- Floating-Point Numbers: **Float**, **Double**
- Characters: **Char**
- Booleans: **Boolean**

Each of these types has its specific size and range, allowing you to choose the most appropriate type for your data. Unlike in Java, where primitive types are not objects, Kotlin treats all of its types, including primitives, as objects. This uniformity allows you to use methods and properties directly on numbers, characters, and booleans, providing more functionality and ease of use.

Example:

```
val byteValue: Byte = 127 // 8-bit signed integer
val shortValue: Short = 32767 // 16-bit signed integer
val intValue: Int = 2147483647 // 32-bit signed integer
```

```
val longValue: Long = 9223372036854775807L // 64-bit signed integer

val floatValue: Float = 3.14F // 32-bit floating point
val doubleValue: Double = 3.141592653589793 // 64-bit floating
point

val charValue: Char = 'A' // Character
val booleanValue: Boolean = true // Boolean
```

Complex Data Types

In addition to primitive types, Kotlin provides several complex data types that are necessary for more advanced programming tasks. These include:

- **Strings:** Used to represent sequences of characters.
- **Arrays:** Collections of elements of a specific type.
- **Lists, Sets, and Maps:** Standard collection types for managing groups of data.

Strings

Strings in Kotlin are immutable sequences of characters. You can create strings using double quotes, and Kotlin provides numerous methods for string manipulation.

Example:

```
val greeting: String = "Hello, Kotlin!"
val length = greeting.length // 13
val upperCaseGreeting = greeting.uppercase() // "HELLO, KOTLIN!"
```

Arrays

In Kotlin, an Array is a container that holds a number of values of a specific type. You can access elements by index, and arrays are zero-indexed.

Example:

```
val numbers: Array<Int> = arrayOf(1, 2, 3, 4, 5)
val firstNumber = numbers[0] // 1
```

Collections

Kotlin's standard library includes collections such as **List**, **Set**, and **Map**. These collections can be mutable or immutable, depending on whether the data they contain can change.

Example:

```
val immutableList: List<String> = listOf("apple", "banana",
"cherry")
val mutableList: MutableList<String> = mutableListOf("apple",
"banana")
mutableList.add("cherry")
```

Type Inference

Type inference is one of Kotlin's most powerful features, allowing the compiler to automatically deduce the type of a variable based on the value assigned to it. This reduces the need for explicit type declarations, making your code more concise and easier to read.

Example:

```
val inferredInt = 10 // The compiler infers that this is an Int
val inferredString = "Kotlin is great!" // The compiler infers
that this is a String
val inferredDouble = 3.14 // The compiler infers that this is a
Double
```

While type inference is a convenient feature, there are cases where you might still want to specify the type explicitly. This can improve code readability, especially in complex scenarios, or prevent ambiguity when the compiler might not infer the type you expect.

Type Conversion

In Kotlin, type conversion must be explicit. This means you need to convert a variable to a different type, if the operation requires it, unlike in some other languages where type conversion is implicit.

Kotlin provides several methods for type conversion:

- `toByte()`
- `toShort()`
- `toInt()`
- `toLong()`
- `toFloat()`
- `toDouble()`
- `toChar()`

Example:

```
val number: Int = 42
val longNumber: Long = number.toLong()
val doubleNumber: Double = number.toDouble()
```

Working with Type Aliases

Kotlin allows you to define type aliases to create more readable and maintainable code, especially when working with complex types.

Example:

```
typealias Username = String
typealias Age = Int

val username: Username = "john_doe"
val age: Age = 30
```

Type aliases do not create new types; they are simply alternate names for the existing types. However, they can make your code more expressive, and easier to understand.

Casting and Type Checking

Kotlin provides several mechanisms for type checking and casting:

Type Checking: You can check if a variable is of a specific type using the '**is**' operator.

Example:

```
fun printType(value: Any) {
   when (value) {
        is Int -> println("This is an Int")
        is String -> println("This is a String")
        else -> println("Unknown type")
   }
}
```

Smart Casts: Kotlin automatically casts a variable to a specific type when it passes a type check.

Example:

```
fun describe(obj: Any): String {
   return when (obj) {
        is String -> "String of length ${obj.length}"
        is Int -> "Integer value $obj"
        else -> "Unknown"
```

```
    }
}
```

Explicit Casting: Use the as keyword for explicit casting.

Example:

```
val obj: Any = "Kotlin"
val str: String = obj as String
```

Be cautious with explicit casting, as it can throw a **`ClassCastException`**, if the object is not of the expected type.

Using Any and Unit Types

In Kotlin, Any is the root of the class hierarchy–every class in Kotlin has Any as a superclass. This makes Any similar to Object in Java. The Unit type in Kotlin corresponds to void in Java, but unlike void, Unit is a type and can be used as a return type in functions.

Example:

```
fun logMessage(message: Any): Unit {
    println("Log: $message")
}
```

In this example, **`logMessage`** can accept any type of argument, and it returns Unit, indicating that the function does not return any meaningful value.

Null Safety and Nullable Types

One of Kotlin's key features is its null safety, designed to prevent null pointer exceptions, which are a common source of bugs in other languages such as Java. In Kotlin, a type cannot hold null unless explicitly declared as nullable by appending a **?** to the type.

Example:

```
var nonNullableString: String = "Kotlin"
// nonNullableString = null // Error: Null cannot be a value of a
non-null type String

var nullableString: String? = "Kotlin"
nullableString = null // This is allowed
```

Kotlin also provides several operators to handle nullable types:

- **Safe Call (`?.`)**: Calls a method or accesses a property, only if the object is not null.
- **Elvis Operator (`?:`)**: Returns a default value, if the expression to the left is null.

- **Non-null Assertion (!!)**: Throws a **NullPointerException**, if the variable is null.

Example:

```
val length = nullableString?.length ?: 0
```

Working with Nullable Types and Null Safety

Null safety is one of Kotlin's most distinguishing features, setting it apart from many other programming languages. Handling null values has been a notorious source of bugs and runtime errors, especially in languages like Java, where **NullPointerException** (NPE) is a common issue. Kotlin's approach to null safety is baked into its type system, providing developers with a robust set of tools to manage null values effectively and avoid these pitfalls. In this chapter, we will explore the nuances of working with nullable types, leveraging Kotlin's null safety features, and adopting best practices to write clean, safe, and efficient codes.

The Concept of Nullable and Non-Nullable Types

Kotlin differentiates between nullable and non-nullable types at the type system level, which means the compiler ensures that you handle null values explicitly. By default, all types in Kotlin are non-nullable, which means a variable cannot hold a null value, unless you explicitly allow it by appending a **?** to the type declaration.

Non-Nullable Types

In Kotlin, a standard type like **String**, **Int**, or **Boolean** cannot hold null. Attempting to assign null to such a variable results in a compilation error.

Example:

```
var nonNullableString: String = "Hello, Kotlin"
// nonNullableString = null // This line would cause a
compile-time error
```

Here, **nonNullableString** is declared as a String, and thus, cannot be assigned a null value.

Nullable Types

To allow a variable to hold null, you must explicitly declare it as nullable by appending

? to its type. This indicates that the variable can either hold a value of the specified type, or be null.

Example:

```
var nullableString: String? = "Hello, Kotlin"
nullableString = null // This is perfectly valid
```

In this example, **nullableString** can hold either a **String** or **null**, making it a nullable type.

Working with Nullable Types

Handling nullable types in Kotlin is straightforward, thanks to a variety of operators and functions that help you manage potential null values without causing runtime errors.

Safe Call Operator (?.): The safe call operator **?.** is one of Kotlin's most powerful tools for dealing with nullable types. It allows you to call methods or access properties on an object, only if that object is not null. If the object is null, the entire expression evaluates to null.

Example:

```
val length: Int? = nullableString?.length
println(length) // Output: null if nullableString is null
```

In this example, if **nullableString** is not null, its length is returned; otherwise, null is returned. This prevents a **NullPointerException** from occurring.

Elvis Operator (?:): The Elvis operator **?:** provides a default value when an expression evaluates to null. It is particularly useful for providing fallback values in cases where a nullable expression might not hold a valid value.

Example:

```
val length: Int = nullableString?.length ?: 0
println(length) // Output: 0 if nullableString is null
```

In this case, if **nullableString** is null, the Elvis operator returns 0 instead of null.

Non-Null Assertion Operator (!!)

The non-null assertion operator **!!** is a way to tell the compiler that you are sure a particular variable is not null. When you use **!!**, the compiler trusts you, but if the variable is actually null, a **NullPointerException** is thrown at runtime.

Example:

```
val length: Int = nullableString!!.length
```

While !! can be useful in certain scenarios, it should be used sparingly. Overusing it can lead to code that is prone to runtime exceptions, negating Kotlin's null safety features.

Advanced Techniques for Handling Nullability

In addition to basic operators, Kotlin provides more advanced techniques for handling nullable types effectively, allowing you to write cleaner and more concise code.

Safe Cast Operator (as?): The safe cast operator **as?** attempts to cast an object to a specific type. If the cast is not possible, it returns **null** instead of throwing a **ClassCastException**.

Example:

```
val obj: Any = "Kotlin"
val str: String? = obj as? String // Safe cast
val num: Int? = obj as? Int // Safe cast returns null
```

In this example, obj is safely cast to **String**, but when attempting to cast it to Int, the safe cast operator returns null.

The let Function: The **let** function is a scoping function that is often used in combination with nullable types. It allows you to execute a block of code only if the variable is not null, and within this block, the variable is non-nullable.

Example:

```
nullableString?.let {
   println("The length of the string is ${it.length}")
}
```

Here, the let function is executed only if **nullableString** is not null. Inside the let block, it refers to the non-nullable value of **nullableString**.

The lateinit Modifier: The **lateinit** modifier is used for variables that cannot be initialized at the point of declaration, but are guaranteed to be initialized before they are used. It is typically used with class properties that are initialized in a constructor or through dependency injection.

Example:

```
lateinit var name: String

fun initializeName() {
   name = "Kotlin"
}
```

```
fun printName() {
    if (::name.isInitialized) {
        println(name)
    } else {
        println("Name has not been initialized")
    }
}
```

In this example, the name is declared with **lateinit**, meaning it will be initialized later, but before it is used.

Nullable Collections

Kotlin's support for nullable types extends to collections, where either the entire collection or individual elements within the collection can be nullable. Understanding how to handle nullable collections is important for working with data structures in Kotlin.

Collections with Nullable Elements: In Kotlin, you can create collections where the elements themselves can be **null**.

Example:

```
val listOfNullableStrings: List<String?> = listOf("Kotlin", null,
"Java")
for (item in listOfNullableStrings) {
    item?.let { println(it) } // Prints only non-null items
}
```

This list contains both non-null and null elements, and the let function is used to safely print only the non-null items.

You can also create collections that themselves can be null. This requires you to handle the possibility that the entire collection might not exist.

Example:

```
val nullableList: List<String>? = null
nullableList?.forEach { println(it) } // Safe call on the
collection
In this case, nullableList is a list that could be null, so the
safe call operator is used to avoid a NullPointerException.
```

Best Practices for Working with Nullable Types

To make the most of Kotlin's null safety features, consider the following best practices:

- **Prefer Non-Nullable Types:** Whenever possible, use non-nullable types to reduce the complexity of your code, and minimize the risk of null-related errors.

- **Use Safe Call and Elvis Operators:** These operators are your go-to tools for handling nullable types safely and concisely.
- **Avoid Overusing !!:** The non-null assertion operator should be a last resort, as it bypasses Kotlin's null safety features, and can lead to runtime exceptions.
- **Leverage let and Scoping Functions**: Use scoping functions such as let, apply, run, and also to handle nullable types in a clean and expressive manner.
- **Document Nullable Types**: Clearly document when a variable or function can return null, so that other developers (and your future self) understand the potential risks, and how to handle them.

Control Flow Statements in Kotlin

Control flow statements are fundamental in any programming language, allowing developers to dictate the flow of program execution based on certain conditions, or the values of expressions. Kotlin, with its concise and expressive syntax, offers several control flow structures that help you write clean, readable, and efficient code. In this chapter, we will explore Kotlin's control flow statements, including if-else, when expressions, loops (**`for`**, **`while`**, and **`do-while`**), and the use of break and continue within these loops.

`If-Else` Statements

The **`if-else`** statement is the most basic control flow structure, allowing your program to execute certain code blocks conditionally. In Kotlin, **`if-else`** can be used both as a statement, and as an expression, making it more flexible compared to some other languages.

Basic `If-Else` Syntax

The basic syntax of an **`if-else`** statement in Kotlin is straightforward. You check a condition, and if it evaluates to true, the code block inside the **`if`** statement is executed. If it evaluates to false, the code block inside the else statement (if present) is executed.

Example:

```
val number = 10

if (number > 0) {
   println("$number is positive")
} else {
   println("$number is not positive")
}
```

In this example, the program checks if the number is greater than 0. If it is, the first block of code is executed; otherwise, the else block is executed.

`If-Else` as an Expression

In Kotlin, **`if-else`** can also be used as an expression, meaning it can return a value. This feature allows you to assign the result of an **`if-else`** statement directly to a variable.

Example:

```
val max = if (number > 0) number else 0
println("The maximum value is $max")
```

Here, the **`if-else`** expression determines whether the number is positive. If it is, the number is assigned to **`max;`** otherwise, max is set to 0.

Nested `If-Else` Statements

Sometimes, you need to check multiple conditions. Kotlin allows you to nest **`if-else`** statements for this purpose, though it is often better to use when expressions (which we will cover next) for better readability.

Example:

```
val number = -10

val result = if (number > 0) {
    "positive"
} else if (number < 0) {
    "negative"
} else {
    "zero"
}

println("The number is $result")
```

In this example, the program checks multiple conditions to determine if the number is positive, negative, or zero, and then prints the appropriate result.

When Expressions

The **`when`** expression in Kotlin is a powerful alternative to **`if-else`** chains, and the traditional switch statement found in other languages. It allows you to evaluate multiple conditions concisely, and is more expressive and flexible.

Basic `when` Usage: The **`when`** expression evaluates a value or condition, and matches it against multiple branches. If a match is found, the corresponding block of the code is executed.

Example:

```
val dayOfWeek = 3

val dayName = when (dayOfWeek) {
    1 -> "Monday"
    2 -> "Tuesday"
    3 -> "Wednesday"
    4 -> "Thursday"
    5 -> "Friday"
    6 -> "Saturday"
    7 -> "Sunday"
    else -> "Invalid day"
}

println("Today is $dayName")
```

Here, the '**`when`**' expression checks the value of **`dayOfWeek`** and assigns the corresponding day name to dayName. If the value does not match any of the specified cases, the '**`else`**' branch is executed.

Advanced `when` Expressions: Kotlin's **`when`** expression can handle more complex scenarios, such as matching multiple conditions, using ranges, or even checking the type of an object.

Example: Matching Multiple Conditions

```
val number = 25

val description = when (number) {
    1, 2, 3 -> "Small number"
    in 4..10 -> "Medium number"
    !in 11..20 -> "Large number"
    else -> "Unknown size"
}

println("The number is a $description")
```

Example: Type Checking with When

```
fun describe(obj: Any): String {
    return when (obj) {
        is Int -> "Integer"
        is String -> "String"
        is Double -> "Double"
```

```
        else -> "Unknown type"
    }
}

println(describe(123)) // Output: Integer
println(describe("Hello")) // Output: String
```

In these examples, **when** is used to match multiple conditions, ranges, and types, making it a versatile tool in your Kotlin programming toolkit.

Loops in Kotlin

Loops allow you to execute a block of code repeatedly, either for a specific number of iterations or until a condition is met. Kotlin provides several types of loops such as: **for**, **while**, and **do-while**.

For Loops: The **for** loop in Kotlin is primarily used to iterate over ranges, arrays, or collections. It provides a concise and readable way to loop through elements.

Example: Iterating over a Range

```
for (i in 1..5) {
    println(i)
}
```

This loop prints the numbers 1 through 5. The **in** keyword is used to define the range.

Example: Iterating over a Collection

```
val fruits = listOf("Apple", "Banana", "Cherry")

for (fruit in fruits) {
    println(fruit)
}
```

Here, the loop iterates over each element in the fruits list, and prints it.

While and Do-While Loops: while and **do-while** loops are used when the number of iterations is not known beforehand, and the loop should continue running as long as a certain condition is true.

While Loop Example:

```
var i = 1

while (i <= 5) {
    println(i)
    i++
}
```

In this example, the loop continues as long as i is less than or equal to 5.

`Do-While` Loop Example:

```
var j = 1

do {
   println(j)
   j++
} while (j <= 5)
```

The **`do-while`** loop is similar to the **`while`** loop, but it guarantees that the loop body is executed at least once, even if the condition is false from the start.

Break and Continue Statements

Within loops, Kotlin provides break and continue statements to control the flow of the loop.

`Break` Statement: The break statement immediately terminates the loop, and the program continues with the next statement after the loop.

Example:

```
for (i in 1..10) {
   if (i == 5) break
   println(i)
}
```

In this example, the loop stops execution when **`i`** equals to 5.

`Continue` Statement: The continue statement skips the current iteration of the loop, and proceeds to the next iteration.

Example:

```
for (i in 1..10) {
   if (i % 2 == 0) continue
   println(i)
}
```

Here, the loop prints only the odd numbers between 1 and 10, skipping the even numbers.

Labels in Kotlin

Kotlin supports labeled breaks and continues, which are useful when dealing with nested loops. A label is essentially a name given to a loop, which you can then use with **`break`** or **`continue`** to specify which loop to exit or continue.

Example:

```
outer@ for (i in 1..5) {
    for (j in 1..5) {
        if (i == 3 && j == 3) break@outer
        println("i = $i, j = $j")
    }
}
```

In this example, the **`break@outer`** statement exits the outer loop when both **`i`** and **`j`** are equal to 3, stopping the entire nested loop structure.

Functions and Return Types in Kotlin

Functions are the fundamental building blocks of any Kotlin program. They encapsulate logic, promote code reusability, and help in organizing code into manageable pieces. In Kotlin, functions are first-class citizens, which means they can be passed around as parameters, returned from other functions, and stored in variables. Understanding how to define and use functions effectively is essential for writing clean, maintainable, and efficient Kotlin code. This chapter will guide you through the various aspects of functions in Kotlin, including function declaration, parameters, return types, inline functions, higher-order functions, and lambda expressions.

Function Basics

In Kotlin, a function is declared using the fun keyword, followed by the function name, parameter list, and the function body. Functions can return values, and the return type must be explicitly declared unless it can be inferred.

Declaring a Function

The basic syntax for declaring a function in Kotlin is:

```
fun functionName(parameter1: Type1, parameter2: Type2, ...):
ReturnType {
    // function body
    return value
}
```

Here is a simple example of a function that takes two integers as parameters, and returns their sum:

Example:

```
fun add(a: Int, b: Int): Int {
    return a + b
}
```

In this example, the function add takes two integers, a and b, and returns their sum. The return type, **Int** is specified after the parameter list.

Function Return Types

In Kotlin, every function must either explicitly declare its return type, or allow it to be inferred by the compiler. If a function does not return any meaningful value, it can return Unit, which is the Kotlin equivalent of void in Java. However, in Kotlin, Unit is a type, and can be omitted when declaring the return type.

Example:

```
fun printMessage(message: String): Unit {
   println(message)
}

// Unit can be omitted
fun printMessage(message: String) {
   println(message)
}
```

Both functions in the example above are equivalent; they take a String parameter and print it to the console.

Parameters in Functions

Kotlin functions can take zero or more parameters. Parameters in Kotlin are always defined with a name and a type. Kotlin also supports several advanced parameter features, such as default values, named arguments, and variable-length argument lists.

Default Parameters: Kotlin allows you to specify default values for function parameters. If a parameter is not provided when the function is called, the default value is used.

Example:

```
fun greet(name: String = "Guest") {
   println("Hello, $name!")
}

greet() // Output: Hello, Guest!
greet("John") // Output: Hello, John!
```

In this example, the greet function has a default parameter value of "**Guest**". If no argument is passed to greet, it uses the default value.

Named Arguments: Named arguments allow you to specify arguments by their parameter names, making function calls more readable, especially when a function has multiple parameters or when using default values.

Example:

```
fun createUser(name: String, age: Int, country: String
= "Unknown") {
    println("Name: $name, Age: $age, Country: $country")
}

createUser(name = "Alice", age = 30)
createUser(name = "Bob", age = 25, country = "USA")
```

In this example, **createUser** is called using named arguments, which makes the function calls clearer and easier to understand.

Vararg Parameters: The **vararg** keyword in Kotlin allows you to pass a variable number of arguments to a function. Inside the function, the **vararg** parameter is treated as an array.

Example:

```
fun sum(vararg numbers: Int): Int {
    return numbers.sum()
}

val result = sum(1, 2, 3, 4)
println(result) // Output: 10
```

Here, the **sum** function takes a variable number of integers, and returns their sum.

Single-Expression Functions

In Kotlin, you can simplify functions that consist of a single expression by using the single-expression syntax. In this case, you can omit the curly braces, and the return keyword.

Example:

```
fun multiply(a: Int, b: Int): Int = a * b

This is equivalent to writing:

fun multiply(a: Int, b: Int): Int {
    return a * b
}
```

Single-expression functions are concise, and often used for simple operations.

Inline Functions

Kotlin provides a feature called inline functions, which are marked with the inline keyword. When a function is inline, the compiler replaces the function call with the actual code from the function. This can lead to performance improvements, especially in cases involving higher-order functions, by avoiding the overhead of function calls.

Inline functions are particularly useful in situations where performance is critical, such as in loops or frequently called functions. They are also beneficial when working with higher-order functions, as they reduce the overhead of function objects and lambda expressions.

Example:

```
inline fun performOperation(a: Int, b: Int, operation: (Int, Int)
-> Int): Int {
   return operation(a, b)
}

val result = performOperation(4, 5) { x, y -> x + y }
println(result) // Output: 9
```

In this example, the **performOperation** function is marked as inline. This means the lambda passed to the function is also inline, potentially improving performance.

Higher-Order Functions and Lambda Expressions

Kotlin treats functions as first-class citizens, meaning you can pass functions as arguments to other functions, return them from functions, or store them in variables. Functions that take other functions as parameters or return functions are known as higher-order functions.

Higher-Order Functions: A higher-order function is a function that takes another function as a parameter or returns a function.

Example:

```
fun operateOnNumbers(a: Int, b: Int, operation: (Int, Int) ->
Int): Int {
   return operation(a, b)
}

val sum = operateOnNumbers(3, 4) { x, y -> x + y }
println(sum) // Output: 7
```

In this example, **operateOnNumbers** is a higher-order function that takes a function as a parameter.

Lambda Expressions: Lambda expressions are anonymous functions that can be passed as arguments to higher-order functions, or used to inline short code blocks.

Example:

```
val sum = { x: Int, y: Int -> x + y }
println(sum(2, 3)) // Output: 5
```

In this example, `sum` is a lambda expression that adds two integers. Lambda expressions are concise and allow for more readable code when used appropriately.

Extension Functions

Kotlin allows you to extend existing classes with new functions using extension functions. This feature is particularly useful when you want to add functionality to a class, without modifying its source code.

Example:

```
fun String.isPalindrome(): Boolean {
    return this == this.reversed()
}

println("madam".isPalindrome()) // Output: true
println("kotlin".isPalindrome()) // Output: false
```

In this example, the **`isPalindrome`** function is an extension function added to the **`String`** class, allowing you to check if a string is a palindrome.

Tail-Recursive Functions

Kotlin supports tail-recursive functions, which are functions that call themselves as the last operation in their execution. Tail recursion can be optimized by the compiler, reducing the risk of stack overflow errors in recursive functions.

Example:

```
tailrec fun factorial(n: Int, accumulator: Int = 1): Int {
    return if (n <= 1) accumulator else factorial(n - 1, n *
accumulator)
}

println(factorial(5)) // Output: 120
```

In this example, the factorial function is tail-recursive, meaning it can be optimized by the compiler to avoid stack overflow.

Exploring Kotlin's String Interpolation

String interpolation is one of Kotlin's most powerful and convenient features. It allows developers to embed variables and expressions directly within string literals, making string manipulation not only easier but also more readable and concise. This feature eliminates the need for complex concatenation, enabling cleaner and more expressive codes.

Basic String Interpolation

In Kotlin, you can embed a variable or an expression within a string using the $ symbol. If the expression is just a simple variable, you can directly use $variableName inside the string. For more complex expressions, you use the **${}** syntax.

Example:

```
val name = "Kotlin"
val greeting = "Hello, $name!"
println(greeting)  // Output: Hello, Kotlin!
```

In the above example, the value of the variable name is directly inserted into the string where $name appears. This makes the code more readable compared to traditional concatenation methods found in other programming languages.

Interpolating Expressions

Kotlin also allows you to embed more complex expressions within strings. This is particularly useful when you need to perform calculations or invoke methods, and include their results directly within a string. To achieve this, you enclose the expression in **${}**.

Example:

```
val items = 5
val pricePerItem = 10
val totalCost = "Total cost: ${items * pricePerItem} dollars"
println(totalCost)  // Output: Total cost: 50 dollars
```

Here, the expression **${items * pricePerItem}** is evaluated, and the result is inserted into the string in place of the expression. This approach is far more concise and readable than the alternative of breaking the string, and manually concatenating the components.

Complex Expressions and Method Calls

String interpolation is not limited to simple arithmetic operations. You can also call methods and use more complex expressions within the **${}** block.

Example:

```
val fruits = listOf("Apple", "Banana", "Cherry")
val message = "The first fruit is ${fruits.first()} and the list
contains ${fruits.size} items."
println(message)  // Output: The first fruit is Apple and the list
contains 3 items.
```

In this example, the **first()** method is called on the fruits list, and the result is embedded in the string. Additionally, the size property of the list is used to dynamically insert the number of items in the list.

Escaping Characters

Sometimes, you might want to include the **$** symbol or a curly brace **{}** within your string without triggering interpolation. In such cases, you need to escape these characters.

Example:

```
val price = 9.99
val text = "The price is \$${price}"
println(text)  // Output: The price is $9.99
```

In the preceding example, the **\$** is used to print the dollar sign, without it being interpreted as the start of an interpolation expression.

Using Triple-Quoted Strings

Kotlin supports triple-quoted strings, which allow you to create multi-line strings or strings that include characters that would normally need escaping, such as double quotes or backslashes. String interpolation works seamlessly within these strings as well.

Example:

```
val name = "Kotlin"
val multiLineText = """
    |Hello, $name!
    |Welcome to the world of Kotlin.
""".trimMargin()

println(multiLineText)
```

The output will be:

Hello, Kotlin!

Welcome to the world of Kotlin.

Triple-quoted strings are particularly useful when dealing with formatted text or JSON strings, where maintaining the original formatting is crucial.

Best Practices

When using string interpolation, it is important to keep a few best practices in mind:

- **Readability**: Always aim to make your code as readable as possible. String interpolation can improve readability, but avoid overly complex expressions inside **${}** blocks.
- **Avoid Overuse**: While string interpolation is powerful, it should be used judiciously. In some cases, using it excessively in a single string can make the code harder to understand.
- **Performance Considerations**: String interpolation is generally efficient, but if performance is a critical concern (for example, in loops or large-scale operations), be mindful of the potential overhead of frequent string manipulation.

Utilizing Ranges and Collections in Kotlin

Kotlin provides powerful and versatile tools for working with ranges and collections, which are essential for handling sequences of data, and organizing information in a structured way. Ranges offer a concise way to define a sequence of values, while collections such as lists, sets, and maps allow for efficient data management and manipulation.

Understanding Ranges in Kotlin

Ranges in Kotlin represent a sequence of values, typically numbers or characters, defined by a start and end point. Ranges are useful for iteration, checking value membership, and creating sequences.

Creating and Using Ranges:

Ranges are created using the **..** operator, which includes both the start and end values:

```
val oneToTen = 1..10
println(oneToTen) // Output: 1..10

You can iterate over ranges using a for loop:
for (i in 1..5) {
   println(i)
}
```

This loop will print numbers 1 through 5. You can also create ranges that exclude the end value using the until function:

```
for (i in 1 until 5) {
    println(i)
}
```

This loop prints numbers from 1 to 4, excluding 5.

Step and Reverse Ranges:

Ranges can be incremented using the **step** function, and they can also be reversed using the **downTo** function:

```
for (i in 1..10 step 2) {
    println(i)
}

for (i in 10 downTo 1) {
    println(i)
}
```

The first loop prints every second number from 1 to 10, while the second loop prints numbers from 10 down to 1.

Working with Collections

Kotlin offers a rich set of collection types, including lists, sets, and maps. These collections can be immutable (read-only) or mutable (modifiable).

Lists: A list is an ordered collection of elements that can contain duplicates. Immutable lists are created using **listOf**, while mutable lists are created using **mutableListOf**:

```
val fruits = listOf("Apple", "Banana", "Cherry")
val mutableFruits = mutableListOf("Apple", "Banana")
mutableFruits.add("Cherry")
```

Immutable lists cannot be modified after they are created, while mutable lists can be updated by adding, removing, or modifying elements.

Sets: A set is an unordered collection of unique elements such as lists, sets can be immutable (**setOf**) or mutable (**mutableSetOf**):

```
val uniqueNumbers = setOf(1, 2, 3)
val mutableNumbers = mutableSetOf(1, 2)
mutableNumbers.add(3)
mutableNumbers.add(1) // No effect, since sets do not allow
duplicates
```

Sets are particularly useful when you need to ensure that no duplicate elements exist in the collection.

Maps: A map is a collection of key-value pairs, where each key maps to exactly one value. Immutable maps are created using **mapOf**, and mutable maps using **mutableMapOf**:

```
val countryCodes = mapOf("US" to "United States", "IN" to "India")
val mutableCountryCodes = mutableMapOf("US" to "United States")
mutableCountryCodes["IN"] = "India"
```

Thus, **maps** are ideal for associating values with unique keys, making them useful for tasks like looking up values, based on a specific identifier.

Common Operations on Collections

Kotlin provides a wide range of operations for manipulating collections, such as filtering, mapping, and reducing.

Filtering: The **filter** function creates a new collection containing only the elements that match a given condition:

```
val numbers = listOf(1, 2, 3, 4, 5)
val evenNumbers = numbers.filter { it % 2 == 0 }
println(evenNumbers) // Output: [2, 4]
```

Mapping: The **map** function transforms each element in a collection into a new element based on a given function:

```
val squares = numbers.map { it * it }
println(squares) // Output: [1, 4, 9, 16, 25]
```

Reducing: The **reduce** function combines all elements in a collection into a single value based on a specified operation:

```
val sum = numbers.reduce { acc, num -> acc + num }
println(sum) // Output: 15
```

Best Practices for Using Ranges and Collections

- **Prefer Immutability:** Use immutable collections whenever possible to avoid unintended modifications.
- **Leverage Kotlin's Standard Library:** Use built-in functions such as **filter**, **map**, and **reduce** to simplify your code.
- **Choose the Right Collection Type:** Use lists for ordered data, sets for unique elements, and maps for key-value associations.

Handling Exceptions and Errors in Kotlin

Handling exceptions and errors is a crucial part of building robust and reliable applications. Kotlin, like many modern programming languages, provides a structured way to handle runtime errors through exceptions. By understanding how to effectively manage exceptions, you can prevent your program from crashing, and provide meaningful feedback to users or log information for developers.

Understanding Exceptions

An exception is an event that occurs during the execution of a program that disrupts the normal flow of instructions. In Kotlin, exceptions are typically used to handle errors that cannot be handled through normal control flow, such as file I/O errors, invalid user input, or network failures.

Kotlin's exception handling is built upon the same principles as Java, but with a more streamlined syntax. All exceptions in Kotlin are objects of classes that inherit from the Throwable class.

The `Try-Catch` Block

The most common way to handle exceptions in Kotlin is by using a **`try-catch`** block. The **`try`** block contains codes that might throw an exception, while the **`catch`** block handles the exception.

Basic Syntax:

```
try {
    // Code that might throw an exception
} catch (e: ExceptionType) {
    // Code to handle the exception
}
```

Example:

```
fun divide(a: Int, b: Int): Int {
    return try {
        a / b
    } catch (e: ArithmeticException) {
        println("Cannot divide by zero")
        0 // Return a default value
    }
}
```

In this example, if **`b`** is zero, an **`ArithmeticException`** is thrown. The **`catch`** block handles this exception by printing an error message, and returning a default value of 0.

Finally Block

In addition to try and catch, Kotlin provides a **finally** block. The **finally** block is executed after the **try** and **catch** blocks, regardless of whether an exception was thrown. This is useful for cleanup operations, such as closing resources.

Example:

```
fun readFile(fileName: String) {
    val file = File(fileName)
    try {
        val content = file.readText()
        println(content)
    } catch (e: IOException) {
        println("Error reading file")
    } finally {
        println("Closing file resources")
        // Code to close resources
    }
}
```

Here, the **finally** block will run even if an exception is thrown, ensuring that the file resources are properly closed.

Throwing Exceptions

You can **throw** exceptions manually using the **throw** keyword. This is often used to signal an error condition that you have detected in your code/s.

Example:

```
fun validateAge(age: Int) {
    if (age < 0) {
        throw IllegalArgumentException("Age cannot be negative")
    }
}
```

In this example, if the **age** is negative, an **IllegalArgumentException** is thrown, providing a clear message about what went wrong.

Custom Exceptions

Kotlin allows you to define custom exceptions by creating a class that inherits from exceptions or one of its subclasses. This is useful when you need to handle specific error conditions in a way that is meaningful to your application.

Example:

```
class InvalidUserInputException(message: String) : Exception
(message)

fun processUserInput(input: String) {
   if (input.isEmpty()) {
       throw InvalidUserInputException("Input cannot be empty")
   }
}
```

Here, **`InvalidUserInputException`** is a custom exception that is thrown when the user input is invalid.

Best Practices for Exception Handling

- **Handle Only What You Can Recover From:** Only catch exceptions that you can actually recover from. Avoid catching generic exceptions unless absolutely necessary.
- **Provide Meaningful Messages:** When throwing or catching exceptions, use clear and descriptive messages to help understand the error.
- **Use Finally for Cleanup**: Always use the finally block to release resources such as files, network connections, or database connections.
- **Log Exceptions**: In production applications, it is crucial to log exceptions to help diagnose and fix issues.

Writing and Running Simple Kotlin Programs

Kotlin is a versatile and easy-to-learn language that allows developers to quickly write and execute simple programs. This topic will guide you through the basics of writing your first Kotlin program, compiling and running it using different methods, and understanding the core structure of Kotlin code.

Setting Up Your Development Environment

Before writing and running Kotlin programs, you need to set up a development environment. There are a few common options:

- **IntelliJ IDEA:** A powerful Integrated Development Environment (IDE) that supports Kotlin out of the box. Download: https://www.jetbrains.com/idea.

- **Android Studio:** Ideal if you are planning to develop Android applications, as it comes with built-in support for Kotlin. Download: https://developer.android.com/studio.
- **Command Line:** For those who prefer working in a terminal, Kotlin can be run directly from the command line using the Kotlin compiler (`kotlinc`). Instructions: https://kotlinlang.org/docs/command-line.html.

Installing Kotlin:

- If you are using IntelliJ IDEA or Android Studio, Kotlin is included by default. For command-line usage, you can download the Kotlin compiler from the official website, and set it up in your PATH.

Writing Your First Kotlin Program

The first step in learning any programming language is writing a simple "`Hello, World!`" program. This will give you a feel for Kotlin's syntax and structure.

`Hello, World!` Example:

```
fun main() {
    println("Hello, World!")
}
```

Explanation:

- `fun`: The keyword used to declare a function in Kotlin.
- `main`: The main function is the entry point of a Kotlin application. It is where the program starts execution.
- `println`: A standard library function that prints a line of text to the console.

This simple program demonstrates the basic structure of a Kotlin application, including function declaration, and calling standard library functions.

Running Kotlin Programs

Depending on your setup, you can run Kotlin programs in several ways:

1. Using IntelliJ IDEA or Android Studio:
   a. Open your Kotlin file in the IDE.
   b. Click the green "`Run`" button next to the main function, or use the "`Run`" menu.
   c. The output ("`Hello, World!`") will be displayed in the console window at the bottom of the IDE.

2. Using the Command Line:

   a. Save your Kotlin code in a file with the .kt extension, such as **`HelloWorld.kt`**.

   b. Open a terminal and navigate to the directory containing your file.

   c. Compile the Kotlin file using the kotlinc compiler:

   ```
   kotlinc HelloWorld.kt -include-runtime -d HelloWorld.jar
   ```

   d. Run the compiled program using the java command:

   ```
   java -jar HelloWorld.jar
   ```

3. Using an Online Kotlin Compiler:

   a. You can also use an online Kotlin compiler, such as play.kotlinlang.org, where you can write and run Kotlin code directly in your browser. This is convenient for quick testing and learning.

Exploring Kotlin's Program Structure

Kotlin programs typically consist of a series of functions and variables organized within files and packages. Here is a breakdown of the basic elements:

- **Functions:** Defined using the fun keyword. Functions can take parameters and return values. The main function is special because it is the entry point of the program.
- **Variables:** Declared using **`val`** (immutable) or **`var`** (mutable). Type inference often allows you to omit explicit type declarations.
- **Comments**: Use **`//`** for single-line comments and **`/* ... */`** for multi-line comments. Comments are ignored by the compiler, and are used to explain and document the code.

Example Program:

```
fun main() {
    val name = "Kotlin"
    greet(name)
}

fun greet(name: String) {
    println("Hello, $name!")
}
```

In this example, the main function calls another function **`greet`**, passing a string as an argument. The **`greet`** function prints a personalized greeting. This demonstrates how functions interact within a program, illustrating the modular nature of the Kotlin code.

Understanding Program Output

When you run a Kotlin program, the output is displayed in the console. Understanding the output helps in debugging and ensuring your program is working as expected.

Example Output:

```
Hello, Kotlin!
```

This output confirms that the program executed successfully, called the `greet` function, and passed the correct argument.

Best Practices for Writing Simple Programs

- **Start Small:** Begin with small programs to build your understanding of Kotlin's syntax and structure.
- **Experiment:** Modify your code to see how changes affect the output. This is a great way to learn.
- **Use Meaningful Names:** Use descriptive names for variables and functions to make your code easy to read and maintain.

Conclusion

In this chapter, *Basics of Kotlin Programming*, you explored the fundamental concepts that form the backbone of Kotlin development. From understanding variable declaration and initialization to mastering control flow, functions, and null safety, you have gained the essential skills needed to write clean, concise, and effective Kotlin code. These basics serve as the foundation upon which all your future Kotlin projects will be built.

As you move forward to the next chapter, *Advanced Kotlin Programming*, you will take your skills to the next level. Prepare to dive into more sophisticated aspects of Kotlin, including higher-order functions, lambda expressions, and advanced collection operations. You will also explore Kotlin's powerful features such as coroutines for asynchronous programming, extension functions, and other advanced techniques that will enable you to create more efficient, scalable, and maintainable applications. This next step will challenge you to push the boundaries of what you can achieve with Kotlin, setting the stage for truly advanced programming capabilities.

CHAPTER 3
Advanced Kotlin Programming

Introduction

Welcome to the Advanced Kotlin Programming chapter, where we take your Kotlin expertise to the next level by exploring more sophisticated and powerful features of the language. In this chapter, we will focus on advanced object-oriented programming techniques, functional programming, and concurrency management, equipping you with the tools to write high-performance, scalable Kotlin applications. The topics covered here will deepen your understanding of Kotlin, and enable you to leverage its full potential in real-world applications.

We begin with Advanced Object-Oriented Programming concepts, delving into inheritance, interfaces, and the use of abstract classes as well as singleton objects to create reusable and maintainable code architectures. These foundational elements will allow you to design more robust object models, and apply the principles of object-oriented programming effectively.

Next, we explore Functional Programming Techniques, a paradigm that Kotlin embraces through higher-order functions and lambdas, providing you with concise, expressive ways to manipulate data and control flow. We will also introduce inline and extension functions, which will help you optimize performance and extend the existing classes with new functionality in a clean and efficient manner.

Concurrency is a critical component of modern application development, and Kotlin's Coroutines and Asynchronous Programming framework offers an elegant solution. You will learn the basics of coroutines, structured concurrency, and how to handle asynchronous tasks without the complexity of traditional threading, making your code more efficient and easier to maintain.

Kotlin's Advanced Type System provides enhanced flexibility for type management. Topics such as generics, variance, sealed classes, and data classes will help you write more reusable and type-safe code. Understanding these concepts will allow you to take full advantage of Kotlin's powerful type system, and write more expressive and error-free programs.

We will also cover Interoperability and Advanced Error Handling, focusing on seamless integration with Java code, and handling exceptions more effectively with custom exceptions and the Result type. This ensures that you can work smoothly across both Kotlin and Java ecosystems, and build robust applications with effective error management.

Finally, we shall explore Practical Applications and Optimization, focusing on building and optimizing Kotlin applications for real-world scenarios. You will also discover best practices, performance tips, and real-world examples to enhance your development process, ensuring that your applications are not only functional but also efficient and scalable.

By the end of this chapter, you will have gained a deep understanding of advanced Kotlin programming, allowing you to build complex and high-performance applications with confidence. So, let us dive in!

Structure

In this chapter, we will cover the following topics:

- Advanced Object-Oriented Programming
    - Inheritance and Interfaces
    - Abstract Classes and Singleton Objects
- Functional Programming Techniques
    - Higher-Order Functions and Lambdas
    - Inline and Extension Functions
    - Scoped Functions (let, apply, run, also, with)
- Coroutines and Asynchronous Programming
    - Coroutine Basics and Builders
    - Structured Concurrency
- Kotlin's Advanced Type System
    - Generics and Variance
    - Sealed and Data Classes
- Interoperability and Advanced Error Handling
    - Working with Java Code
    - Custom Exceptions and Result Type

- Practical Applications and Optimization
  - Building and Optimizing Kotlin Applications
  - Best Practices and Real-World Examples

Advanced Object-Oriented Programming

In this section, we move beyond the basics, and explore the advanced features of Object-Oriented Programming (OOP) in Kotlin. While Kotlin is designed to be concise and expressive, it fully supports traditional OOP principles, allowing you to build robust, scalable, and maintainable applications. Here, we will delve into topics such as inheritance, interfaces, abstract classes, and singleton objects, which are essential for designing complex systems, and achieving code reusability and modularity.

Inheritance and Interfaces

Inheritance and interfaces are two fundamental concepts in Object-Oriented Programming (OOP) that help structure complex systems, promote code reuse, and enforce consistent behavior across different classes. Kotlin, as a modern language, supports both inheritance and interfaces with some unique features that enhance flexibility and simplicity.

We will start by examining inheritance–one of the core pillars of OOP–which allows classes to inherit properties and behavior from other classes, promoting code reuse and the creation of more flexible designs. You will learn how Kotlin manages class hierarchies, and how to override functions as well as properties effectively.

We will also cover interfaces, which allow you to define contracts that classes must adhere to, encouraging the design of loosely coupled, flexible systems. Unlike in some other languages, Kotlin interfaces can contain default method implementations, providing greater versatility.

Inheritance in Kotlin

Inheritance allows a class to acquire properties and behavior (methods) from another class. In Kotlin, every class can have a superclass from which it inherits. By default, all classes in Kotlin are final, meaning they cannot be subclassed unless explicitly marked with the open keyword.

Basic Syntax of Inheritance:

```
open class Animal {
    fun eat() {
        println("Eating...")
    }
```

```
}

class Dog : Animal() {
    fun bark() {
        println("Woof!")
    }
}

fun main() {
    val dog = Dog()
    dog.eat()  // Inherited method from Animal class
    dog.bark() // Dog's own method
}
```

In the preceding example:

a. The **Animal** class is marked as open, allowing it to be subclassed.

b. The **Dog** class inherits from **Animal** using the: **Animal()** syntax, gaining access to the **eat()** method, while also defining its own method, **bark()**.

Overriding Methods: When a subclass needs to modify the behavior of a superclass, it can override methods using the **override** keyword. The superclass method must be marked as open to allow overriding.

```
open class Animal {
    open fun sound() {
        println("Some sound")
    }
}

class Dog : Animal() {
    override fun sound() {
        println("Woof!")
    }
}

fun main() {
    val dog = Dog()
    dog.sound() // Outputs: Woof!
}
```

Here, the **Dog** class overrides the **sound()** method of the **Animal** class to provide its own implementation.

Calling Superclass Methods

If the subclass wants to invoke a method from the superclass, it can use the **super** keyword.

```
open class Animal {
   open fun sound() {
        println("Some sound")
   }
}

class Cat : Animal() {
   override fun sound() {
        super.sound()  // Calls Animal's sound()
        println("Meow!")
   }
}

fun main() {
   val cat = Cat()
   cat.sound() // Outputs: Some sound \n Meow!
}
```

In this case, **Cat** calls the **sound()** method of the superclass Animal, before adding its own behavior.

Interfaces in Kotlin

Interfaces in Kotlin are a powerful way to define a contract that classes must adhere to. Unlike abstract classes, interfaces can be implemented by any class, regardless of its position in the class hierarchy. An interface can contain both abstract methods (which need to be implemented by subclasses) and default method implementations.

Defining an Interface:

```
interface Animal {
   fun sound() // Abstract method
   fun breathe() {
        println("Breathing...")
   }
}

class Dog : Animal {
   override fun sound() {
        println("Woof!")
   }
}

fun main() {
   val dog = Dog()
```

```
    dog.sound()   // Outputs: Woof!
    dog.breathe() // Outputs: Breathing...
}
```

In the example:

a. The **sound()** method is abstract and must be implemented by the **Dog** class.

b. The **breathe()** method has a default implementation in the interface, which can be used directly or overridden by the implementing class.

Multiple Inheritance with Interfaces: Kotlin allows a class to implement multiple interfaces, which can help in achieving more flexible and modular designs. When implementing multiple interfaces, you can override methods from different interfaces in the same class.

```
interface Walkable {
   fun walk() {
       println("Walking...")
   }
}

interface Runnable {
   fun run() {
       println("Running...")
   }
}

class Human : Walkable, Runnable

fun main() {
   val person = Human()
   person.walk() // Outputs: Walking...
   person.run()  // Outputs: Running...
}
```

In this example, the Human class implements both **Walkable** and **Runnable** interfaces, and inherits the behavior from both.

Resolving Conflicts in Multiple Interfaces: When multiple interfaces contain methods with the same signature, Kotlin requires the class implementing these interfaces to resolve the conflict by overriding the method, and explicitly choosing which implementation to use.

```
interface FirstInterface {
   fun display() {
       println("From FirstInterface")
   }
}
```

```
interface SecondInterface {
    fun display() {
        println("From SecondInterface")
    }
}

class MyClass : FirstInterface, SecondInterface {
    override fun display() {
        super<FirstInterface>.display() // Choose FirstInterface
implementation
    }
}

fun main() {
    val obj = MyClass()
    obj.display() // Outputs: From FirstInterface
}
```

In this case, **MyClass** implements both **FirstInterface** and **SecondInterface** as well as resolves the conflict by explicitly calling the implementation from FirstInterface.

When to Use Inheritance vs. Interfaces

- Use inheritance when there is a clear "is-a" relationship between classes, and you need to reuse common behavior or state between them.
- Use interfaces when you want to define a contract that can be implemented by different classes, possibly from unrelated hierarchies. Interfaces are especially useful when multiple inheritance is needed (since Kotlin does not support multiple inheritance with classes but does with interfaces).

Abstract Classes and Singleton Objects in Kotlin

In Kotlin, abstract classes and singleton objects provide powerful mechanisms for structuring your code. Abstract classes allow you to define common behavior that must be extended and customized by subclasses, while singleton objects ensure that a class has only one instance, which is particularly useful for managing global state or utility functions. Both of these concepts are integral to designing robust and maintainable systems in Kotlin.

Abstract Classes

An abstract class is one that cannot be instantiated directly. It is designed to be subclassed, allowing child classes to inherit its functionality, while also requiring them to implement certain abstract methods. Abstract classes can contain both fully implemented methods and abstract methods that do not have a body, and must be overridden in subclasses.

Defining an Abstract Class:

```
abstract class Animal {
   abstract fun sound(): String
   fun eat() {
       println("Eating...")
   }
}

class Dog : Animal() {
   override fun sound(): String {
       return "Woof!"
   }
}

fun main() {
   val dog = Dog()
   println(dog.sound())  // Outputs: Woof!
   dog.eat()             // Outputs: Eating...
}
```

In this example:

a. **`Animal`** is an abstract class with an abstract method **`sound()`**, which must be overridden by any subclass.

b. The **`Dog`** class extends **`Animal`** and provides a concrete implementation of the **`sound()`** method, while also inheriting the **`eat()`** method.

Key Features of Abstract Classes:

- **Cannot Be Instantiated Directly:** Abstract classes are meant to be extended, and cannot be instantiated on their own. This helps to define common functionality, without creating objects of the abstract class.
- **Mix of Abstract and Non-Abstract Methods:** Abstract classes can contain both abstract methods, which must be implemented by subclasses, and fully defined methods that can be used as-is or overridden, if necessary.
- **Providing Shared Behavior:** Abstract classes are useful when you want to provide shared behavior to multiple subclasses, while allowing customization through abstract methods.

Example:

```
abstract class Shape {
   abstract fun area(): Double
   fun printArea() {
       println("The area is: ${area()}")
   }
}

class Circle(val radius: Double) : Shape() {
   override fun area(): Double {
       return Math.PI * radius * radius
   }
}

fun main() {
   val circle = Circle(5.0)
   circle.printArea()  // Outputs: The area is: 78.53981633974483
}
```

In this case, the Shape abstract class provides a blueprint for any shape, defining the **`area()`** method as abstract, while implementing the **`printArea()`** method to be used by subclasses like Circle.

When to Use Abstract Classes

- Use an abstract class when you want to share common behavior among multiple subclasses, but you also need certain methods to be implemented in a specific way by each subclass.
- Abstract classes are ideal when you have a base class with common functionality that subclasses should inherit, while requiring them to provide their own implementation of certain methods.

Singleton Objects

A singleton is a class that allows only one instance of itself to be created. In Kotlin, singletons are declared using the **`object`** keyword. This is particularly useful when you need a globally accessible instance, such as for utility classes, configuration management, or state management.

Defining a Singleton Object:

```
object DatabaseConnection {
   val url = "jdbc://localhost:5432/mydb"

   fun connect() {
       println("Connecting to $url")
   }
```

```
}

fun main() {
    DatabaseConnection.connect()  // Outputs: Connecting to
jdbc://localhost:5432/mydb
}
```

In this example:

a. The **DatabaseConnection** object is a singleton, meaning that there is only one instance of it in the application.

b. You can directly access the **connect()** method and url property, without creating an instance.

Thread Safety Note: Kotlin's object declarations are thread-safe by design. The instance is initialized lazily on first access, and the compiler ensures safe publication across threads. This makes object ideal for concurrent environments, without additional synchronization.

Key Features of Singleton Objects:

- **Single Instance:** A singleton object in Kotlin has only one instance, which is created the first time, it is accessed. This ensures that there is a single point of access to the object's data and behavior.
- **Global State:** Singleton objects are often used to manage global states such as configuration settings, logging utilities, or database connections.
- **No Constructors:** Unlike regular classes, you do not use constructors to instantiate singleton objects. The object is automatically initialized the first time, it is accessed.

Companion Objects: In addition to top-level singleton objects, Kotlin also supports companion objects, which allow you to define static-like methods and properties within a class. A companion object is tied to a class, and is used for functionality related to the class, rather than instances of the class.

Example of Companion Object:

```
class User(val name: String) {
    companion object {
        fun createGuestUser(): User {
            return User("Guest")
        }
    }
}
```

```
fun main() {
    val guest = User.createGuestUser()
    println(guest.name)  // Outputs: Guest
}
```

In this example:

a. The **User** class has a companion object that contains a **createGuestUser()** function.

b. Companion objects allow you to write static-like functionality within a class, while still maintaining the structure of object-oriented design.

Singleton Objects vs Companion Objects:

a. Singleton Objects are independent, globally accessible objects that exist as a single instance throughout the application.

b. Companion Objects are tied to a specific class, and provide functionality that is related to that class, such as factory methods or utility functions.

When to Use Singleton Objects:

- Use singleton objects when you need one and only one instance of a class, such as for logging, database connections, or managing a configuration.
- Singleton objects are ideal for utility classes that provide common functionality across your application, without requiring multiple instances.

Functional Programming Techniques

Kotlin is not only an object-oriented language but also a language that embraces functional programming principles. Functional Programming (FP) is a paradigm that treats computation as the evaluation of mathematical functions, and avoids changing states or mutable data. In Kotlin, functional programming techniques provide a more declarative and concise way to write the code that is often more readable, maintainable, and testable.

In this section, we will explore essential functional programming concepts in Kotlin, including higher-order functions, lambdas, inline functions, and extension functions. These techniques allow you to write clean and efficient code by treating functions as first-class citizens, and taking advantage of Kotlin's powerful standard library.

Higher-Order Functions and Lambdas

One of the core concepts in functional programming is higher-order functions. These are functions that take other functions as parameters or return functions. Kotlin treats functions as first-class citizens, meaning you can pass functions around just like any other value.

Example of a Higher-Order Function:

```
fun calculate(a: Int, b: Int, operation: (Int, Int) -> Int): Int {
    return operation(a, b)
}

fun main() {
    val sum = calculate(4, 5) { x, y -> x + y }
    println(sum)  // Outputs: 9
}
```

In this example:

a. Calculate a higher-order function that accepts another function (operation) as a parameter.

b. The lambda expression { **x, y -> x + y** } defines the operation (addition in this case), and is passed as an argument.

Lambda Expressions

In Kotlin, lambda expressions are anonymous functions that are concise, and can be passed as arguments to higher-order functions. They allow for more expressive code.

Syntax of Lambda Expressions:

```
val multiply = { a: Int, b: Int -> a * b }
println(multiply(3, 4))  // Outputs: 12
```

- The lambda starts with parameters (**a**, **b**), followed by the **->** symbol, and ends with the body of the function (**a * b**).
- Lambda expressions are often used with collection operations such as **map**, **filter**, and **reduce** in Kotlin.

Example with map function:

```
val numbers = listOf(1, 2, 3, 4, 5)
val squares = numbers.map { it * it }
println(squares)  // Outputs: [1, 4, 9, 16, 25]
```

In this case, the **map** function applies the lambda **{it * it }** to each element in the list, returning a new list of squared values.

Function Types and Type Inference

Kotlin has a specific syntax for defining function types. A function type **(Int, Int)**

-> Int describes a function that takes two integers, and returns an integer. Kotlin can also infer function types based on the context.

Example:

```
val operation: (Int, Int) -> Int = { a, b -> a + b }
println(operation(10, 20))  // Outputs: 30
```

Inline Functions

Kotlin provides **inline** functions as a way to improve performance when using higher-order functions, especially with lambdas. Normally, passing a lambda to a function incurs overhead in creating a function object. However, with the inline keyword, the function body (including lambdas) is copied directly into the call site, reducing the overhead.

Example of Inline Function:

```
inline fun performOperation(a: Int, b: Int, operation: (Int, Int)
-> Int): Int {
    return operation(a, b)
}

fun main() {
    val result = performOperation(3, 4) { x, y -> x * y }
    println(result) // Outputs: 12
}
```

Here, the **performOperation** function is marked as inline, which means that at compile-time, the lambda **{x, y -> x * y }** will be inlined into the function body, avoiding the overhead of creating function objects.

Advantages of Inline Functions:

- **Performance Gains:** Avoids the creation of additional function objects when using lambdas.
- **Reduced Overhead:** Especially useful when calling higher-order functions frequently such as in loops or performance-critical sections of code.

Extension Functions

Kotlin allows you to add new functionality to existing classes, without modifying their code using extension functions. Extension functions are a great way to enhance the functionality of classes, especially for adding utility methods that can be used throughout your codebase.

Example of Extension Function:

```
fun String.isPalindrome(): Boolean {
   return this == this.reversed()
}

fun main() {
   val word = "madam"
   println(word.isPalindrome())  // Outputs: true
}
```

In this example:

a. The **isPalindrome** extension function adds functionality to the String class without modifying its source code.

b. This makes the code cleaner, more modular, and reusable.

Extension Functions with Collections

Kotlin's standard library provides many extension functions for collections that make working with lists, sets, and maps easier and more expressive.

Example:

```
fun List<Int>.average(): Double {
   return if (this.isEmpty()) 0.0 else this.sum().toDouble() /
this.size
}

fun main() {
   val numbers = listOf(1, 2, 3, 4, 5)
   println(numbers.average())  // Outputs: 3.0
}
```

Here, the average function is added as an extension to the List class, making it simple to compute the average of a list of integers.

Scoped Functions in Kotlin

Kotlin offers a set of powerful functions known as **scoped functions** to enhance code readability, conciseness, and manage object context. These include: let, run, with, apply, and also. They help in performing operations within a certain context or scope, avoiding boilerplate, and making the code more expressive.

Although they look similar, each scoped function serves a slightly different purpose depending on:

- **What is returned (result or context object)**

- **What is this or what does it refer to within the scope**

Why Scoped Functions?

Scoped functions are often used for:

- Object configuration
- Null safety
- Temporary scope access
- Logging or side effects

They help write fluid and chainable code, while maintaining readability.

let

The **let** function is often used for **null** checks, or to execute a block with the object as it.

```
val name: String? = "Kotlin" name?.let { println("Name is $it")
// Only prints if name is not null }
```

- Uses it as the context object
- Returns the **result** of the lambda

Best for: Null safety and chaining operations

run

run executes a block of code, and returns its result. It uses this as the context.

```
val length = "Kotlin".run { println("The word is $this") length }
// returns 6
```

- Uses this inside the block.
- Returns the **result** of the lambda.

Best for: Combining initialization and computation

with

Unlike others, **with** is not an extension function. It's called with the object as an argument.

```
val builder = StringBuilder() val result = with(builder)
{ append("Hello, ") append("World!") toString() }
```

- Uses this inside the block
- Returns the **result**

Best for: Object transformations or grouped actions

`apply`

`apply` runs the block, and returns the **object itself**, using this.

```
val person = Person().apply { name = "John" age = 30 }
```

- Uses this for configuration
- Returns the **object**

Best for: Object configuration

`also`

Similar to let, but returns the object, instead of the lambda result. Uses it as the reference.

```
val list = mutableListOf("A", "B").also { it.add("C") println
("Updated list: $it") }
```

- Uses it
- Returns the **object**

Best for: Logging, debugging, or performing side-effects

Summary

Scoped functions are a hallmark of Kotlin's expressive power. By using them appropriately, you can:

- Avoid boilerplate
- Improve readability
- Chain operations cleanly
- Write safer null-aware code

Thus, understanding when and why to use each scoped function will help you build more idiomatic Kotlin applications.

Combining Functional Programming Techniques

Kotlin allows you to combine higher-order functions, lambdas, and extension functions to create a powerful, expressive code. The use of these functional programming techniques can make your code shorter and more efficient, reducing boilerplate and improving readability.

Example: Using Extension Functions and Lambdas Together:

```
fun List<Int>.filterAndSquare(predicate: (Int) -> Boolean):
List<Int> {
    return this.filter(predicate).map { it * it }
}

fun main() {
    val numbers = listOf(1, 2, 3, 4, 5)
    val result = numbers.filterAndSquare { it % 2 == 0 }
    println(result)  // Outputs: [4, 16]
}
```

In this example:

a. The **filterAndSquare** extension function combines filtering and mapping in a functional style.

b. It uses a lambda predicate to filter the list, and then maps the filtered values to their squares, providing clean and concise code.

Coroutines and Asynchronous Programming

As applications become more complex and performance-critical, the need for efficient handling of long-running tasks such as network requests, file I/O, or computationally intensive operations increases. Traditional approaches like threading can be difficult to manage and introduce complexity in code. Kotlin's coroutines provide an elegant and lightweight solution for handling asynchronous programming in a non-blocking way. They allow you to write asynchronous code that looks and feels synchronous, offering greater clarity and easier management of concurrency.

In this section, we will explore Coroutine Basics and Builders to understand how coroutines work, and how to launch them, followed by an introduction to Structured Concurrency, which ensures that coroutines run predictably, and are properly managed within their scopes.

Coroutine Basics and Builders

A coroutine is essentially a task that can be suspended and resumed at a later time, without blocking the main thread. Unlike traditional threads, coroutines are lightweight, and can handle thousands of concurrent operations without the overhead associated with threads. They allow for a more efficient way to write an asynchronous code.

Coroutine Builders

Kotlin provides several builders that allow you to launch coroutines easily. The most commonly used coroutine builders are launch, async, and runBlocking. Each of these builders serves different purposes depending on whether you need to return a value or wait for a coroutine to complete.

launch

This builder is used to fire off a coroutine that runs in the background, and does not return any result. It is perfect for tasks where you do not need a **return** value, such as performing I/O operations or updating UI elements asynchronously.

Example of launch:

```
import kotlinx.coroutines.*

fun main() = runBlocking {
   launch {
       delay(1000L)  // Simulate a long-running task
       println("Coroutine completed!")
   }
   println("Main function continues...")
}
```

In this example:

a. The launch coroutine starts a background task that is delayed for 1 second, using the **delay()** function (a suspending function).

b. The main function continues its execution, without being blocked by the coroutine.

async

This builder is similar to launch, but it is used when you need to return a result. It allows you to execute tasks concurrently, and retrieve their results using the **await()** function. It is particularly useful when you need to run multiple tasks in parallel, and aggregate their results.

Example of async:

```
import kotlinx.coroutines.*

fun main() = runBlocking {
   val result = async {
       delay(1000L)
       42  // Return result after delay
   }
   println("Result: ${result.await()}")  // Outputs: Result: 42
}
```

Here, the async builder is used to start a coroutine that returns a result after 1 second. The **await()** function suspends the execution until the result is ready, ensuring non-blocking behavior.

runBlocking

This builder blocks the current thread, while the coroutine is running, and is often used in main functions or tests where you need to wait for coroutines to complete. Unlike launch or async, **runBlocking** is typically used for short-lived tasks where blocking the thread is acceptable.

Example of runBlocking:

```
import kotlinx.coroutines.*

fun main() = runBlocking {
    println("Start of runBlocking")
    delay(1000L)  // Delay for 1 second
    println("End of runBlocking")
}
```

In this case, the **runBlocking** function keeps the main thread alive, until the coroutine has completed its execution.

Suspending Functions

A core concept in Kotlin coroutines is the suspending function, which is a function that can be paused and resumed without blocking the thread. Suspending functions are marked with the suspend keyword, and can only be called from within a coroutine or another suspending function.

Example of a Suspending Function:

```
suspend fun fetchData(): String {
    delay(1000L)  // Simulate network request
    return "Data fetched!"
}

fun main() = runBlocking {
    val data = fetchData()
    println(data)
}
```

In this example:

a. The **fetchData()** function is marked as suspend because it uses the **delay()** function to simulate a network request.

b. It returns a string once the delay is complete, and this behavior is non-blocking.

Structured Concurrency

Kotlin promotes structured concurrency, a model which ensures that coroutines are scoped and managed predictably. In structured concurrency, all coroutines are attached to a coroutine scope, which defines their lifecycle. When the scope is completed or cancelled, all coroutines within that scope are automatically cancelled as well, preventing memory leaks, and ensuring that coroutines do not run indefinitely.

Structured concurrency helps prevent errors like orphaned tasks or incomplete processes by providing clear lifecycle boundaries for coroutines. By using scopes, you can ensure that coroutines run within defined limits, and that their completion or failure is handled correctly.

Coroutine Scopes

A coroutine scope controls the lifecycle of a coroutine. The most common scopes include:

- **`GlobalScope`:** A global, application-wide scope that is often used for long-running coroutines that are independent of the application lifecycle. However, using GlobalScope should be done with caution, as it does not tie coroutines to any specific lifecycle.
- **`CoroutineScope`:** A custom scope that is usually tied to a specific component's lifecycle, such as a UI element or a background worker in an Android app. You can define and manage your own coroutine scope, ensuring that all coroutines within that scope are properly managed.
- **`runBlocking` Scope:** This is a blocking scope that is often used in testing or simple programs. It blocks the current thread, while the coroutines inside it are running.

Structured Concurrency in Action

```
fun main() = runBlocking {
    launch {
        delay(500L)
        println("Task 1 completed")
    }

    launch {
        delay(1000L)
```

```
            println("Task 2 completed")
        }

        println("Both tasks launched")
    }
```

In this example:

a. Two coroutines are launched in the runBlocking scope.

b. The first coroutine is delayed for 500 milliseconds, and the second is delayed for 1 second. Both are launched simultaneously within the same scope.

c. The scope (**`runBlocking`**) ensures that the main thread waits until both coroutines have completed before exiting.

Coroutine Contexts and Dispatchers

Coroutine scopes can be run on different dispatchers to control the thread on which they execute. Kotlin provides several dispatchers for different types of tasks:

- **`Dispatchers.Default`**: Used for CPU-intensive tasks.
- **`Dispatchers.IO`**: Used for I/O operations such as reading/writing files or network requests.
- **`Dispatchers.Main`**: Used for updating the UI, especially in Android applications.

Example of Using Dispatchers:

```
fun main() = runBlocking {
    launch(Dispatchers.IO) {
        println("Running on IO Dispatcher")
        delay(1000L)
        println("Task completed on IO Dispatcher")
    }
}
```

In this example, the coroutine is launched on the Dispatchers.IO context, which is optimized for I/O-bound tasks. By using the appropriate dispatcher, you can improve the performance and efficiency of your application.

Watch Out: Improper use of coroutines–such as launching too many, forgetting to cancel them, or using the wrong dispatcher (example, doing blocking work on Dispatchers.Main)–can lead to memory leaks, UI freezes, or thread exhaustion. Always structure coroutine usage carefully, especially in long-lived or UI-bound components.

Kotlin's Advanced Type System

Kotlin's advanced type system provides features that improve code safety, flexibility, and readability. It offers developers the ability to write more reusable and expressive code, allowing for better management of complex types. Two key aspects of Kotlin's type system that are particularly powerful are Generics and Variance as well as Sealed and Data Classes. These features enable developers to handle a variety of use cases, from type safety to creating classes that model specific, fixed states.

Generics and Variance

Generics allow you to write flexible and reusable code by letting your classes, interfaces, and functions work with any type, while still ensuring type safety at compile time. Generics are used extensively in Kotlin collections (such as `List<T>`, `Set<T>`, and `Map<K, V>`), making them an essential tool for any Kotlin developer.

Generics Basics

A generic class or function can operate on different types, without sacrificing type safety. By using generics, you can avoid code duplication, and ensure that your code works for a variety of types.

Example of a Generic Class:

```
class Box<T>(val value: T) {
    fun getValue(): T = value
}

fun main() {
    val intBox = Box(123)
    val stringBox = Box("Hello Kotlin")

    println(intBox.getValue())  // Outputs: 123
    println(stringBox.getValue())  // Outputs: Hello Kotlin
}
```

In this example:

a. The class **Box** is generic, and can hold any type T.

b. This flexibility allows us to create a **Box<Int>** and **Box<String>**, without code duplication.

Variance in Generics

Kotlin provides variance annotations (**in**, **out**) to control how types relate to each other in a hierarchy. Variance ensures that generic types behave predictably in different situations, particularly when dealing with subtype relationships.

- **Covariance (out keyword):** Used when a generic class can only produce values of type T. Covariant types are said to *"preserve the subtype relationship,"* meaning that if **Dog** is a subclass of **Animal**, then **Box<Dog>** can be used wherever **Box<Animal>** is expected.

```
class Box<out T>(val value: T) {
    fun getValue(): T = value
}

fun handleAnimalBox(animalBox: Box<Animal>) {
    println(animalBox.getValue())
}

fun main() {
    val dogBox = Box(Dog())
    handleAnimalBox(dogBox)  // Outputs: Dog instance
}
```

- **Contravariance (in keyword):** Used when a generic class can only consume values of type T. Contravariant types reverse the subtype relationship, meaning that if Dog is a subclass of Animal, then **Box<Animal>** can be used wherever **Box<Dog>** is expected.

```
class Box<in T> {
    fun setValue(value: T) { /* Store value */}
}

fun handleDogBox(dogBox: Box<Dog>) {
    // Box<Animal> can be used as Box<Dog>
}

fun main() {
    val animalBox = Box<Animal>()
    handleDogBox(animalBox)
}
```

In this example:

a. out allows **Box<Dog>** to be used in a **Box<Animal>**, maintaining type safety when producing values.

b. in allows **Box<Animal>** to be used in place of **Box<Dog>**, maintaining type safety when consuming values.

Invariant (No Variance): When neither in nor out is used, the generic type is invariant, meaning that **Box<Dog>** is not a subtype or supertype of **Box<Animal>**, even if **Dog** is a subclass of Animal.

Sealed and Data Classes

Sealed classes and data classes are two special types of classes in Kotlin that are widely used for different purposes–sealed classes help model restricted hierarchies, while data classes are used for storing immutable data with useful utility methods.

Sealed Classes

A **sealed** class is used to represent a restricted class hierarchy, where a class can have a fixed set of subclasses. Sealed classes are particularly useful for representing finite states or choices, making them perfect for handling scenarios like modeling responses, states in a user interface, or results in a computation.

Sealed classes ensure that all possible subclasses are known at compile time, which allows Kotlin to enforce exhaustive expressions, ensuring that all cases are handled.

Example of Sealed Class:

```
sealed class Result {
   data class Success(val data: String) : Result()
   data class Failure(val error: Throwable) : Result()
}

fun handleResult(result: Result) {
   when (result) {
      is Result.Success -> println("Success: ${result.data}")
      is Result.Failure -> println("Error: ${result.error.message}")
   }
}

fun main() {
   val success = Result.Success("Operation completed")
   val failure = Result.Failure(Exception("Something went wrong"))

   handleResult(success)  // Outputs: Success: Operation completed
   handleResult(failure)  // Outputs: Error: Something went wrong
}
```

In this example:

a. The Result sealed class has two possible states: Success and Failure, each represented by a data class.

b. The when expression ensures that all cases of Result are handled at compile time.

Benefits of Sealed Classes:

- **Exhaustive when Statements:** The Kotlin compiler ensures that all possible subclasses are covered in a when expression, making the code more reliable.
- **Type Safety:** By restricting the hierarchy, sealed classes provide a clear and safe way to model states or events.
- **Better Readability:** Sealed classes clearly define the limited options available, improving code readability.

Data Classes

Data classes in Kotlin are used for classes that are primarily meant to hold data. Kotlin generates several useful methods for data classes automatically, such as **`equals()`**, **`hashCode()`**, **`toString()`**, and **`copy()`**, which makes working with immutable data simpler and more efficient.

Defining a Data Class:

```
data class User(val name: String, val age: Int)

fun main() {
    val user = User("John", 25)
    println(user)  // Outputs: User(name=John, age=25)

    val updatedUser = user.copy(age = 26)
    println(updatedUser)  // Outputs: User(name=John, age=26)
}
```

In this example:

a. The **`User`** class is a data class with two properties, name and age.

b. The **`copy()`** function allows you to create a new instance of **`User`** by copying the original data, and updating only the specified fields.

Features of Data Classes:

- **Automatic Generation of Utility Methods: `equals()`, `hashCode()`**, and **`toString()`** are generated automatically.
- **`copy()` Function:** Enables easy creation of new instances with modified properties.
- **Destructuring:** Data classes support destructuring declarations, allowing you to break down an object into its individual components easily.

Example of Destructuring:

```
val (name, age) = user
println("Name: $name, Age: $age")  // Outputs: Name: John, Age: 25
```

Interoperability and Advanced Error Handling

One of Kotlin's strongest features is its full interoperability with Java, which allows Kotlin developers to easily integrate Kotlin code with the existing Java codebases, making the transition from Java to Kotlin seamless. Kotlin's ability to work with Java classes, interfaces, and methods, while maintaining Kotlin's concise syntax and null-safety features, offers significant benefits.

Additionally, advanced error handling in Kotlin enables you to manage exceptions in a more robust and expressive way. Thus, by leveraging custom exceptions and the Result type, you can ensure cleaner and more controlled error-handling mechanisms.

In this section, we will explore Working with Java Code and Custom Exceptions, and the Result Type in Kotlin.

Working with Java Code

Kotlin's design is heavily influenced by its interoperability with Java. This means that Kotlin can call Java code, and Java can call Kotlin code with minimal effort. This is especially useful for projects with large Java codebases where adopting Kotlin gradually is desirable.

Calling Java Code from Kotlin

Kotlin code can directly call Java classes, methods, and use Java libraries. Kotlin retains its strong type system and null-safety mechanisms, even when interacting with Java.

Example: Calling Java Methods from Kotlin

Consider a simple Java class:

```
// Java Class
public class Calculator {
    public int add(int a, int b) {
        return a + b;
    }
}
```

You can use this Java class in Kotlin, without any additional setup:

```
fun main() {
    val calculator = Calculator()
    val result = calculator.add(5, 10)
```

```
        println("Result: $result")  // Outputs: Result: 15
    }
```

In this example:

a. The Java class **Calculator** is directly instantiated and used in Kotlin.

b. Kotlin's syntax remains concise, and there is no need for extra configuration to call Java methods.

Null Safety with Java Interoperability

One of Kotlin's core features is its null-safety, which helps prevent **NullPointerException** errors. However, Java does not have built-in null-safety, so when calling Java methods, Kotlin marks Java types as platform types–a type that could be nullable or non-nullable. Kotlin leaves it up to the developer to handle nullability carefully when interacting with Java.

Example: Handling Platform Types

Suppose you have a Java method that might return null:

```
public class UserManager {
    public String getUserName() {
        return null;  // Could return null
    }
}
```

In Kotlin, you must handle the potential null value:

```
fun main() {
    val userManager = UserManager()
    val userName: String? = userManager.userName  // Kotlin treats
it as a nullable String
    println(userName?.length ?: "Unknown")  // Safe call to avoid
NullPointerException
}
```

In this case:

a. Kotlin treats the return type from the Java method as a nullable **String?**.

b. The safe call (**?.**) and Elvis operator (**?:**) ensure that null is handled safely.

Calling Kotlin from Java

Calling Kotlin code from Java is straightforward, but there are some Kotlin-specific features that you need to be aware of, such as default arguments and top-level functions.

Example: Kotlin Code with Default Arguments

```
// Kotlin Code
class Calculator {
   @JvmOverloads
   fun add(a: Int, b: Int = 10): Int {
       return a + b
   }
}
```

The **@JvmOverloads** annotation allows Java to call Kotlin functions with default parameters:

```
// Java Code
public class Main {
   public static void main(String[] args) {
       Calculator calculator = new Calculator();
       System.out.println(calculator.add(5));  // Outputs: 15
   }
}
```

Without **@JvmOverloads**, Java would not be able to call the **add()** method with just one argument, as Java does not support default arguments in the same way Kotlin does.

Custom Exceptions and the Result Type

Kotlin provides powerful tools for managing exceptions and handling errors gracefully. While Kotlin supports the same exception-handling mechanisms as Java, such as try-catch blocks and throw expressions, it also introduces the Result type, and allows developers to define custom exceptions for more specific error scenarios.

Custom Exceptions

Just like in Java, Kotlin allows you to create custom exceptions by extending the Exception class. Custom exceptions provide a clear way to handle application-specific errors, making your error-handling code more meaningful and tailored to your domain.

Example of a Custom Exception:

```
class InvalidUserInputException(message: String) : Exception
(message)

fun getUserAge(age: Int) {
   if (age < 0) {
       throw InvalidUserInputException("Age cannot be negative")
   }
```

```
    println("User age is $age")
}

fun main() {
    try {
        getUserAge(-5)
    } catch (e: InvalidUserInputException) {
        println("Error: ${e.message}")  // Outputs: Error: Age
cannot be negative
    }
}
```

In this example:

a. The **InvalidUserInputException** is a custom exception that extends the **Exception** class.

b. It is thrown when invalid user input is encountered (negative age in this case), and the error is caught and handled in the try-catch block.

Result Type

The **Result** type is a built-in Kotlin feature that allows you to encapsulate the result of an operation, which could either be a success or a failure. This type is especially useful for avoiding exceptions, and working with predictable, functional error handling. The **Result** type is preferred in situations where throwing exceptions might not be the most efficient or clean approach.

Example of Using Result Type:

```
fun divide(a: Int, b: Int): Result<Int> {
    return if (b == 0) {
        Result.failure(ArithmeticException("Cannot divide by
zero"))
    } else {
        Result.success(a / b)
    }
}

fun main() {
    val result = divide(10, 0)

    result.fold(
        onSuccess = { value -> println("Result: $value") },
        onFailure = { error -> println("Error: ${error.message}")
}
    )
}
```

In this example:

a. The **`divide()`** function returns a Result type, which can either be a successful division or a failure due to dividing by zero.

b. The **`fold()`** function is used to handle both success and failure cases in a clean and predictable manner.

Advantages of the Result Type

- **Predictable Handling of Errors:** By returning a **`Result`** type, the function avoids throwing exceptions, and callers can handle success or failure in a controlled manner.
- **Functional Programming Approach:** The **`Result`** type integrates well with Kotlin's functional programming style, allowing you to handle results with map, flatMap, and fold, without relying on exceptions.
- **Avoids Uncaught Exceptions:** With **`Result`**, you do not need to worry about uncaught exceptions breaking your code flow, as all error handling is localized within the result.

Practical Applications and Optimization

Building efficient, scalable applications requires not just writing good code but also ensuring that it performs optimally, and adheres to the best practices. In Kotlin, you can leverage the language's concise syntax, powerful type system, and coroutine-based concurrency to create highly efficient applications. However, understanding how to optimize your Kotlin code and following established best practices is essential for building maintainable, high-performance applications.

In this section, we will discuss Building and Optimizing Kotlin Applications, and explore the Best Practices and Real-World Examples that illustrate how Kotlin can be used to build modern, efficient software.

Building and Optimizing Kotlin Applications

Kotlin provides several features and tools that make building high-performance applications straightforward. However, it is important to apply optimization techniques to ensure that your applications run efficiently, particularly in resource-constrained environments such as mobile or server-side applications.

Optimizing Performance with Kotlin

- **Use Coroutines for Asynchronous Tasks:** One of the most powerful features of Kotlin is coroutines which allow you to perform non-blocking operations efficiently. By using coroutines instead of traditional threads, you can handle a large number of concurrent tasks, without the overhead of thread management.

When building an application, especially in Android development or server-side applications using Ktor or Spring Boot, using coroutines can significantly enhance performancc by reducing the time spent waiting for I/O-bound tasks (like network requests or database operations).

Example of Optimizing Network Requests with Coroutines:

```
suspend fun fetchUserData(): User {
    return withContext(Dispatchers.IO) {
        // Simulate a network request or database operation
        delay(1000L)
        User("John Doe", 28)
    }
}
```

In this example:

a. The **`fetchUserData`** function performs an I/O-bound operation in a background thread using coroutines and the **`Dispatchers.IO`** context.

b. This ensures that the main thread remains free for other tasks, improving the overall performance.

- **Minimize Object Creation:** Kotlin's data classes and immutable types help reduce the overhead of object creation. However, excessive creation of objects in performance-critical areas, such as in loops or during frequently called methods, can lead to unnecessary memory allocation and garbage collection.

  Where possible, reuse existing objects or use Kotlin's lazy initialization to defer object creation until it is needed.

Example of Using Lazy Initialization:

```
val expensiveObject: ExpensiveClass by lazy {
    ExpensiveClass()
}
```

In this example:

a. The **`expensiveObject`** will only be created when it is first accessed, avoiding unnecessary memory allocation during application startup.

- **Use Inline Functions for Higher-Order Functions:** Kotlin's inline functions help avoid the overhead associated with higher-order functions. Normally, higher-order functions involve creating additional objects, such as function objects or lambda expressions, which can lead to performance degradation.

Inline functions, however, eliminate this overhead by inserting the function code directly at the call site.

Example of Inline Function:

```
inline fun performOperation(a: Int, b: Int, operation: (Int, Int)
-> Int): Int {
    return operation(a, b)
}
```

Here, **performOperation** is marked as inline, meaning the lambda passed as operation will be inlined, avoiding the cost of creating function objects.

- **Leverage Kotlin's Collections API Efficiently:** Kotlin's standard library provides a rich set of utilities for working with collections, such as map, filter, and reduce. While these functions are highly expressive, it is important to avoid chaining too many of these operations in performance-critical code, as they can lead to the creation of temporary collections.

  For large datasets or performance-sensitive operations, consider using Kotlin's sequence API, which processes elements lazily to avoid the overhead of creating intermediate collections.

Example of Using Sequences for Efficient Collection Processing:

```
val numbers = listOf(1, 2, 3, 4, 5)
val result = numbers.asSequence()
    .map { it * it }
    .filter { it > 10 }
    .toList()
```

In this example:

a. The **asSequence()** function transforms the list into a sequence, allowing operations like map and filter to be performed lazily, avoiding the creation of intermediate collections.

- **Optimize Memory Usage with Data Classes:** Data classes in Kotlin are a great way to manage and store immutable data, but they can also help reduce boilerplate and memory usage by generating optimized **equals()**, **hashCode()**, **toString()**, and **copy()** methods.

  When working with large datasets or collections of objects, using data classes can ensure that your application efficiently handles comparison and storage of objects.

Example of Data Class Optimization:

```
data class User(val name: String, val age: Int)
```

Data classes automatically handle memory-efficient storage and easy-to-use comparison as well as copying functions.

Best Practices and Real-World Examples

Thus, to build maintainable, scalable, and efficient applications in Kotlin, it is vital to follow the best practices that ensure code quality, performance, and readability. Here are some key best practices and real-world examples of Kotlin usage in modern application development.

Best Practices for Kotlin Development

- **Favor Immutability**
  - Always prefer immutable data structures (`val` over `var`). Immutability ensures that once a value is assigned, it cannot be changed, making code easier to reason about and less prone to bugs.
  - Kotlin's type system encourages immutability through val declarations, data classes, and read-only collections.
- **Use Extension Functions for Clean Code**
  - Extension functions allow you to add new functionality to the existing classes, without modifying their source code. Use them to encapsulate utility methods, making your code cleaner and more modular.

Example of Extension Function:

```
fun String.isPalindrome(): Boolean {
    return this == this.reversed()
}

fun main() {
    val word = "madam"
    println(word.isPalindrome())  // Outputs: true
}
```

- **Handle Null Safety Explicitly:** Kotlin's null-safety features are one of its key strengths. Always use the appropriate null-safety operators (`?.`, `?:`, `!!`, and `let`) to prevent NullPointerException errors. Avoid using the non-null assertion (`!!`) unless absolutely necessary, as it can lead to unexpected crashes.

  Example of Safe Call Operator:

```
val userName: String? = null
println(userName?.toUpperCase() ?: "Unknown User")  // Outputs:
Unknown User
```

- **Adopt Functional Programming Practices:** Kotlin's support for functional programming allows you to write concise, expressive, and bug-free code by using higher-order functions, lambdas, and immutability. Avoid using imperative loops where functional alternatives (like map, filter, reduce) are available.

Example of Functional Approach:

```
val numbers = listOf(1, 2, 3, 4, 5)
val evenSquares = numbers.filter { it % 2 == 0 }.map { it * it }
```

This code is concise, expressive, and leverages Kotlin's functional programming style.

- **Leverage Kotlin's Coroutine Scope and Structured Concurrency:** Always ensure that coroutines are managed within appropriate scopes to avoid memory leaks and unpredictable behavior. Use GlobalScope sparingly, and prefer using structured concurrency with CoroutineScope or Android's lifecycle-aware scopes for better resource management.

Example of Coroutine Scope:

```
class MyActivity : AppCompatActivity(), CoroutineScope {
   private val job = Job()

   override val coroutineContext: CoroutineContext
      get() = Dispatchers.Main + job

   override fun onDestroy() {
      super.onDestroy()
      job.cancel()  // Cancel all coroutines when the activity
is destroyed
   }
}
```

Real-World Examples of Kotlin Applications

In this section, we explore how Kotlin is being leveraged in real-world scenarios across various domains. From powering popular Android applications to serving as the backbone of high-performance backend systems, Kotlin has proven its versatility and robustness. The following examples highlight practical implementations of Kotlin in both mobile and server-side development, showcasing how its modern features and ecosystem enable developers to build efficient, scalable, and maintainable applications across platforms.

Android Development with Kotlin

Thus, Kotlin is now the preferred language for Android development. Major apps such as Pinterest, Trello, and Evernote have adopted Kotlin for their mobile development due to its concise syntax, null-safety, and full Android Studio support.

Example: Using coroutines to handle network requests and UI updates asynchronously in an Android app, ensure smooth user interactions.

Backend Development with Ktor

Kotlin's lightweight server-side framework, Ktor enables developers to build scalable and asynchronous web applications. By leveraging Kotlin's coroutines, Ktor provides a non-blocking architecture, making it suitable for building high-performance APIs.

Example: Building a REST API with Ktor that handles multiple client requests concurrently, while maintaining efficient resource usage.

Conclusion

Hence, this chapter provided a comprehensive understanding of Kotlin's advanced features, empowering developers to write high-performance, maintainable, and scalable applications. By mastering advanced object-oriented techniques, developers can create reusable, modular, and scalable systems, while functional programming approaches allow for more concise and expressive code. The integration of Kotlin coroutines simplifies asynchronous programming, reducing complexity and enhancing performance.

Furthermore, Kotlin's advanced type system–including generics, sealed classes, and data classes–provides robust tools for type safety and handling complex data structures. The chapter also emphasizes interoperability with Java and introduces custom exception handling through Kotlin's Result type, ensuring that developers can handle errors effectively, while maintaining compatibility with existing Java codebases.

As we conclude this chapter, you are now equipped with the tools to write advanced Kotlin code for sophisticated applications.

In the next chapter, "*Understanding Kotlin Multiplatform*", we will explore Kotlin's capability to write code that can run on multiple platforms, such as Android, iOS, web, and desktop. This approach will allow you to share common code across platforms, improving efficiency, and reducing the development time. So, let us dive into the world of Kotlin Multiplatform, and learn how to build truly cross-platform applications!

CHAPTER 4

Understanding Kotlin Multiplatform

Introduction

In this chapter, we will delve into **Kotlin Multiplatform**, an innovative approach that enables developers to write shared code for multiple platforms such as Android, iOS, Web, and Desktop. We will cover the **fundamentals of Kotlin Multiplatform architecture**, including how to structure projects to maximize code reuse, while accommodating platform-specific needs.

Structure

In this chapter, we will cover the following topics:

- Introduction to Kotlin Multiplatform
    - Overview and Key-Concepts
    - Benefits and Challenges of Adopting a Multiplatform Strategy
- Project Structure and Architecture
    - Understanding Shared and Platform-Specific Code
    - Project Structure Breakdown
- Setting Up a Multiplatform Project
    - Development Environment Setup
    - Creating a Multiplatform Project in IntelliJ IDEA
    - Gradle Configuration for Multiplatform Projects
- Code Sharing across Platforms
    - Writing Shared Code in the Common Module
    - Handling Platform-Specific Code with Expect/Actual Mechanism
    - Sharing Common Libraries across Platforms

  - Handling Platform-Specific Implementations
  - Best Practices for Code Sharing
- Tools and Libraries for Multiplatform Development
  - Development Tools
  - Popular Multiplatform Libraries
  - Additional Tools for Multiplatform Development
  - Best Practices for Using Multiplatform Libraries
- Practical Implementation

Introduction to Kotlin Multiplatform

Kotlin Multiplatform is a revolutionary approach to software development that enables developers to write shared code for different platforms, including Android, iOS, Web, and Desktop. The core idea behind Kotlin Multiplatform is to maximize code reuse across platforms, while allowing flexibility for platform-specific implementations where necessary.

Overview and Key Concepts

Kotlin Multiplatform allows developers to write the code once, and share it across various platforms. By separating platform-specific and shared logic, it enables a clear distinction between the parts of the codebase that can be reused, and those that are platform-specific.

For example, business logic, data models, and algorithms can often be shared across platforms, while UI components and platform-specific APIs (such as camera access or file storage) may need custom implementations. The ability to target multiple platforms from a single codebase significantly reduces code duplication and maintenance efforts.

Unlike traditional cross-platform UI frameworks such as Flutter or React Native, Kotlin Multiplatform takes a different approach by focusing on sharing business logic and core code, while preserving the native UI layer for each platform. This enables developers to deliver a seamless user experience that feels fully native, without compromising on development efficiency.

Key Concepts

- **Shared Code and Platform-Specific Code:** Kotlin Multiplatform uses the concept of expect/actual to separate shared logic from platform-specific code. Developers write shared logic in a common module and implement platform-specific code in platform modules.

- **`expect` keyword:** Declares a function or class that will have platform-specific implementations.
- **`actual` keyword:** Defines platform-specific implementations of those expected declarations.

- **Supported Platforms**: Kotlin Multiplatform currently supports a wide range of platforms:
  - **Mobile**: Android and iOS.
  - **Web**: Using Kotlin/JS.
  - **Desktop**: Using Kotlin/Native for Windows, macOS, and Linux.
  - **Backend**: JVM for server-side development.

  Each of these platforms can share common code, while enabling native functionality where needed.

- **Advantages of Kotlin Multiplatform:**
  - **Code Reusability:** Write once, run anywhere. Business logic, data handling, and network calls can be written in a common module, and shared across platforms.
  - **Consistency Across Platforms:** A single codebase ensures that functionality is consistent across all platforms.
  - **Efficient Development:** Kotlin Multiplatform reduces the need for duplicating efforts across different platforms, speeding up development, and reducing maintenance.
  - **Interoperability:** Kotlin's seamless interoperability with Java makes it easy to integrate the existing libraries and frameworks in JVM-based **projects.**

- **Challenges of Kotlin Multiplatform:**
  - **Learning Curve:** The concept of writing platform-agnostic code, while accounting for platform-specific nuances can take time to master.
  - **Library Support:** While Kotlin Multiplatform has a growing ecosystem, not all popular libraries support it natively, requiring developers to adapt or find alternatives.
  - **Performance Considerations:** Although Kotlin Multiplatform aims to maximize performance, certain platform-specific optimizations may require additional attention to ensure native performance levels.

With this overview, developers can understand why Kotlin Multiplatform is gaining traction in the industry, and how it can transform their development workflow. Next, we will cover Project Structure and Architecture in Kotlin Multiplatform to explore how to organize the shared and platform-specific code efficiently.

Benefits and Challenges of Adopting a Multiplatform Strategy

Kotlin Multiplatform offers a powerful and flexible approach for developing applications that run on multiple platforms, such as Android, iOS, Web, and Desktop, using a shared codebase. However, like any development strategy, it comes with both benefits and challenges. Hence, understanding these pros and cons is crucial for making an informed decision about whether to adopt a multiplatform strategy for your project.

Benefits of a Multiplatform Strategy

- **Code Reusability:** One of the most significant advantages of adopting a multiplatform strategy is the ability to reuse code across multiple platforms. Instead of writing separate business logic for Android, iOS, Web, and other platforms, you can share a common codebase that handles non-UI logic like data processing, networking, and validation. This leads to:
    - Reduced duplication of efforts.
    - Easier maintenance, since bugs and improvements can be addressed in one place.
    - Faster development cycles, as much of the logic only needs to be written once.
- **Consistency across Platforms:** By sharing business logic and other core components, you ensure that the behavior of your app remains consistent across platforms. This consistency is particularly important in applications where maintaining the same user experience and functionality across different devices is critical. Code reuse also minimizes discrepancies that could arise from implementing similar logic multiple times in different languages.
- **Reduced Development and Maintenance Costs:** With a shared codebase, developers can focus more on writing core functionality, rather than duplicating efforts for each platform. This can lead to:
    - **Lower development costs:** Fewer resources are needed to build and maintain the application across platforms.
    - **Lower maintenance costs:** Fixes and updates can be made centrally in the shared code, reducing the need to fix the same issue multiple times.

- **Faster Time to Market:** Since you can share significant portions of the codebase, the development process is generally faster. Teams can focus on building the unique parts of the application (such as platform-specific UI) while the shared code is reused across platforms. This is particularly useful for startups and projects with tight deadlines, where getting to market quickly is a priority.
- **Seamless Integration with Native Code:** Kotlin Multiplatform is designed to interoperate seamlessly with the native code, allowing developers to call platform-specific APIs (such as Android's Jetpack Compose or iOS's SwiftUI) while sharing the business logic. This flexibility ensures that you do not have to compromise on using native features or optimizing performance.
- **Community and Ecosystem Support:** Kotlin Multiplatform has a rapidly growing ecosystem with tools, libraries, and community support. JetBrains continues to improve and update the platform, and many popular libraries (like Ktor for networking and SQLDelight for databases) already support multiplatform development. This helps developers build multiplatform applications using familiar tools and frameworks.

Challenges of a Multiplatform Strategy

- **Learning Curve:** While Kotlin Multiplatform simplifies the development of cross-platform applications, there is still a learning curve, particularly for developers who are new to Kotlin or to multiplatform strategies. Understanding how to structure projects, manage shared and platform-specific code, and effectively use the expect/actual mechanism can take time to master.
- **Limited UI Code Sharing:** While you can share most of the business logic, UI code is typically platform-specific. This means developers need to write and maintain separate UIs for each platform (for example, Jetpack Compose for Android, SwiftUI for iOS). Although the business logic can be shared, the platform-specific UI work can still add to the development effort.
    - **Platform-Specific Nuances:** Even with shared code, there will always be platform-specific nuances that need to be addressed. For example, managing different lifecycle events, handling platform-specific user interactions, or accessing native APIs requires knowledge of each platform's unique behavior. These differences can sometimes increase the complexity of the project, as platform-specific edge cases need to be handled individually.
    - **Library Support:** While the Kotlin Multiplatform ecosystem is growing rapidly, not all third-party libraries support multiplatform development yet. This can limit your options, particularly if you are reliant on libraries that are platform-specific. In such cases, you may need to write or find workarounds, which could increase development complexity.

  - **Build Configuration Complexity:** Multiplatform projects typically require more complex build configurations than single-platform projects. Managing dependencies, platform-specific configurations, and ensuring that builds work correctly across all platforms can be challenging. Developers need to be familiar with Gradle and platform-specific build tools (like Xcode for iOS) to manage these aspects effectively.
  - **Performance Considerations:** While Kotlin Multiplatform aims to deliver native performance, certain platform-specific optimizations may still be necessary to achieve optimal performance. Developers may need to carefully tune their platform-specific implementations or use platform-specific libraries to ensure that the application runs efficiently on each platform. Additionally, some shared code may not perform as well as the purely native code in certain scenarios, especially if native APIs are heavily involved.

Summary

Adopting a multiplatform strategy with Kotlin Multiplatform offers significant benefits, such as increased code reusability, faster development, and lower costs. However, it also comes with challenges, particularly in terms of managing platform-specific code, navigating the learning curve, and dealing with platform-specific nuances. For many teams, the advantages of shared business logic outweigh the complexities, but it is essential to carefully evaluate whether Kotlin Multiplatform aligns with the specific goals and constraints of your project.

Thus, by weighing the benefits and challenges, development teams can make an informed decision about whether a multiplatform strategy is right for their project.

Project Structure and Architecture

Kotlin Multiplatform introduces a flexible project architecture that allows developers to maximize code reuse, while maintaining the flexibility to implement platform-specific functionality. Understanding how to structure a Kotlin Multiplatform project is key to leveraging its full potential. In this section, we will cover the architecture of a Kotlin Multiplatform project, and how to organize code between shared and platform-specific modules.

Understanding Shared and Platform-Specific Code

In a typical Kotlin Multiplatform project, the codebase is divided into two main types:

- **Common (Shared) Code:** This contains platform-agnostic code that can be reused across multiple platforms. Typically, this includes business logic, data handling, algorithms, and networking logic. The shared code is written in the common module, which is platform-independent and does not directly access platform-specific APIs.

- **Platform-Specific Code:** This part of the project contains code that is specific to a particular platform, such as Android, iOS, Web, or Desktop. Examples include code that interacts with the camera, location services, or user interface (UI) frameworks such as Jetpack Compose for Android or SwiftUI for iOS. Platform-specific code is housed in platform modules.

The ability to write common logic, and separate platform-specific logic allows Kotlin Multiplatform projects to share most of the code, while still accessing native capabilities when required.

Project Structure Breakdown

A Kotlin Multiplatform project typically follows a hierarchical structure where:

- **Common Module:** Contains shared code that runs on all platforms. It defines the business logic, models, utility functions, and any other logic that can be reused across platforms.
- **Platform Modules:** These modules contain code that is specific to each platform. For instance, Android and iOS may need to implement different ways to access the file system or network capabilities.

Here is a breakdown of the common structure:

```
project-root/
├── commonMain/                 # Shared code for all platforms
│   ├── kotlin/                 # Common Kotlin code
│   └── resources/              # Shared resources (optional)
├── androidMain/                # Android-specific code
│   └── kotlin/                 # Kotlin code targeting Android
├── iosMain/                    # iOS-specific code
│   └── kotlin/                 # Kotlin code targeting iOS
├── webMain/                    # Web-specific code (optional)
│   └── kotlin/                 # Kotlin code targeting JS
├── desktopMain/                # Desktop-specific code (optional)
│   └── kotlin/                 # Kotlin code targeting Native (macOS,
Linux, Windows)
└── build.gradle.kts            # Build configuration
```

Organizing Common and Platform Modules

Each Kotlin Multiplatform project consists of a commonMain module that holds shared code, and specific modules such as **`androidMain`**, **`iosMain`**, **`webMain`**, and **`desktopMain`** for platform-specific code.

- **Common Module (commonMain):** This module contains the shared logic that can be used across all platforms. You typically define classes, functions, data models, and core logic here. The common module avoids direct references to platform APIs, and instead uses expect/actual declarations to define platform-specific behavior.

- **Platform Modules (androidMain, iosMain, and so on):** These modules contain the actual implementations of the code that was declared using the expect keyword in the common module. For example, if the common module defines an expected function to retrieve a file, the platform module would provide the actual implementation of that function for Android, iOS, Web, and many more.

Expect/Actual Mechanism

Kotlin Multiplatform uses the expect/actual mechanism to handle platform-specific code. This allows developers to write a common logic, while deferring platform-specific functionality to individual platform modules.

- **expect:** Declares a function or a class in the common module, indicating that the actual implementation will be provided in platform-specific modules.
- **actual:** Provides the platform-specific implementation for the expected declaration.

Example:

In the common module:

```
// commonMain
expect fun getPlatformName(): String

In the Android-specific module:
// androidMain
actual fun getPlatformName(): String {
   return "Android"
}

In the iOS-specific module:

// iosMain
actual fun getPlatformName(): String {
   return "iOS"
}
```

This expect/actual mechanism ensures that the platform-specific logic can be neatly abstracted, while still allowing shared code to call those platform-specific functions when necessary.

Modularizing the Codebase

Modularization is crucial in Kotlin Multiplatform projects to ensure clean separation of concerns and easy maintenance. The key benefits of modularization include:

- **Encapsulation:** Keep platform-specific code isolated, while promoting reusability of the shared logic.
- **Scalability:** Makes the codebase easier to scale and manage, especially in larger projects.
- **Maintenance:** Reduces the maintenance burden by localizing changes to specific modules.

Thus, a well-organized Kotlin Multiplatform project minimizes platform dependencies in the shared code, keeps platform-specific functionality modular, and promotes code reuse across the different platforms.

Therefore, with a clear understanding of the project structure, and how shared and platform-specific modules are organized, the next step is to dive into Setting Up a Multiplatform Project, and learn how to configure the project environment.

Setting Up a Multiplatform Project

Setting up a Kotlin Multiplatform project involves configuring the development environment, and properly managing dependencies for the different platforms you plan to target. This section will guide you through setting up a basic Kotlin Multiplatform project using Gradle, configuring platform-specific modules, and managing dependencies effectively.

Development Environment Setup

Before creating a Kotlin Multiplatform project, ensure that you have the following tools installed:

- **IntelliJ IDEA or Android Studio:** Both of these IDEs support Kotlin Multiplatform development. IntelliJ IDEA is preferred if you are focusing on non-Android platforms as well.
- **Kotlin Multiplatform Plugin:** Install the Kotlin plugin in IntelliJ IDEA or Android Studio. This enables support for Kotlin/Native, Kotlin/JS, and Kotlin Multiplatform development.

Creating a Multiplatform Project in IntelliJ IDEA

You can create a Kotlin Multiplatform project, either from scratch or by using the project templates provided by IntelliJ IDEA or Android Studio.

1. Open IntelliJ IDEA, and select New Project.
2. Choose Kotlin Multiplatform as the project type.
3. Select the platforms you wish to target (JVM, Android, iOS, JavaScript, and so on.). You can always add more platforms later.
4. Configure the project settings such as project name, location, and Gradle options.

Once the project is generated, the basic structure will include the common module for shared code and platform-specific modules for Android, iOS, and so on.

Gradle Configuration for Multiplatform Projects

Kotlin Multiplatform projects are managed using Gradle, which supports various plugins and tools to configure the project for each platform. Here is a basic Gradle setup for a Kotlin Multiplatform project:

In your **`build.gradle.kts`** file, the Kotlin Multiplatform plugin is applied, and platforms are configured for Android, iOS, and JVM targets:

```
plugins {
    kotlin("multiplatform") version "1.5.21"
}

kotlin {
    // Common code shared across all platforms
    sourceSets {
        val commonMain by getting {
            dependencies {
                // Add dependencies that are common across all
platforms
            }
        }

        // Android-specific code
        android()
        sourceSets["androidMain"].dependencies {
            implementation("androidx.core:core-ktx:1.6.0")
        }

        // iOS-specific code
        ios()
        sourceSets["iosMain"].dependencies {
            // Add iOS-specific dependencies here
        }
```

```
        // Optional: Add other targets like JS or Desktop
    }
}

android {
    // Standard Android configuration
    compileSdkVersion(30)
    defaultConfig {
        minSdkVersion(21)
        targetSdkVersion(30)
    }
}
```

Managing Dependencies across Platforms

Kotlin Multiplatform allows you to manage dependencies separately for each platform or share them across all platforms. Here is how you can handle different types of dependencies:

- **Common Dependencies:** Shared dependencies that are used in the common module for all platforms.
- **Platform-Specific Dependencies:** Libraries and frameworks that are only used by a specific platform (for example, Android, iOS, or JavaScript).

In the **commonMain** source set, you define dependencies that are available across all platforms. In platform-specific source sets like androidMain or iosMain, you define platform-specific dependencies.

Example of dependency setup:

```
kotlin {
    sourceSets {
        val commonMain by getting {
            dependencies {
                implementation("org.jetbrains.kotlin:kotlin-
stdlib-common")
                implementation("io.ktor:ktor-client-core:1.6.1")
// Shared networking library
            }
        }
        val androidMain by getting {
            dependencies {
                implementation("org.jetbrains.kotlin:kotlin-
stdlib")
                implementation("io.ktor:ktor-client-an-
droid:1.6.1")  // Android-specific Ktor client
```

```
                }
            }
            val iosMain by getting {
                dependencies {
                    implementation("io.ktor:ktor-client-ios:1.6.1")
    // iOS-specific Ktor client
                }
            }
        }
    }
```

This way, you can ensure that shared libraries such as **ktor-client-core** are available across all platforms, while platform-specific versions like **ktor-client-android** or **ktor-client-ios** handle specific implementations for Android and iOS.

Targeting Multiple Platforms

Kotlin Multiplatform supports various targets. Here is how to configure the most common targets:

- **Android Target:**

```
android {
    compileSdkVersion(30)
    defaultConfig {
        minSdkVersion(21)
        targetSdkVersion(30)
    }
}
```

- **iOS Target:**

```
ios {
    binaries {
        framework {
            baseName = "SharedCode"
        }
    }
}
```

- **JS and Web Target:**

```
js(IR) {
    browser {
        commonWebpackConfig {
            cssSupport.enabled = true
        }
    }
}
```

- **Desktop Target (Kotlin/Native):**

```
jvm("desktop") {
    // Add JVM desktop-specific configurations
}
```

Each platform target can be customized based on the platform-specific needs. For example, the Android target can specify **compileSdkVersion**, while the iOS target can configure binary formats such as **.framework** for integrating into an Xcode project.

Running and Testing Multiplatform Projects

Once your project is set up, you can run and test it for different platforms using the respective platform environments:

- **Android:** You can run the project directly on an Android device or emulator through Android Studio.
- **iOS:** The iOS module can be compiled to a framework that you can import into Xcode for testing on a simulator or a real device.
- **JS:** For Kotlin/JS, you can run and test web applications in a browser.
- **Desktop:** Kotlin/Native can be compiled and run as a desktop application.

Testing multiplatform code is similar to writing regular unit tests. You can add tests in the commonTest source set for shared logic, and platform-specific tests in the androidTest, iosTest, and so on.

With this setup, you are ready to start building your Kotlin Multiplatform project. The next section will cover Code Sharing across Platforms, explaining how to write reusable shared code and manage platform-specific implementations using Kotlin's **expect/actual** mechanism.

Code Sharing across Platforms

The essence of Kotlin Multiplatform lies in the ability to share as much code as possible across multiple platforms, while still retaining the flexibility to implement platform-specific functionality where needed. In this section, we will explore how to write shared code, handle platform-specific functionality using the expect/actual mechanism, and create reusable code that works across Android, iOS, Web, Desktop, and many more.

Writing Shared Code in the Common Module

The commonMain module in a Kotlin Multiplatform project is where shared business logic, data models, utilities, and core algorithms are placed. The code written in this module is platform-agnostic, which means it can be reused across different platforms without modification. Here are some typical components of the shared code:

- **Business Logic**: This includes shared functionalities such as authentication, data processing, and business rules that are the same across platforms.
- **Data Models:** Shared data classes, such as models representing users, products, or any other domain-specific entities.
- **Utility Functions:** Common utilities like string manipulation, date formatting, and error handling that are not platform-specific.

Example of Shared Code in the Common Module:

```
// Shared data model
data class User(val id: String, val name: String, val email: String)

// Shared business logic
fun validateEmail(email: String): Boolean {
   val emailPattern = "[a-zA-Z0-9._-]+@[a-z]+\\.+[a-z]+"
   return email.matches(emailPattern.toRegex())
}

// Shared utility function
fun formatDate(timestamp: Long): String {
   return java.text.SimpleDateFormat("yyyy-MM-dd").format(Date(timestamp))
}
```

In this example, the `User` data class, `validateEmail` function, and `formatDate` utility function are platform-agnostic, and can be reused across all platforms.

Handling Platform-Specific Code with `expect/actual` Mechanism

Kotlin Multiplatform provides the **`expect/actual`** mechanism to define platform-specific code, while keeping the shared code platform-independent. The **`expect`** keyword is used in the shared code to declare functions or classes whose implementations will differ based on the platform. The actual keyword is then used in the platform-specific modules to provide the platform-specific implementation of the expected code.

Example of `expect/actual` Usage

Step 1: Declare an expected function in the shared code (common module):

```
// commonMain
expect fun getPlatformName(): String
```

Step 2: Provide platform-specific implementations using actual in the platform-specific modules:

Android implementation:

```
// androidMain
actual fun getPlatformName(): String {
   return "Android"
}

iOS implementation:
// iosMain
actual fun getPlatformName(): String {
   return "iOS"
}
```

Step 3: Use the shared function in the common code, without worrying about the platform:

```
// commonMain
fun printPlatform() {
   println("Running on ${getPlatformName()}")
}
```

When the project is compiled, the correct platform-specific implementation will be used based on the target platform (Android, iOS, Web, and so on).

Sharing Common Libraries across Platforms

In many cases, you may want to use third-party libraries that are supported across multiple platforms. Kotlin Multiplatform has a growing ecosystem of libraries that can be used in the shared code.

Here are some examples of popular multiplatform libraries:

- **Ktor (Networking):** Provides an asynchronous HTTP client for making network requests. It has platform-specific implementations for Android, iOS, and other targets.
- **`kotlinx.serialization` (Serialization):** A multiplatform serialization library that allows you to serialize and deserialize objects across platforms.
- **SQLDelight (Database):** A Kotlin Multiplatform library for working with SQL databases like SQLite across multiple platforms.
- **Koin (Dependency Injection):** A lightweight, multiplatform library for dependency injection.

Example of Using Ktor in Shared Code:

```
// commonMain
import io.ktor.client.*
import io.ktor.client.request.*

val httpClient = HttpClient()

suspend fun fetchUserData(userId: String): User {
   return httpClient.get("https://api.example.com/user/$userId")
}
```

Ktor's **`HttpClient`** works across all platforms. However, platform-specific configurations (for example, Android or iOS) can be handled in the platform modules using actual implementations, if necessary.

Handling Platform-Specific Implementations

While much of your business logic can be shared, some features require platform-specific implementations. Kotlin Multiplatform enables you to define platform-specific implementations for APIs or functionality that cannot be shared. Examples of platform-specific functionality include:

- **User Interfaces:** Each platform has its own UI framework (for example, Jetpack Compose for Android, SwiftUI for iOS).
- **File Handling:** File system access may differ between Android and iOS.
- **Networking Configurations:** Networking libraries may require platform-specific setup (for example, handling SSL certificates differently on Android and iOS).

Example of Platform-Specific File Handling:

In the common module:

```
// commonMain
expect fun readFile(fileName: String): String
```

In the Android-specific module:

```
// androidMain
actual fun readFile(fileName: String): String {
   val file = File(context.filesDir, fileName)
   return file.readText()
}
```

In the iOS-specific module:

```
// iosMain
actual fun readFile(fileName: String): String {
```

```
    val path = NSBundle.mainBundle.pathForResource(fileName,
ofType: null)
    return NSString.stringWithContentsOfFile(path, encoding
= NSUTF8StringEncoding, error = null) as String
}
```

In this example, the **readFile** function is defined in the common module, but its actual implementation differs between Android and iOS.

Best Practices for Code Sharing

- **Maximize Shared Code:** Strive to share as much code as possible. Business logic, models, and utilities are often prime candidates for code sharing.
- **Use expect/actual Strategically:** Only use the **expect/actual** mechanism for code that truly needs to be platform-specific, such as file handling or device-specific features.
- **Encapsulate Platform-Specific Code:** Keep platform-specific code contained within platform modules. Use clean interfaces in the common module to abstract platform-specific behavior.
- **Avoid Overusing Platform-Specific Code**: While Kotlin Multiplatform makes it easy to write platform-specific code, try to minimize its usage to ensure code reusability and maintainability.

By leveraging shared code and platform-specific implementations via the **expect/actual** mechanism, Kotlin Multiplatform allows developers to build efficient, maintainable, and scalable projects.

Tools and Libraries for Multiplatform Development

Kotlin Multiplatform development benefits from a growing ecosystem of tools and libraries that help streamline the development process, enhance productivity, and support a wide variety of use cases, such as networking, dependency injection, serialization, and testing. In this section, we will cover the essential tools and popular libraries that can be used to build robust multiplatform applications.

Development Tools

To effectively develop Kotlin Multiplatform projects, several tools are necessary for setup, coding, building, and testing across multiple platforms:

- **IntelliJ IDEA/Android Studio:** These Integrated Development Environments (IDEs) offer excellent support for Kotlin Multiplatform projects. They provide powerful features such as code completion, debugging, testing, and Gradle integration. IntelliJ IDEA, in particular, is the go-to tool for multiplatform development since it supports a wide range of platforms, while Android Studio is best suited if Android is your primary target.

- **Gradle:** Kotlin Multiplatform projects use Gradle for build automation. Gradle manages platform-specific build tasks, dependencies, and configuration for Android, iOS, JavaScript, and other targets. Multiplatform-specific Gradle tasks simplify the process of building and testing across different environments.
- **Kotlin Multiplatform Plugin:** The Kotlin Multiplatform plugin is a critical component that enables multiplatform support in IntelliJ IDEA and Android Studio. It allows developers to define multiple targets (Android, iOS, JVM, JS, and so on.) within a single project, and configure platform-specific behavior through Gradle.
- **Xcode (for iOS development):** When targeting iOS, Xcode is essential for compiling and running iOS applications. Kotlin Multiplatform generates frameworks that can be included in an Xcode project for iOS development and testing.

Popular Multiplatform Libraries

Several libraries are available to handle common tasks such as networking, serialization, database management, and dependency injection across multiple platforms. These libraries are designed to work seamlessly in Kotlin Multiplatform projects.

Networking: Ktor

Ktor is a Kotlin framework for building asynchronous servers and clients. It has native multiplatform support, allowing developers to write networking code once, and run it on Android, iOS, Web, and other platforms.

Features of Ktor:

- Supports HTTP requests, WebSockets, and much more.
- Multiplatform support with platform-specific client implementations (for example, Ktor Client for Android, iOS and so on).
- Integration with Kotlin Coroutines for asynchronous programming.

Example:

```
val client = HttpClient()

suspend fun fetchData(): String {
   return client.get("https://api.example.com/data")
}
```

Serialization: kotlinx.serialization

`Kotlinx.serialization` is a powerful and multiplatform serialization library for Kotlin. It supports serialization and deserialization of objects into various formats such as JSON, ProtoBuf, and many more. It can be used across Android, iOS, Web, and JVM environments.

Features of `kotlinx.serialization`:

- Easy-to-use annotations for data class serialization.
- Support for multiple formats such as JSON, CBOR, ProtoBuf, and so on.
- Integration with Kotlin's type system, allowing safe and efficient serialization.

Example:

```
import kotlinx.serialization.*
import kotlinx.serialization.json.*

@Serializable
data class User(val id: Int, val name: String)

val jsonString = Json.encodeToString(User(1, "Alice"))
val user = Json.decodeFromString<User>(jsonString)
```

Database: SQLDelight

SQLDelight is a multiplatform library for working with databases such as SQLite across Android, iOS, and other platforms. It generates typesafe Kotlin APIs from your SQL statements, making it easier to query databases in a multiplatform environment.

Features of SQLDelight:

- Multiplatform database support (Android, iOS, JVM).
- SQL-first approach, where you write SQL queries, and Kotlin types are generated from them.
- Built-in support for SQLite, PostgreSQL, and MySQL.

Example:

```
-- schema.sql
CREATE TABLE user (
   id INTEGER PRIMARY KEY,
   name TEXT
);
```

```
// UserDao.kt
val users = database.userQueries.selectAll().executeAsList()
```

Dependency Injection: Koin

Koin is a lightweight and simple-to-use Dependency Injection (DI) framework designed specifically for Kotlin. It supports Kotlin Multiplatform projects, and simplifies the process of managing dependencies across different modules.

Features of Koin:

- No proxy generation, reflection, or bytecode manipulation–Koin is built using Kotlin's DSL and extension functions.
- Multiplatform support.
- Provides a simple and easy-to-use syntax for declaring and resolving dependencies.

Example:

```
// Declare a module
val appModule = module {
    single { UserRepository() }
}

// Start Koin with modules
startKoin {
    modules(appModule)
}
```

Testing: Kotlin Test

Kotlin's testing library (kotlin-test) is multiplatform, and provides tools to write unit tests for both shared code and platform-specific code. Kotlin-test integrates with popular testing frameworks such as JUnit for JVM targets and XCTest for iOS.

Features of kotlin-test:

- Multiplatform support for unit tests in common, Android, iOS, and JVM modules.
- Provides common assertions and test DSL.
- Integration with platform-specific testing tools such as JUnit and XCTest.

Example:

```
// Shared test code
@Test
fun testUserValidation() {
```

```
        assertTrue(validateEmail("test@example.com"))
    }
```

Additional Tools for Multiplatform Development

Beyond the core tools and libraries mentioned above, other tools can also assist in building and managing Kotlin Multiplatform projects:

- **Multiplatform Mobile (KMM Plugin):** Kotlin Multiplatform Mobile (KMM) plugin for Android Studio simplifies the development of mobile applications that target both Android and iOS.
- **Cocoapods Plugin:** For iOS developers, the Cocoapods plugin simplifies the integration of Kotlin Multiplatform code into Xcode by generating iOS frameworks, and handling dependency management via Cocoapods.
- **Moko Libraries:** Moko provides several multiplatform libraries for common use cases such as localization, resources management, networking, and more, tailored specifically for Kotlin Multiplatform.

Best Practices for Using Multiplatform Libraries

- **Choose Libraries that Support Multiplatform:** When selecting third-party libraries, prefer those that have built-in support for Kotlin Multiplatform. This ensures that you can reuse them across multiple platforms.
- **Centralize Dependencies in the Common Module:** Where possible, define dependencies in the common module to ensure that they are shared across all platforms. Only use platform-specific dependencies in platform modules when necessary.
- **Regularly Update Libraries:** As the Kotlin Multiplatform ecosystem evolves, library updates may include new features or critical fixes. Keeping libraries up to date to ensure compatibility and performance improvements.

With these tools and libraries, you can streamline the development of Kotlin Multiplatform projects, and enhance the maintainability and scalability of your applications.

Practical Implementation

In this section, we will build a simple Kotlin Multiplatform app that demonstrates the core principles of multiplatform development, including code sharing, platform-specific implementations, and the use of popular multiplatform libraries. The example app will be a basic application that fetches and displays user data from an API, using shared business logic for networking and data handling, with platform-specific implementations for the user interface.

Overview of the App

We will build a simple multiplatform app that:

1. Fetches user data from a public API using shared networking code.
2. Displays the user data in a list format.
3. Implements platform-specific UIs for Android and iOS.
4. Utilizes shared business logic for fetching and processing data.

The app will use Ktor for networking and **`kotlinx.serialization`** for handling JSON responses in the shared code. The UI will be implemented separately for Android (using Jetpack Compose) and iOS (using SwiftUI).

Project Setup

We will start by setting up a basic Kotlin Multiplatform project with support for Android and iOS.

1. **Create a new project in IntelliJ IDEA or Android Studio.**

   Select Kotlin Multiplatform, and configure the project for Android and iOS.

2. **Configure build.gradle.kts to include the necessary dependencies:**
   - Ktor for networking.
   - **`kotlinx.serialization`** for JSON parsing.
   - Platform-specific dependencies for Android and iOS.

Here is an example `build.gradle.kts` file for our project:

```
plugins {
    kotlin("multiplatform") version "1.5.31"
    kotlin("plugin.serialization") version "1.5.31"
    id("com.android.application")
}

kotlin {
    android()
    ios()

    sourceSets {
        val commonMain by getting {
            dependencies {
                implementation("io.ktor:ktor-client-core:1.6.3")
```

```
                implementation("io.ktor:ktor-client-serialization
:1.6.3")
                implementation("org.jetbrains.kotlinx:kotlinx-
serialization-json:1.3.0")
            }
        }

        val androidMain by getting {
            dependencies {
                implementation("io.ktor:ktor-client-an-
droid:1.6.3")
                implementation("androidx.compose.ui:ui:1.0.3")  //
For Jetpack Compose
            }
        }

        val iosMain by getting {
            dependencies {
                implementation("io.ktor:ktor-client-ios:1.6.3")
            }
        }
    }
}

android {
    compileSdkVersion(30)
    defaultConfig {
        minSdkVersion(21)
        targetSdkVersion(30)
    }
}
```

Creating Shared Business Logic

Now that the project is set up, let us create the shared business logic for fetching user data from an API.

Step 1: Define a data model for the user

In the commonMain module, we define a data model that will represent the user fetched from the API:

```
import kotlinx.serialization.Serializable

@Serializable
data class User(val id: Int, val name: String, val username:
String, val email: String)
```

Step 2: Set up networking with Ktor

We create a function to fetch user data from a public API (for example, https://jsonplaceholder.typicode.com/users):

```
import io.ktor.client.*
import io.ktor.client.features.json.*
import io.ktor.client.features.json.serializer.*
import io.ktor.client.request.*

val client = HttpClient {
   install(JsonFeature) {
        serializer = KotlinxSerializer()
   }
}

suspend fun fetchUsers(): List<User> {
   return client.get("https://jsonplaceholder.typicode.com/us-
ers")
}
```

This function uses Ktor's **`HttpClient`** to make a GET request, and fetch a list of users from the API. The data is automatically deserialized into the User data class, using kotlinx.serialization.

Implementing Platform-Specific User Interfaces

Now that we have the shared logic for fetching users, we will move on to implementing platform-specific user interfaces for Android and iOS.

Android Implementation with Jetpack Compose: For Android, we will use Jetpack Compose to create a simple UI that displays the list of users fetched from the API.

Step 1: Create a Composable Function for User List

In the **`androidMain`** module, we will create a composable function to display the list of users:

```
import androidx.compose.foundation.layout.*
import androidx.compose.foundation.lazy.LazyColumn
import androidx.compose.foundation.lazy.items
import androidx.compose.material.Text
import androidx.compose.runtime.*
import androidx.compose.ui.Modifier
import androidx.compose.ui.unit.dp
import kotlinx.coroutines.CoroutineScope
import kotlinx.coroutines.Dispatchers
import kotlinx.coroutines.launch
```

```
@Composable
fun UserList() {
   var users by remember { mutableStateOf(listOf<User>()) }

   // Fetch users from the API
   LaunchedEffect(Unit) {
       users = fetchUsers()
   }

   // Display the list of users
   LazyColumn(modifier = Modifier.fillMaxSize()) {
       items(users) { user ->
           UserRow(user)
       }
   }
}

@Composable
fun UserRow(user: User) {
   Column(modifier = Modifier.padding(16.dp)) {
       Text(text = "Name: ${user.name}")
       Text(text = "Username: ${user.username}")
       Text(text = "Email: ${user.email}")
   }
}
```

This code creates a **UserList** composable that fetches the user data, and displays it in a list using **LazyColumn**. The **LaunchedEffect** block is used to launch the network request in a coroutine.

Step 2: Set up the Main Activity

In the Android **MainActivity**, we will use Jetpack Compose to display the **UserList**:

```
import android.os.Bundle
import androidx.activity.ComponentActivity
import androidx.activity.compose.setContent

class MainActivity : ComponentActivity() {
   override fun onCreate(savedInstanceState: Bundle?) {
       super.onCreate(savedInstanceState)
       setContent {
           UserList()
       }
   }
}
```

iOS Implementation with SwiftUI: For iOS, we will use SwiftUI to display the list of users. Kotlin Multiplatform allows us to fetch the users in the shared code, and we will pass this data to SwiftUI for rendering.

Step 1: Create a SwiftUI View

In the **iosMain** module, we create a SwiftUI view to display the list of users:

```
import SwiftUI
import shared

struct UserListView: View {
   @State private var users = [User]()

   var body: some View {
   List(users, id: \.id) { user in
       VStack(alignment: .leading) {
   Text("Name: \(user.name)")
   Text("Username: \(user.username)")
   Text("Email: \(user.email)")
}
}
   .onAppear {
       fetchUsers()
   }
}

   func fetchUsers() {
       UserRepository().fetchUsers { fetchedUsers in
               self.users = fetchedUsers
       }
   }
}
```

In this view, we use SwiftUI's List to display the users. The **fetchUsers** function interacts with the shared Kotlin code, and the data is passed to SwiftUI for display.

Step 2: Connect the SwiftUI View to the iOS App

In your iosApp project, replace the default content view with UserListView:

```
@main
struct iOSApp: App {
   var body: some Scene {
   WindowGroup {
       UserListView()
   }
}
}
```

Testing and Running the App

- **Android:** Build and run the Android app in an emulator or a real device using Android Studio. The app should display the list of users fetched from the API.
- **iOS:** Build and run the iOS app in an Xcode simulator or on a real device. The list of users should appear in a SwiftUI list.

Summary

In this example, we demonstrated how to:

- Share business logic across platforms using Kotlin Multiplatform.
- Use popular multiplatform libraries such as Ktor and kotlinx.serialization.
- Implement platform-specific user interfaces, using Jetpack Compose for Android and SwiftUI for iOS.

By following this approach, you can build maintainable and scalable apps that target multiple platforms, while maximizing code reuse.

Conclusion

In this chapter, we explored Kotlin Multiplatform's core concepts, architecture, and benefits for cross-platform development. We examined how the platform enables code reuse across Android, iOS, Web, and Desktop, leveraging shared business logic, while maintaining flexibility for platform-specific implementations. The **`expect/actual`** mechanism plays a crucial role in seamlessly integrating platform-specific functionality. We also reviewed the essential tools and libraries, such as Ktor for networking and kotlinx.serialization for serialization, which support multiplatform development.

Thus, Kotlin Multiplatform offers significant benefits in terms of development efficiency, code consistency, and reduced maintenance costs. However, developers need to navigate challenges such as the learning curve, platform-specific nuances, and managing UI implementations separately for each platform. With the right approach, these challenges can be overcome, making Kotlin Multiplatform an ideal solution for many cross-platform applications.

Now that we have a strong understanding of Kotlin Multiplatform's architecture and code-sharing mechanisms, it is time to dive into the practical aspects of Building a Multiplatform Project. In the next chapter, we will guide you step-by-step through setting up a multiplatform project, configuring the necessary build tools, managing dependencies, and writing reusable code that runs on Android, iOS, and other platforms. This chapter will focus on building a real-world application to showcase the potential of Kotlin Multiplatform in practice.

CHAPTER 5
Building a Multiplatform Project

Introduction

In this chapter, we take the foundational knowledge of Kotlin Multiplatform, and put it into practice by building a fully functional multiplatform project. Kotlin Multiplatform empowers developers to write shared business logic, while allowing flexibility for platform-specific implementations, enabling applications to run seamlessly on Android, iOS, and other platforms.

Structure

In this chapter, we will cover the following topics:

- Configuring IDE for Multiplatform Development
- Configuring Gradle for Multiplatform
- Project Structure and Best Practices
- Implementing Platform-Specific Features
- Tips and Best Practices
- Hands-on Example: Building and Running a Simple Multiplatform Application

Configuring IDE for Multiplatform Development

The goal of this chapter is to provide a step-by-step guide to set up, develop, and test a Kotlin Multiplatform project. By the end of this chapter, you will have a clear understanding of how to create a project structure that supports multiple platforms, manage shared and platform-specific dependencies, and implement reusable logic, while addressing platform-specific needs.

This chapter begins with the setup process, detailing how to configure the development environment, and initialize a new Kotlin Multiplatform project. We then move on to managing dependencies across shared and platform-specific modules, writing shared business logic, and handling platform-specific functionality, using the `expect/actual` mechanism. Finally, we demonstrate how to run, test, and debug the application on different platforms, providing practical insights into real-world development scenarios.

Whether you are a seasoned Kotlin developer or new to multiplatform development, this chapter equips you with the tools and knowledge necessary to build robust and maintainable multiplatform applications.

Setting Up the Development Environment

To begin building a Kotlin Multiplatform project, it is essential to set up a well-configured development environment. This involves installing the necessary tools, and configuring your IDE for smooth multiplatform development. This section provides a detailed guide for setting up your environment to target Android, iOS, and other platforms.

Installing Tools (IDE, SDKs)

Kotlin Multiplatform development requires a few key tools for targeting different platforms. The following is a checklist of tools, and their setup instructions:

IntelliJ IDEA/Android Studio: Both *IntelliJ* IDEA and *Android Studio* provide excellent support for Kotlin Multiplatform. Choose IntelliJ IDEA, if your focus includes non-Android targets such as iOS and Web. Use Android Studio, if you are primarily targeting Android and iOS.

Download and Install IntelliJ IDEA:

1. Visit the IntelliJ IDEA download page. (https://www.jetbrains.com/idea/).
2. Choose the Ultimate Edition (recommended) or the Community Edition (limited features for multiplatform projects).
3. Install the application, and ensure that the Kotlin plugin is installed (it typically comes pre-installed).

Download and Install Android Studio:

1. Visit the Android Studio download page. (https://developer.android.com/studio).
2. Follow the installation instructions for your platform (Windows, macOS, or Linux).

3. Ensure that the Kotlin plugin is enabled under **`Settings`** > **`Plugins`** > **`Kotlin`**.

Xcode for iOS Development: Xcode is required for building and testing iOS targets in Kotlin Multiplatform.

Download and Install Xcode:

1. Open the *Mac App Store.*
2. Search for Xcode, and install it.
3. After installation, open Xcode and agree to the license agreement. Install the required command-line tools (Xcode may prompt this automatically).

Gradle: Gradle is the build system used in Kotlin Multiplatform projects. It manages dependencies, builds shared and platform-specific modules, and coordinates project configurations.

Install Gradle (Optional for IntelliJ IDEA/Android Studio): IntelliJ IDEA and Android Studio manage Gradle internally, so no manual installation is necessary. However, if you prefer using Gradle from the command line:

1. Visit the Gradle installation page.
2. Download and install the latest version.
3. Verify the installation by running: **`gradle --version`**.

Kotlin Multiplatform Plugin: The Kotlin plugin is required to enable multiplatform development features.

- **Verify Kotlin Plugin Installation in IntelliJ IDEA:**
    1. Go to **`File`** > **`Settings`** > **`Plugins`** (on macOS: **`IntelliJ IDEA`** > **`Preferences`** > **`Plugins`**).
    2. Search for "**`Kotlin`**", and ensure that it is installed and enabled.
    3. Restart IntelliJ IDEA, if prompted.
- **Update the Kotlin Plugin:** Always ensure that the Kotlin plugin is up to date to access the latest features and fixes.

Cocoapods for iOS Dependency Management: For iOS, you may need Cocoapods to manage dependencies for Kotlin Multiplatform projects.

Install Cocoapods:

1. Open a terminal and run: **`sudo gem install cocoapods`**
2. Verify installation with: **`pod --version`**

Java Development Kit (JDK): Kotlin relies on the JDK for development, hence, ensure that you have a JDK version compatible with Kotlin (for example, JDK 11 or 17).

Download and Install JDK:

1. Visit the OpenJDK page (https://openjdk.org/) or download from vendors such as Oracle or Amazon Corretto.
2. Set the environment variable `JAVA_HOME` to point to the JDK installation directory.

Configuring IDE for Multiplatform Development

Once the necessary tools are installed, configure the IDE to streamline multiplatform development.

Setting Up IntelliJ IDEA for Multiplatform Development

1. **Create a New Kotlin Multiplatform Project**:
   a. Open IntelliJ IDEA.
   b. Select `New Project` > `Kotlin Multiplatform`.
   c. Configure platforms (for example, Android, iOS, and JVM).
   d. Finish the project setup.
2. **Install Additional Plugins (Optional)**:
   a. For iOS, install the *Kotlin Native Debugger* plugin for better debugging support.
   b. For Web (Kotlin/JS), ensure that the `JavaScript Debugger` plugin is enabled.
3. **Configure Gradle**:
   a. IntelliJ IDEA automatically manages Gradle.
   b. Check `Settings` > `Build, Execution, Deployment` > `Gradle` to ensure that the Gradle JVM is set to the installed JDK.

Setting Up Android Studio for Multiplatform Development

1. **Enable Kotlin Multiplatform Mobile (KMM):**

   a. Android Studio includes KMM support via the Kotlin plugin. Ensure that it is enabled under `Settings` > `Plugins` > `Kotlin`.

2. **Configure iOS Target**:

   a. Install the Cocoapods plugin, if using Android Studio for iOS targets.

   b. Set up the iOS *framework* to sync with Xcode for testing on simulators or devices.

3. **Configure Build Settings**:

   a. Navigate to `File` > `Project Structure` > `Modules`.

   b. Ensure that multiplatform modules are correctly recognized for Android and iOS targets.

Setting Up Xcode for Multiplatform Development

1. **Generate iOS Framework**:

   - Use Gradle to generate the iOS framework from the Kotlin project:

     ```
     ./gradlew assembleDebugFramework
     ```

2. **Integrate Framework in Xcode**:

   a. Open your Xcode project.

   b. Add the generated Kotlin framework to the *Linked Frameworks* and *Libraries section*.

3. **Run the iOS Application**:

   a. Select a simulator or device from Xcode.

   b. Build and run the application.

Testing the Setup

1. **Verify Gradle Sync:** Open the project in IntelliJ IDEA or Android Studio, and ensure that the Gradle sync completes successfully.

2. **Build for Android and iOS:** Use the Gradle tasks to build and test both Android and iOS targets:
   - For Android: `./gradlew assembleDebug`
   - For iOS: `./gradlew linkDebugFrameworkIos`

With the tools installed and the IDE configured, you are now ready to start building a Kotlin Multiplatform project. In the next section, we will create the project structure, manage dependencies, and begin writing shared and platform-specific code.

Configuring Gradle for Multiplatform

Gradle is the build tool used in Kotlin Multiplatform projects to manage dependencies, compile source code, and target multiple platforms. Setting up Gradle properly is crucial for a seamless multiplatform development experience. In this section, we will configure Gradle, add the required Kotlin Multiplatform plugins, and manage dependencies effectively.

Gradle Setup

Gradle requires specific configurations to support Kotlin Multiplatform projects. Below are the steps to set up Gradle for a multiplatform project.

Apply the Kotlin Multiplatform Plugin

The Kotlin Multiplatform plugin is essential for enabling support for multiple platforms (Android, iOS, Web, etc.) in your project.

Example: Adding the plugin to the `build.gradle.kts` file:

```
plugins {
   // Replace with the latest Kotlin version
   kotlin("multiplatform") version "1.5.31"
   // For Android-specific builds
       id("com.android.application")
     }
```

Configure Targets for Platforms

Gradle allows you to define multiple targets, such as Android, iOS, Web, and Desktop. Each target corresponds to a specific platform your project will support.

Example: Basic target configuration for Android and iOS:

```
kotlin {
    android()  // Target Android
    ios {        // Target iOS
        binaries {
            framework {
                baseName = "SharedCode"
  // Name of the framework generated for iOS
            }
        }
    }
}
```

Specify the Source Sets

Source sets define the shared and platform-specific code directories in your project. Gradle uses commonMain, androidMain, and iosMain as default conventions for shared and platform-specific code.

Example: Configuring source sets:

```
kotlin {
    sourceSets {
    val commonMain by getting {
            dependencies {
                implementation("io.ktor:ktor-client-core:1.6.3")
// Shared dependency
            }
        }
    val androidMain by getting {
            dependencies {
                implementation("io.ktor:ktor-client-an-
droid:1.6.3")  // Android-specific dependency
            }
        }
    val iosMain by getting {
            dependencies {
                implementation("io.ktor:ktor-client-ios:1.6.3")
// iOS-specific dependency
            }
        }
    }
}
```

Adding Multiplatform Plugins

Plugins in Gradle simplify tasks like dependency management, framework generation for iOS, and platform-specific builds. Here are the common plugins used in Kotlin Multiplatform projects.

Kotlin Multiplatform Plugin

The Kotlin Multiplatform plugin enables the core functionality for multiplatform development.

Adding the plugin:

```
plugins {
   kotlin("multiplatform") version "1.5.31"
}
```

Android Plugin

The Android plugin is required to build and package the Android application.

Adding the Android plugin:

```
plugins {
   id("com.android.application")
}
```

Configure the Android-specific settings:

```
android {
   compileSdk = 31
   defaultConfig {
       minSdk = 21
       targetSdk = 31
   }
}
```

Cocoapods Plugin (Optional for iOS)

The Cocoapods plugin simplifies integrating Kotlin frameworks into Xcode projects when targeting iOS.

Adding the Cocoapods plugin:

```
kotlin {
   ios {
       binaries.framework {
           baseName = "SharedCode"
       }
```

```
        }
        cocoapods {
            summary = "Description of the library"
            homepage = "Link to the project homepage"
            ios.deploymentTarget = "14.0"
            podfile = project.file("../iosApp/Podfile")
        }
    }
```

Dependency Management

Managing dependencies in Kotlin Multiplatform projects involves specifying common dependencies for shared code and platform-specific dependencies for platform modules.

Adding Shared Dependencies

Shared dependencies are added to the **commonMain** source set and are available across all platforms.

Example: Adding shared dependencies:

```
kotlin {
    sourceSets {
    val commonMain by getting {
            dependencies {
                implementation("io.ktor:ktor-client-core:1.6.3")
// Shared HTTP client
                implementation("org.jetbrains.kotlinx:kotlinx-
serialization-json:1.3.0")  // Shared JSON serialization
            }
        }
    }
}
```

Adding Platform-Specific Dependencies

Platform-specific dependencies are added to platform-specific source sets, such as **androidMain** or **iosMain**.

Example: Adding platform-specific dependencies:

```
kotlin {
    sourceSets {
    val androidMain by getting {
            dependencies {
```

```
                implementation("io.ktor:ktor-client-android
:1.6.3") // Android HTTP client
                implementation("androidx.core:core-ktx:1.6.0")
// Android KTX
            }
        }
    val iosMain by getting {
            dependencies {
                implementation("io.ktor:ktor-client-ios:1.6.3")
// iOS HTTP client
            }
        }
    }
}
```

Managing Dependency Versions

Centralizing dependency versions ensures consistency across all platforms.

Example: Using a gradle.properties file to define versions:

```
ktor_version=1.6.3
serialization_version=1.3.0
Referencing these versions in build.gradle.kts:
dependencies {
   implementation("io.ktor:ktor-client-core:$ktor_version")
implementation("org.jetbrains.kotlinx: kotlinx-serialization
-json: $serialization_version")
}
```

Resolving Version Conflicts

Gradle automatically resolves version conflicts, but it is a good practice to ensure that all modules use consistent dependency versions.

Project Structure and Best Practices

When building a Kotlin Multiplatform project, maintaining a clean and scalable project structure is essential. This section covers how to organize shared and platform-specific code and implement modularization for maximum code reuse.

Organizing Shared and Platform-Specific Code

Kotlin Multiplatform uses a source set hierarchy to distinguish shared and platform-specific code. A well-organized project structure ensures efficient code reuse and platform-specific flexibility.

Project Structure:

```
project-root/
├── commonMain/              # Shared business logic, data models, and
│   └── kotlin/              utilities
├── androidMain/             # Android-specific code
│   └── kotlin/
├── iosMain/                 # iOS-specific code
│   └── kotlin/
├── commonTest/              # Shared test cases
├── androidTest/             # Android-specific tests
├── iosTest/                 # iOS-specific tests
```

Best Practices:

1. Shared Code (**`commonMain`**): Place platform-independent logic here, such as networking, data processing, and shared models.
2. Platform-Specific Code (**`androidMain`**, **`iosMain`**): Include platform-specific APIs (for example, file handling or lifecycle management) using the expect/actual mechanism.

Example: Using **`expect/actual`** for platform-specific functionality:

- Shared code (**`commonMain`**): **`expect fun getPlatformName(): String`**
- Android implementation (**`androidMain`**): **`actual fun getPlatformName(): String = "Android"`**
- iOS implementation (**`iosMain`**): **`actual fun getPlatformName(): String = "iOS"`**

Modularization and Code Reuse

Modularization improves maintainability, scalability, and performance by separating the shared and platform-specific features into independent modules.

Key Strategies for Modularization

1. **Separate Business Logic and UI**: Keep shared business logic in **`commonMain`**, while defining platform-specific UIs in androidMain or iosMain.
2. **Reusable Modules**: Create independent shared modules for features that can be reused across multiple projects, such as:
   - **Networking Module:** Handles API calls and error processing.
   - **Authentication Module:** Manages user login and token storage.

Example: Creating a Networking Module

Networking module (`commonMain`):

```
val client = HttpClient()
suspend fun fetchUsers(): List<User> {
   return client.get("https://api.example.com/users")
}
```

Usage in app module (`commonMain`):

```
val users = fetchUsers()
```

Best Practices for Modularization:

1. Define modules by feature or layer (for example, data, domain, and ui).
2. Keep dependencies minimal between modules to improve build times.
3. Use Gradle's api and implementation keywords to control dependency visibility.

Implementing Platform-Specific Features

While Kotlin Multiplatform enables shared business logic across platforms, certain features rely on platform-specific functionality. This section covers setting up platform modules and integrating platform-specific APIs to handle unique requirements for Android, iOS, and other targets.

Setting Up Platform Modules

Platform modules (**`androidMain`**, **`iosMain`**, and so on.) are used for platform-specific implementations. These modules extend the shared logic by integrating APIs or features unique to each platform.

Project Structure with Platform Modules

```
project-root/
├── commonMain/                # Shared code
├── androidMain/               # Android-specific code
├── iosMain/                   # iOS-specific code
```

Each platform module inherits shared logic from commonMain, while adding platform-specific functionality.

Example: Configuring Platform Modules in Gradle

```
kotlin {
   android()  // Android target
   ios {       // iOS target
       binaries {
```

```
                framework {
                    baseName = "SharedCode"
                }
            }
        }
    }
```

Best Practices for Setting Up Platform Modules

1. Keep platform modules lightweight and focused on platform-specific tasks.
2. Delegate as much logic as possible to the shared module to maximize code reuse.
3. Use expect/actual to integrate platform-specific functionality where necessary.

Working with Platform-Specific APIs

Platform modules allow direct access to native APIs, enabling the implementation of features like file handling, UI interactions, and hardware access.

Accessing Android-Specific APIs

In the androidMain module, you can integrate Android-specific APIs such as context, permissions, or sensors.

Example: File Handling in Android

```
import java.io.File
actual fun readFile(fileName: String): String {
    val file = File(context.filesDir, fileName)
    return file.readText()
}
```

Accessing iOS-Specific APIs

In the iosMain module, you can use iOS-specific APIs such as CoreData, Foundation, or UIKit.

Example: File Handling in iOS

```
import platform.Foundation.*
actual fun readFile(fileName: String): String {
    val path = NSBundle.mainBundle.pathForResource(fileName, ofType
= null)
    return NSString.stringWithContentsOfFile(path, encoding =
NSUTF8StringEncoding, error = null) as String
}
```

Example: Using Platform-Specific UI Components

Android (Jetpack Compose):

@Composable

```
fun PlatformSpecificButton(onClick: () -> Unit) {
   Button(onClick = onClick) {
       Text("Android Button")
   }
}
```

iOS (SwiftUI): Use Kotlin Multiplatform's generated framework in SwiftUI:

```
import SharedCode
struct ContentView: View {
   var body: some View {
   Text("iOS Button")
}
}
```

Best Practices for Platform-Specific APIs:

- **Encapsulate Platform Logic:** Keep platform-specific logic modular and minimal to maintain clarity as well as reduce maintenance overhead.
- **Use Abstractions:** Abstract platform-specific implementations with shared interfaces for consistency in the commonMain module.
- **Test Individually:** Ensure that platform-specific implementations are independently tested to validate functionality.

Tips and Best Practices

Building a successful Kotlin Multiplatform project requires attention to code quality, maintainability, and effective sharing of functionality across platforms. This section focuses on ensuring code quality, and sharing logic effectively, while maintaining flexibility for platform-specific implementations.

Ensuring Code Quality

Maintaining high code quality is critical for the success and scalability of any project, particularly in a multiplatform environment where shared code impacts multiple platforms.

Writing Clean and Modular Code

- Follow SOLID principles (for example, Single Responsibility Principle) to keep functions and classes focused on a single purpose.

- Use modularization to separate responsibilities (for example, networking, data handling, and UI logic).

Example: Modularizing Shared Logic

- Keep networking, data models, and utility functions in separate modules or packages within the **`commonMain`**.

Testing Shared and Platform-Specific Code

- Write unit tests for shared logic in the commonTest module to validate core functionality.
- Use platform-specific test modules (for example, **`androidTest`** and **`iosTest`**) to ensure that platform-dependent features work as expected.

Example: Unit Testing Shared Code

```
@Test
fun testEmailValidation() {
    assertTrue(validateEmail("test@example.com"))
}
```

Best Practices:

- Use testing libraries such as kotlin-test for shared tests and platform-specific frameworks like JUnit (Android) or XCTest (iOS) for platform modules.
- Aim for high test coverage in commonMain to reduce redundancy in platform-specific tests.

Static Analysis and Linting

- Integrate static code analysis tools such as Detekt for Kotlin to enforce code standards, and detect potential issues.
- Use platform-specific linters (for example, Android Lint) to catch platform-specific code quality issues.

Example: Adding Detekt to Gradle

```
plugins {
    id("io.gitlab.arturbosch.detekt") version "1.18.1"
}
detekt {
    config = files("detekt-config.yml")
}
```

Consistent Dependency Management

- Define dependency versions in a central location (for example, **`gradle.properties`**) to maintain consistency across modules.
- Use Gradle's dependency constraints to prevent version conflicts.

Example: Using a **`gradle.properties`** file to define versions:

```
ktor_version=1.6.3
serialization_version=1.3.0
```

Referencing these versions in **`build.gradle.kts`**:

```
dependencies {
   implementation("io.ktor:ktor-client-core:$ktor_version")
implementation("org.jetbrains.kotlinx: kotlinx-serializa-
tion-json: $serialization_version")
}
```

Techniques for Effective Code Sharing

Maximizing code reuse is the cornerstone of Kotlin Multiplatform development. Proper techniques ensure that the shared code is efficient and maintainable.

Define Shared Abstractions

Use interfaces and abstract classes in **`commonMain`** to define shared abstractions for platform-specific implementations.

Example: Shared Abstraction

- Shared Interface in **`commonMain`**:

```
interface Logger {
   fun log(message: String)
}
```

Platform Implementations:

- Android (**`androidMain`**):

```
actual class LoggerImpl : Logger {
   override fun log(message: String) {
        Log.d("Logger", message)
   }
}
```

iOS (iosMain):

```
actual class LoggerImpl : Logger {
   override fun log(message: String) {
        println("Logger: $message")
   }
}
```

Avoid Platform-Specific Code in `commonMain`

- Keep **`commonMain`** free from platform dependencies.
- Use the **`expect/actual`** mechanism for platform-specific code.

Example: Abstracting File Access

- Shared Declaration in **`commonMain`**
  ```
  expect fun readFile(fileName: String): String
  ```
- Platform-Specific Implementations: Android and iOS handle file access using actual implementations in their respective modules.

Use Multiplatform Libraries

Leverage libraries that support Kotlin Multiplatform, such as:

  - Ktor for networking.
  - kotlinx.serialization for data serialization.
  - SQLDelight for database operations.

Example: Shared Networking with Ktor

```
val client = HttpClient()
suspend fun fetchUsers(): List<User> {
    return client.get("https://api.example.com/users")
}
```

Minimize `expect/actual` Code

While the **`expect/actual`** mechanism is powerful, overusing it can complicate the codebase. Strive to implement most functionality in commonMain, and limit platform-specific code to the essential features.

Centralize Configuration in Gradle

Consolidate Gradle configurations to simplify project management:

- Use **`sourceSets`** to manage dependencies and shared logic.
- Declare shared settings in the root build.gradle.kts file.

Example: Centralized Gradle Configurations

```
kotlin {
    android()
    ios()
    sourceSets {
        val commonMain by getting {
```

```
                dependencies {
                    implementation("io.ktor:ktor-client-core:1.6.3")
                }
            }
        }
    }
```

Hands-on Example: Building and Running a Simple Multiplatform Application

In this section, we will create a simple Kotlin Multiplatform application that demonstrates shared logic, platform-specific implementations, and the process of building and running on both Android and iOS platforms.

Project Overview

We will build an application that:

1. Fetches and displays a list of users from a public API.
2. Shares the networking and data logic in the commonMain module.
3. Implements platform-specific user interfaces in the androidMain and iosMain modules.

Step 1: Setting Up the Project

Create a New Multiplatform Project

a. Open IntelliJ IDEA or Android Studio.

b. Select **`New Project`** > **`Kotlin Multiplatform`** > **`Multiplatform Mobile`**.

c. Configure targets for Android and iOS.

Verify Project Structure: The generated structure should look like this:

```
project-root/
├── commonMain/          # Shared code
├── androidMain/         # Android-specific code
├── iosMain/             # iOS-specific code
├── build.gradle.kts     # Gradle build file
└── settings.gradle.kts
```

Add Dependencies, update the `build.gradle.kts` file to include ktor for networking, and `kotlinx.serialization` for JSON parsing:

```
kotlin {
   sourceSets {
       val commonMain by getting {
           dependencies {
               implementation("io.ktor:ktor-client-core:1.6.3")
               implementation("io.ktor:ktor-client-serialization
:1.6.3")
               implementation("org.jetbrains.kotlinx:kotlinx-
serialization-json:1.3.0")
           }
       }
       val androidMain by getting {
           dependencies {
               implementation("io.ktor:ktor-client-android
:1.6.3")
           }
       }
       val iosMain by getting {
           dependencies {
               implementation("io.ktor:ktor-client-ios:1.6.3")
           }
       }
   }
}
```

Step 2: Writing Shared Logic

In the commonMain module, implement the shared networking logic to fetch the user data.

Define the Data Model, and use `kotlinx.serialization` to create a serializable data model:

```
import kotlinx.serialization.Serializable

@Serializable
data class User(val id: Int, val name: String, val email: String)
```

Create the Networking Function, and use ktor to fetch data from a public API:

```
import io.ktor.client.*
import io.ktor.client.features.json.*
import io.ktor.client.features.json.serializer.*
import io.ktor.client.request.*
```

```
val client = HttpClient {
   install(JsonFeature) {
      serializer = KotlinxSerializer()
   }
}

suspend fun fetchUsers(): List<User> {
   return client.get("https://jsonplaceholder.typicode.com/users")
}
```

Step 3: Implementing Platform-Specific UIs

Android Implementation

a. Create a Composable Function in the **androidMain** module, and create a Jetpack Compose UI to display the list of users:

```
import androidx.compose.foundation.layout.*
import androidx.compose.foundation.lazy.LazyColumn
import androidx.compose.foundation.lazy.items
import androidx.compose.material.Text
import androidx.compose.runtime.*
import androidx.compose.ui.Modifier
import androidx.compose.ui.unit.dp

@Composable
fun UserList() {
   var users by remember { mutableStateOf(emptyList<User>()) }

   LaunchedEffect(Unit) {
       users = fetchUsers()
   }

   LazyColumn(modifier = Modifier.fillMaxSize().padding(16.dp)) {
       items(users) { user ->
           Text("Name: ${user.name}")
           Text("Email: ${user.email}")
           Spacer(modifier = Modifier.height(8.dp))
       }
   }
}
```

b. Set Up Main Activity in the **androidMain** module, and use the **UserList** composable in your **MainActivity**:

```
import android.os.Bundle
import androidx.activity.ComponentActivity
import androidx.activity.compose.setContent
```

```
class MainActivity : ComponentActivity() {
    override fun onCreate(savedInstanceState: Bundle?) {
        super.onCreate(savedInstanceState)
        setContent {
            UserList()
        }
    }
}
```

iOS Implementation

1. Create a SwiftUI View in the **iosMain** module, integrate the shared Kotlin framework into a SwiftUI view:

```
import SwiftUI
import SharedCode

struct UserListView: View {
    @State private var users: [User] = []

    var body: some View {
    List(users, id: \.id) { user in
        VStack(alignment: .leading) {
    Text("Name: \(user.name)")
    Text("Email: \(user.email)")
}
}
    .onAppear {
        fetchUsers()
    }
}


    func fetchUsers() {
        let repository = UserRepository()
        repository.fetchUsers { fetchedUsers in
                self.users = fetchedUsers
        }
    }
}
```

2. Connect the View in the iOS App, and replace the default SwiftUI ContentView with UserListView in your iOS project:

```
import SwiftUI

@main
struct iOSApp: App {
    var body: some Scene {
```

```
        WindowGroup {
            UserListView()
        }
    }
}
```

Step 4: Running the Application

Running on Android

1. Open the project in Android Studio.
2. Select an emulator or a physical Android device.
3. Build and run the application to display the user list.

Running on iOS

1. Generate the iOS framework using Gradle:

   ```
   ./gradlew linkDebugFrameworkIos
   ```

2. Open the iOS project in Xcode.
3. Run the application on a simulator, or physical iOS device.

Conclusion

In this chapter, we covered the essentials of creating a Kotlin Multiplatform project, from setting up the development environment, and configuring Gradle to writing shared business logic as well as implementing platform-specific features. By leveraging Kotlin Multiplatform's structured project architecture, we demonstrated how to maximize code reuse in the commonMain module, while maintaining flexibility for platform-specific implementations in androidMain and iosMain. This approach ensures scalable, maintainable, and efficient cross-platform development.

In the next chapter, we will explore the powerful ecosystem of Kotlin Multiplatform libraries and tools. From networking with Ktor to serialization with **`kotlinx.serialization`**, we will delve into how these libraries simplify development, and enhance the capabilities of your multiplatform projects. We will also discuss the necessary tools for debugging, testing, and optimizing your applications.

CHAPTER 6

Utilizing Multiplatform Libraries and Tools

Introduction

This chapter introduces you to essential libraries and tools that enhance Kotlin Multiplatform development. By leveraging these tools, you can create efficient, maintainable, and scalable applications. We will cover key libraries such as **Ktor** for web development, **Koin** for dependency injection, and **kotlinx.serialization** for data handling. Additionally, we will explore tools such as the **Kotlin Multiplatform Mobile (KMM) plugin** and **Jetpack Compose** for building user interfaces. By the end of this chapter, you will be well-equipped to integrate these tools into your projects seamlessly.

Structure

In this chapter, we will cover the following topics:

- Introduction to Multiplatform Libraries
- Ktor for Web Applications
- Koin for Dependency Injection
- `kotlinx.serialization` for Data Handling
- Kotlin Multiplatform Mobile (KMM) Plugin
- Jetpack Compose for UI Development
- Additional Tools and Resources

Introduction to Multiplatform Libraries

Kotlin Multiplatform libraries serve as foundational tools that simplify and streamline development across Android, iOS, Web, and Desktop platforms. By enabling shared code, these libraries significantly reduce duplication, and promote consistency throughout a codebase, allowing developers to maintain uniform behavior and centralized business logic. This shared approach not only speeds up development but also enhances scalability, as modular libraries adapt easily to evolving project needs. Among the standout benefits are improved code reusability, simplified maintenance, and overall time and cost efficiency.

The Kotlin ecosystem offers a rich set of multiplatform libraries to support various development tasks. Libraries like Ktor provide powerful tools for handling networking and web APIs, while Koin offers a lightweight solution for dependency injection. kotlinx.serialization handles data serialization with formats like JSON and ProtoBuf, integrating smoothly with networking tools. SQLDelight facilitates database management by generating type-safe Kotlin APIs from SQL schemas, and Multiplatform Settings that enables seamless handling of user preferences across platforms. Together, these libraries empower developers to create scalable and maintainable applications that leverage the full potential of Kotlin Multiplatform.

Importance and Benefits

Kotlin Multiplatform libraries play a critical role in streamlining development across multiple platforms. These libraries enable developers to share code effectively, improve consistency, and reduce duplication, making the development process more efficient and manageable.

Key Benefits

- **Code Reusability:**
  - Write shared logic once, and use it across Android, iOS, Web, and Desktop platforms.
  - Reduce duplication, leading to faster development and easier maintenance.
- **Consistency:**
  - Shared libraries ensure uniform behavior across all platforms, minimizing discrepancies.
  - Maintain consistent features and updates by consolidating business logic in one place.

- **Scalability:**
  - Multiplatform libraries are designed to handle a growing codebase with ease.
  - Their modular nature supports adding or updating features across platforms seamlessly.
- **Time and Cost Efficiency:**
  - Accelerate development cycles by leveraging pre-built solutions.
  - Reduce the resources required for implementing and maintaining platform-specific features.

Overview of Popular Libraries

Kotlin's ecosystem offers several powerful multiplatform libraries, each tailored to handle specific aspects of development:

- **Ktor:**
  - A robust networking framework for building HTTP clients and servers.
  - Provides cross-platform support for web communication and APIs.
  - Includes features such as routing, JSON serialization, and WebSocket support.
- **Koin:**
  - A lightweight dependency injection library that simplifies managing dependencies.
  - Offers an intuitive DSL for declaring and injecting dependencies across platforms.
- **`kotlinx.serialization`:**
  - A library for serializing and deserializing data in JSON, ProtoBuf, CBOR, and other formats.
  - Enables type-safe, efficient data handling across platforms.
  - Works seamlessly with Ktor for API responses and requests.
- **SQLDelight:**
  - A multiplatform library for database management and SQL queries.
  - Generates type-safe Kotlin APIs from SQL schemas, ensuring database consistency and safety.
  - Provides support for Android, iOS, and other platforms.

- **Multiplatform Settings:**
  - Facilitates managing application preferences in a shared codebase.
  - Works seamlessly for storing and retrieving user settings across Android and iOS.

Library	Purpose	Key Features
Ktor	Networking and web APIs	HTTP client/server, WebSockets
Koin	Dependency injection	Lightweight, intuitive DSL
`kotlinx.serialization`	Data serialization/deserialization	JSON, ProtoBuf, type safety
SQLDelight	Database management	Type-safe SQL APIs
Multiplatform Settings	Application preferences	Cross-platform key-value storage

Table 6.1: *Summary Table*

These libraries, along with many others in the Kotlin ecosystem, empower developers to build robust, scalable, and maintainable multiplatform applications with ease.

Ktor for Web Applications

Ktor is a powerful, asynchronous framework for building web applications and HTTP clients in Kotlin. It is designed to be lightweight and highly customizable, making it ideal for multiplatform projects.

Setting Up Ktor

To use Ktor in a Kotlin Multiplatform project, follow these steps:

1. **Add Dependencies:**
   a. Include the Ktor dependency in your **`commonMain`** source set for shared code:
   ```
   implementation("io.ktor:ktor-client-core:2.0.0")
   ```
   b. Add platform-specific dependencies:
      - `Android: ktor-client-android`
      - `iOS: ktor-client-ios`
   ```
   implementation("io.ktor:ktor-client-android:2.0.0") // For Android
   implementation("io.ktor:ktor-client-ios:2.0.0")     // For iOS
   ```

2. **Configure Plugins**:

   a. Install Ktor plugins like **JsonFeature** for JSON serialization:

   ```
   val client = HttpClient {
       install(JsonFeature) {
           serializer = KotlinxSerializer()
       }
   }
   ```

3. **Set up Gradle**: Ensure your **build.gradle.kts** includes Kotlin Multiplatform plugin setup and Ktor dependencies.

Building Simple Web Apps

Ktor simplifies creating web applications with its modular structure. Here is how you can create a simple web app:

1. **Define an HTTP Client:** Create a shared HTTP client for making network requests:

   ```
   val client = HttpClient {
       install(JsonFeature) {
           serializer = KotlinxSerializer()
       }
   }
   ```

2. **Routing:** Use Ktor's routing feature to define endpoints for your application:

   ```
   fun Application.module() {
       routing {
           get("/") {
               call.respondText("Welcome to Ktor!")
           }
       }
   }
   ```

3. **Run the Application:** Deploy and run the server to handle incoming requests. Use **embeddedServer** for local testing:

   ```
   fun main() {
       embeddedServer(
           Netty,
           port = 8080,
           module = Application::module
       ).start(wait = true)
   }
   ```

Handling Requests

Efficient request handling is crucial for web applications. Ktor provides flexible tools for managing incoming and outgoing HTTP requests:

1. **Making a GET Request:** Use the **`client.get`** method to fetch data from an API:

   ```
   suspend fun fetchPosts(): List<Post> {
      return client.get("https://api.example.com/posts")
   }
   ```

2. **Sending a POST Request:** Use the **`client.post`** method to send data to a server:

   ```
   suspend fun sendPost(post: Post): HttpResponse {
      return client.post("https://api.example.com/posts") {
          contentType(ContentType.Application.Json)
          body = post
      }
   }
   ```

3. **Handling JSON Responses:** Leverage **`kotlinx.serialization`** for parsing responses:

   ```
   @Serializable
   data class Post(val id: Int, val title: String, val body: String)
   val posts: List<Post> = Json.decodeFromString(jsonResponse)
   ```

4. **Error Handling**: Handle exceptions gracefully to ensure robust networking:

   ```
   try {
      val posts = fetchPosts()
      println("Posts fetched successfully: $posts")
   } catch (e: Exception) {
      println("Error fetching posts: ${e.message}")
   }
   ```

Ktor's flexibility and multiplatform support make it an excellent choice for building web applications and APIs. Its integration with Kotlin's features ensures a seamless development experience across platforms.

Koin for Dependency Injection

Koin is a lightweight and practical **Dependency Injection (DI)** framework for Kotlin, designed to simplify dependency management in your projects. It provides an easy-to-use DSL to declare and inject dependencies, making your code modular, testable, and scalable.

Dependency Injection

Dependency Injection is a design pattern that promotes loose coupling by injecting dependencies into objects, rather than instantiating them internally. This approach:

- Simplifies testing by allowing you to replace dependencies with mock objects.
- Improves code reusability and maintainability by separating object creation from usage.
- Facilitates modular architecture, enabling easy swapping of implementations.

Example without DI:

```
class Repository {
    fun fetchData() = "Data from repository"
}

class ViewModel {
    private val repository = Repository() // Direct dependency

    fun getData() = repository.fetchData()
}
```

Example with DI:

```
class ViewModel(private val repository: Repository) {
    fun getData() = repository.fetchData()
}
```

With DI, **Repository** can be injected into **ViewModel**, making it more flexible and testable.

Setting Up Koin

Koin provides a simple setup process to integrate DI into your Kotlin project:

1. **Add Dependencies**: Add the Koin core dependency to your **commonMain** source set in a multiplatform project:

   ```
   implementation("io.insert-koin:koin-core:3.3.0")
   ```

   Add platform-specific dependencies, if needed:

   - Android: **koin-android**
   - iOS: **koin-core**

2. **Define a Module**: A **`module`** is a container for your dependency declarations. Use Koin's DSL to declare singleton, factory, or scoped dependencies:

   ```
   val appModule = module {
      // Singleton instance
      single { Repository() }

      // Factory (new instance per injection)
      factory { ViewModel(get()) }
   }
   ```

3. **Start Koin**: Initialize Koin in your application's entry point, such as the main function or **`Application`** class:

   ```
   fun main() {
      startKoin {
         modules(appModule) // Load the module
      }
   }
   ```

Managing Dependencies

Koin allows you to manage dependencies efficiently with a simple and intuitive API.

Declaring Dependencies

- **Singleton:** A single instance is created and shared throughout the app.
  ```
  single { Repository() }
  ```
- **Factory:** A new instance is created each time it is requested.
  ```
  factory { ViewModel(get()) }
  ```
- **Scoped:** A dependency tied to a specific lifecycle (for example, session or activity).
  ```
  scope(named("MyScope")) {
     scoped { SessionManager() }
  }
  ```

Injecting Dependencies

Inject dependencies into your classes using **`get()`** or by **`inject()`**:

```
class ViewModel(private val repository: Repository) {
   fun getData() = repository.fetchData()
}

val viewModel: ViewModel = get()
```

```
Alternatively, use property delegation:

val viewModel: ViewModel by inject()
```

Testing with Koin

Koin simplifies unit testing by allowing you to declare test-specific modules. Use **startKoin** to load mock dependencies:

```
val testModule = module {
    single { MockRepository() as Repository }
}

@Before
fun setup() {
    startKoin {
        modules(testModule)
    }
}
```

Modularizing Dependencies

Break down dependencies into multiple modules to maintain clean and scalable code:

```
val networkModule = module {
    single { NetworkClient() }
}

val repositoryModule = module {
    single { Repository(get()) } // Inject NetworkClient
}

val appModules = listOf(networkModule, repositoryModule)
startKoin { modules(appModules) }
```

Koin's simplicity and Kotlin-first design make it a perfect fit for managing dependencies in multiplatform projects. Its modular approach ensures that your code remains maintainable and scalable, while adhering to the best practices for dependency injection.

kotlinx.serialization for Data Handling

kotlinx.serialization is a multiplatform library for serializing and deserializing data to and from various formats like JSON, ProtoBuf, CBOR, and more. It enables type-safe and efficient data handling across platforms, making it a perfect fit for Kotlin Multiplatform projects.

Setting Up kotlinx.serialization

To use **kotlinx.serialization** in your project, follow these steps:

1. **Add Dependencies:** Include the library in your commonMain source set:

```
implementation("org.jetbrains.kotlinx:kotlinx-serialization
-json:1.5.0")
```

2. **Apply the Serialization Plugin:** Enable the Kotlin serialization plugin in your **build.gradle.kts** file:

```
plugins {
   kotlin("plugin.serialization") version "1.8.10"
}
```

3. **Configure the Build Script**: Ensure that your project is properly configured for multiplatform support, including platform-specific targets like Android and iOS.

Serializing and Deserializing Data

kotlinx.serialization simplifies converting data classes to and from JSON and other formats.

1. **Define a Serializable Data Class**: Annotate your Kotlin data classes with **@ Serializable**:

```
@Serializable
data class User(val id: Int, val name: String)
```

2. **Serialize Data**: Convert a Kotlin object into a JSON string using the **encodeToString** method:

```
val user = User(1, "John Doe")
val json = Json.encodeToString(user)
println(json) // Output: {"id":1,"name":"John Doe"}
```

3. **Deserialize Data**: Convert a JSON string back into a Kotlin object using the **decodeFromString** method:

```
val json = "{"id":1,"name":"John Doe"}"
val user = Json.decodeFromString<User>(json)
println(user) // Output: User(id=1, name=John Doe)
```

Working with JSON

kotlinx.serialization provides flexible JSON handling, allowing you to customize parsing and serialization behavior.

1. **Configuring JSON Settings**: You can configure **Json** settings for specific use cases, such as ignoring unknown keys, or enabling lenient parsing:

```
val json = Json {
   isLenient = true
   ignoreUnknownKeys = true
}
```

2. **Handling Default Values**: Set default values in your data classes to handle missing keys during deserialization:

```
@Serializable
data class User(val id: Int, val name: String = "Unknown")

val json = "{"id":1}"
val user = Json.decodeFromString<User>(json)
println(user) // Output: User(id=1, name=Unknown)
```

3. **Nested Structures**: Serialize and deserialize nested data structures easily:

```
@Serializable
data class Address(val street: String, val city: String)

@Serializable
data class Person(val name: String, val address: Address)

val json = """
    {
        "name": "Alice",
        "address": {
            "street": "Main St",
            "city": "Metropolis"
        }
    }
""".trimIndent()

val person = Json.decodeFromString<Person>(json)
println(person)

// Output: Person(name=Alice, address=Address(street=Main St,
city=Metropolis))
```

4. **Custom Serializers**: Use custom serializers for special data types like dates and **enums**:

```
@Serializable
data class Event(
   @Serializable(with = LocalDateSerializer::class) val date:
LocalDate
```

```
)

object LocalDateSerializer : KSerializer<LocalDate> {
    override val descriptor = PrimitiveSerialDescriptor(
        "LocalDate",
        PrimitiveKind.STRING
    )
    override fun serialize(encoder: Encoder, value: LocalDate) {
        encoder.encodeString(value.toString())
    }

    override fun deserialize(decoder: Decoder): LocalDate {
        return LocalDate.parse(decoder.decodeString())
    }
}
```

`kotlinx.serialization`'s flexibility and ease of use make it an essential tool for managing data in Kotlin Multiplatform projects. Hence, whether you are working with simple objects or complex nested structures, its features ensure efficient and type-safe serialization and deserialization.

Kotlin Multiplatform Mobile (KMM) Plugin

Kotlin Multiplatform Mobile (KMM) is a powerful tool that enables developers to share business logic across Android and iOS, while maintaining platform-specific flexibility for UI and other native features. By using KMM, you can significantly reduce development time, and maintain a single source of truth for your application logic.

Setting Up KMM

To set up Kotlin Multiplatform Mobile in your project, follow these steps:

1. **Install the KMM Plugin**

   a. Ensure that you have the latest version of IntelliJ IDEA, or Android Studio installed.

   b. Install the Kotlin Multiplatform plugin from the IDE's plugin marketplace.

2. **Create a Multiplatform Project:** Use the project wizard in IntelliJ IDEA or Android Studio:

   a. Select **`New Project`** -> **`Kotlin Multiplatform Mobile`**.

   b. Configure targets for both Android and iOS.

   c. The wizard will generate a project with shared and platform-specific modules.

3. **Configure Build Scripts**: In your **build.gradle.kts**, enable targets for Android and iOS:

```
kotlin {
   android()
   ios()
}
```

4. **Add Dependencies**: Add dependencies in **commonMain** for shared logic, and platform-specific dependencies in **androidMain** and **iosMain**:

```
sourceSets {
    val commonMain by getting {
        dependencies {
            implementation("org.jetbrains.kotlinx:kotlinx-corou-
tines-core:1.6.0")
        }
    }

    val androidMain by getting {
        dependencies {
            implementation("androidx.lifecycle:lifecycle-run-
time-ktx:2.4.0")
        }
    }

    val iosMain by getting {
        dependencies {
            implementation("io.ktor:ktor-client-ios:2.0.0")
        }
    }
}
```

5. **Sync and Build: Sync** your Gradle files, and ensure that your project builds successfully for both Android and iOS targets.

Managing Multiplatform Code

KMM provides an efficient way to manage shared and platform-specific code.

1. **Shared Code in commonMain**: Write shared logic in the **commonMain** source set to maximize code reuse:

```
expect fun getPlatformName(): String

fun greet(): String = "Hello from ${getPlatformName()}"
```

2. **Platform-Specific Code with `expect/actual`**: Use **`expect`** declarations in **`commonMain`**, and provide **`actual`** implementations in platform-specific modules.

   ```
   commonMain:
   expect fun getPlatformName(): String

   androidMain:
   actual fun getPlatformName(): String = "Android"

   iosMain:
   actual fun getPlatformName(): String = "iOS"
   ```

3. **Accessing Native APIs:** Integrate platform-specific features like sensors, file systems, or native UI components directly in platform modules.

   Example for Android (`androidMain`):

   ```
   actual fun getDeviceModel(): String {
      return android.os.Build.MODEL
   }
   ```

   Example for iOS (`iosMain`):

   ```
   actual fun getDeviceModel(): String {
      return UIDevice.currentDevice.model
   }
   ```

4. **Testing Shared Code**: Write unit tests in the **`commonTest`** source set to ensure the correctness of shared logic.

   ```
   @Test
   fun testGreet() {
      assertEquals("Hello from Android", greet())
   }
   ```

5. **Debugging KMM Projects**
   - Use Android Studio for debugging Android code and Xcode for debugging iOS code.
   - For shared code, ensure that breakpoints in **`commonMain`** are set up correctly in the IDE.

Kotlin Multiplatform Mobile simplifies cross-platform development, while providing the flexibility to use native features when needed. By following these practices, you can build maintainable and efficient applications for both Android and iOS.

Jetpack Compose for UI Development

Jetpack Compose is a modern, declarative UI framework for building user interfaces in Kotlin. It simplifies UI development by allowing developers to describe the UI using composable functions, making the code more readable, reusable, and maintainable.

Introduction to Jetpack Compose

Key Features of Jetpack Compose

- **Declarative UI:** Define the UI as a set of composable functions that describe how it should look and behave.
- **Code Reusability:** Composable functions promote modular design, making the UI components reusable across different parts of the application.
- **State Management:** Jetpack Compose integrates seamlessly with state management tools, allowing dynamic UI updates.
- **Cross-Platform Potential:** With Kotlin Multiplatform, you can use Jetpack Compose to share UI components across Android and other platforms in the future.

Benefits

- **Concise Code:** Reduces boilerplate code compared to traditional XML-based layouts.
- **Customizability:** Easy to customize and extend components.
- **Integration:** Works well with the existing Android components, allowing gradual migration.

Building Cross-Platform UI

Jetpack Compose simplifies building a consistent UI across platforms. While Jetpack Compose is primarily for Android, its integration into Kotlin Multiplatform projects allows sharing UI logic and components.

Creating a Composable Function

Define reusable UI components as composable functions using the `@Composable` annotation:

```
@Composable
fun Greeting(name: String) {
    Text(text = "Hello, $name!")
}
```

Using Composable Functions

Use **composable** functions within other composables to build complex layouts:

```
@Composable
fun GreetingCard(name: String) {
   Column {
       Greeting(name = name)
       Button(onClick = { /* Handle click */ }) {
           Text("Click Me")
       }
   }
}
```

Previewing Composables

Use Android Studio's Compose Preview to visualize the UI without running the app:

```
@Preview(showBackground = true)
@Composable
fun PreviewGreetingCard() {
   GreetingCard(name = "Kotlin")
}
```

Integrating with Shared Code

Jetpack Compose can leverage shared logic from Kotlin Multiplatform projects to create dynamic and data-driven UIs.

Using Shared ViewModels

Access shared view models or business logic in **commonMain** to populate the UI:

```
@Composable
fun UserProfile(viewModel: UserViewModel) {
   val user = viewModel.user.collectAsState(
       initial = User("Loading...")
   )

   Column {
       Text(text = "Name: ${user.value.name}")
       Button(onClick = { viewModel.fetchNewUser() }) {
           Text("Refresh")
       }
   }
}
```

Combining Platform-Specific and Shared Code

Compose works seamlessly with platform-specific implementations. For example, you can define shared components in **`commonMain`**, and extend them in **`androidMain`** for Android-specific behavior.

Shared Code (`commonMain`):

```
expect fun getPlatformName(): String
```

Platform-Specific Code (`androidMain`):

```
actual fun getPlatformName(): String = "Android"
```

Composable Function:

```
@Composable
fun PlatformGreeting() {
    Text(text = "Hello from ${getPlatformName()}!")
}
```

Handling State across Platforms

Jetpack Compose integrates well with state management tools like **`StateFlow`** or **`LiveData`**. Use shared state logic to ensure consistent UI behavior on all platforms.

Jetpack Compose offers a powerful, modern approach to building UIs with Kotlin. Its integration with Kotlin Multiplatform makes it a key tool for creating cohesive, cross-platform applications with shared logic and dynamic behavior.

Additional Tools and Resources

This section highlights additional libraries and tools that can enhance your Kotlin Multiplatform development experience. Staying updated with the latest developments in the Kotlin ecosystem is also critical to ensuring that your projects use the best practices and tools available.

SQLDelight

- **Purpose:** A multiplatform library for database management and SQL queries.
- **Key Features:**
  - Generates type-safe Kotlin APIs from SQL statements.
  - Supports Android, iOS, and other platforms.
  - Simplifies database operations, while ensuring type safety.

- **Example Usage:**

```
// Define SQL Schema
CREATE TABLE user (
   id INTEGER NOT NULL PRIMARY KEY,
   name TEXT NOT NULL
);

// Access Database
val database = UserDatabase(driver)
val userQueries = database.userQueries

// Query Operations
userQueries.insertUser(id = 1, name = "Alice")
val user = userQueries.selectUserById(1).executeAsOne()
```

Multiplatform Settings

- **Purpose**: A library for managing key-value storage in a multiplatform project.
- **Key Features**:
  - o Abstracts shared preferences (Android) and user defaults (iOS).
  - o Supports encrypted storage for sensitive data.
- **Example Usage:**

```
val settings = Settings()
settings.putString("username", "JohnDoe")

val username = settings.getString(
   "username",
   defaultValue = "Guest"
)
```

Ktor

- While covered earlier, Ktor deserves a mention here as a versatile framework for networking in multiplatform projects, especially when paired with **`kotlinx.serialization`** for data handling.

Kodein-DI

- An alternative dependency injection library, offering a multiplatform-compatible and lightweight solution for managing dependencies.

Staying Updated with Multiplatform Development

The Kotlin ecosystem is rapidly evolving, with regular updates, new libraries, and best practices emerging. To stay ahead, consider the following resources:

- **Official Kotlin Blog and Documentation**
    - **Blog:** Kotlin Blog [https://blog.jetbrains.com/kotlin/]
    - **Documentation:** Kotlin Documentation [https://kotlinlang.org/docs/home.html]
- **Community Forums and Discussions**
    - **Reddit:** Join the r/Kotlin [https://www.reddit.com/r/Kotlin/] subreddit for discussions and news.
    - **Slack:** Participate in the Kotlin Slack Channel [https://slack.kotlinlang.org/].
- **YouTube Channels and Tutorials**
    - Follow JetBrains' official YouTube channel for webinars, tutorials, and updates on Kotlin Multiplatform.
    - Explore independent creators offering guides on tools like Ktor, SQLDelight, and Jetpack Compose.
- **GitHub Projects:** Explore open-source Kotlin Multiplatform projects on GitHub to understand the practical use cases and best practices.
- **Conferences and Meetups:** Attend `KotlinConf` and other developer meetups to connect with the community, and learn about the latest trends.

Thus, leveraging these additional tools and staying engaged with the Kotlin community will help you make the most of Kotlin Multiplatform development, keeping your projects up-to-date and competitive.

Conclusion

This chapter introduced essential libraries and tools that make Kotlin Multiplatform development more efficient and effective. By integrating these libraries into your projects, you can simplify common tasks such as networking, dependency injection, and data serialization, while maintaining clean and maintainable code. The tools discussed, such as Jetpack Compose for UI development and the Kotlin Multiplatform Mobile (KMM) plugin, empower you to create robust cross-platform applications.

In addition, exploring additional libraries like SQLDelight and Multiplatform Settings, as well as staying updated with the latest trends and resources in the Kotlin ecosystem, ensures that your projects remain competitive and well-supported. By leveraging these tools and maintaining an active presence in the Kotlin community, you can build scalable, high-performance applications that stand the test of time.

As you move forward, remember that the foundation laid by these tools and libraries will serve as a stepping stone for tackling more complex multiplatform challenges. Continue experimenting, learning, and building with Kotlin Multiplatform to unlock its full potential!

CHAPTER 7
Android Development with Kotlin Multiplatform

Introduction

This chapter provides an in-depth look at developing Android applications using Kotlin Multiplatform. You will learn how to set up your Android Studio environment to support multiplatform development, integrate shared code, and utilize Android-specific APIs and libraries. The chapter will guide you through building a fully functional Android app, focusing on practical implementation, efficient code reuse, and best practices. We will cover handling UI with Jetpack Compose, managing platform-specific code, and debugging as well as testing your applications on Android. By the end of this chapter, you will have the skills and knowledge to effectively develop, and maintain Android applications using Kotlin Multiplatform, leveraging shared code to enhance productivity and consistency across projects.

Structure

In this chapter, we will cover the following topics:

- Setting Up Android Studio for Multiplatform
- Integrating Shared Code in Android Projects
- Using Android-Specific APIs and Libraries
- Handling UI with Jetpack Compose
- Managing Platform-Specific Code
- Building a Sample Android App
- Debugging and Testing on Android
- Best Practices for Android Development

Setting Up Android Studio for Multiplatform

To effectively develop Android applications using Kotlin Multiplatform, you need to ensure that your Android Studio environment is properly set up. This involves installing necessary plugins, setting up dependencies, and configuring project settings to accommodate multiplatform capabilities. This section details the process of preparing your development environment for Kotlin Multiplatform.

Installing Plugins and Dependencies

Installing plugins and dependencies is a crucial step to ensure a smooth development experience when working with Kotlin Multiplatform in Android Studio. The right plugins enhance functionality, improve code management, and enable the integration of specific features necessary for building applications that target multiple platforms. In the following sections, we will cover the essential steps to install Android Studio, enable the Kotlin plugin, install the Kotlin Multiplatform plugin, integrate Cocoapods for iOS targets, and optionally add IDE support plugins for enhanced coding practices. By following these steps, you will set up a robust development environment tailored for Kotlin Multiplatform development.

1. **Install Android Studio:**
   a. Download the latest version of Android Studio from the official website (https://developer.android.com/studio).
   b. Follow the installation instructions specific to your operating system (Windows, macOS, or Linux).
2. **Enable Kotlin Plugin:**
   a. Open Android Studio and navigate to **`File`** > **`Settings`** (or **`Preferences`** on macOS).
   b. In the **`Plugins`** section, search for the Kotlin plugin. Ensure that it is installed and up to date. If it is not installed, find it in the Marketplace, and install it.
3. **Install Kotlin Multiplatform Plugin:** For Kotlin Multiplatform, make sure that you include the Kotlin Multiplatform, and the appropriate Android plugin in your **`build.gradle.kts`** file:

```
plugins {
   kotlin("multiplatform") version "1.6.10" // Use the latest
stable version
```

```
    id("com.android.application")
}
```

4. **Cocoapods Integration (for iOS targets)**: If your project will also target iOS, include the Cocoapods plugin. You can set it up in your **`build.gradle.kts`** file as well:

```
kotlin {
    ios {
        binaries {
            framework {
                baseName = "SharedCode"
            }
        }
    }
}
```

5. **IDE Support Plugins (Optional)**: You might also want to install additional plugins for code quality and other features, such as Ktlint or Detekt, to help maintain code integrity as you build your project.

Configuring Project Settings

Configuring project settings is a vital step in establishing a Kotlin Multiplatform project, as it lays the groundwork for effective development across multiple platforms. Proper configuration ensures that shared and platform-specific code can coexist seamlessly, enabling developers to leverage the strengths of each platform, while maintaining code reusability. In the ensuing sections, we will guide you through the process of creating a new multiplatform project, setting up Android-specific Gradle configurations, defining source sets for shared and platform-specific code, syncing Gradle files, running basic setup commands, and adjusting iOS application settings if applicable. By following these guidelines, you will be well-equipped to optimize your development environment, and maximize your productivity in building Kotlin Multiplatform applications.

1. **Create a New Multiplatform Project:**
   a. Start a new project by selecting New Project from the welcome screen in Android Studio.

   b. Choose Kotlin Multiplatform Mobile, and follow the wizard to specify project details such as project name, package name, and save location.

2. **Setting up Android-specific Gradle Configurations**: When setting up the Android module in your build.gradle.kts, ensure that you define your Android configurations clearly:

```
android {
    compileSdk = 31
    defaultConfig {
        applicationId = "com.example.mymultiplatformapp"
        minSdk = 21
        targetSdk = 31
        versionCode = 1
        versionName = "1.0"
    }
}
```

3. **Defining Source Sets:** Configure your source sets correctly to separate shared and platform-specific code. This ensures that the shared logic can be utilized seamlessly across all target platforms.

```
kotlin {
    sourceSets {
        val commonMain by getting {
            dependencies {
                implementation("io.ktor:ktor-client-core:1.6.3")
            }
        }
        val androidMain by getting {
            dependencies {
                implementation("io.ktor:ktor-client-android
:1.6.3")
                implementation("androidx.core:core-ktx:1.6.0")
            }
        }
        val iosMain by getting {
            dependencies {
                implementation("io.ktor:ktor-client-ios:1.6.3")
            }
        }
    }
}
```

4. **Syncing the Gradle Files:** Click on the Sync Now link that appears at the top of the editor after making changes to your **`build.gradle.kts`** files. This will resolve dependencies, and prepare your project for development.

5. **Running Basic Setup**: Once the project is fully set up, run some basic build commands (such as **`./gradlew`** tasks from the terminal) to ensure that everything is configured correctly, and to view available Gradle tasks.

6. **iOS Application Settings (If Applicable):** If targeting iOS, after linking the iOS framework, ensure that those settings are adjusted properly in Xcode.

Make sure to configure your app's Info.plist, and build settings to match your requirements.

By completing these steps, you will create a robust Android Studio environment ready to develop applications using Kotlin Multiplatform, allowing for effective use of shared code alongside platform-specific features. This setup is foundational for leveraging the best of Kotlin in a multiplatform landscape.

Integrating Shared Code in Android Projects

One of the key advantages of Kotlin Multiplatform is the ability to share code across different platforms, which enhances code reuse and maintainability. In Android projects, you can integrate shared modules containing business logic to achieve consistency and efficiency. This section explores how to integrate shared code into your Android projects, focusing on sharing business logic, and accessing shared modules.

Sharing Business Logic

Sharing business logic across platforms is a core principle of Kotlin Multiplatform development, enabling developers to maximize code reuse and maintain consistency in application behavior. By efficiently identifying and implementing common business logic, you can streamline development across various platforms, while adhering to the "Don't Repeat Yourself" (DRY) paradigm. In the following sections, we will explore how to identify common business logic, create shared logic in the commonMain source set, implement interfaces for platform-specific functionalities, and conduct testing of the shared logic to ensure reliability and correctness. Mastering these practices will empower you to build robust applications that share essential components and maximize development efficiency.

1. **Identify Common Business Logic:** Assess your application to determine which aspects can be shared, such as data manipulation, business rules, and algorithms. This reduces redundancy, and promotes DRY principles across platforms.

2. **Create Shared Logic in the `commonMain`:** Write shared business logic in the **`commonMain`** source set, ensuring that the code is designed to be platform-independent.

```
fun calculateDiscountedPrice(
    originalPrice: Double,
    discountRate: Double
): Double {
```

```
    return originalPrice - (originalPrice * discountRate)
}
```

3. **Implementing Interfaces for Platform Specifics:** Create interfaces in the shared code for any platform-specific functionality that cannot be implemented in commonMain. Implement these interfaces in the androidMain source set for Android-specific behavior.

```
interface Logger {
    fun log(message: String)
}

Implementation in Android:

actual class AndroidLogger : Logger {
    actual override fun log(message: String) {
        Log.d("AndroidLogger", message)
    }
}
```

4. **Testing Shared Logic:** Write unit tests for your shared business logic in the commonTest source set. This ensures that your shared code behaves correctly and consistently.

```
class DiscountCalculatorTest {

    @Test
    fun testCalculateDiscountedPrice() {
        assertEquals(
                90.0,
                calculateDiscountedPrice(100.0, 0.10),
                0.0
        )
    }
}
```

Accessing Shared Modules

Accessing shared modules is a crucial aspect of developing applications using Kotlin Multiplatform, allowing you to leverage common business logic across different platforms. This process involves several key steps that ensure seamless integration of shared code into your Android projects. We will explore the following essential subtopics that guide you through configuring build scripts, utilizing shared code, debugging interactions, handling platform-specific cases, and synchronizing updates in your shared code. Understanding these concepts will empower you to create efficient and maintainable applications that utilize shared code effectively.

1. **Configuring Build Scripts:** Update the Android module's **build.gradle.kts** file to include the shared code module as a dependency. This enables the Android application to access shared business logic.

```
dependencies {
   implementation(project(":shared")) // Ensure the shared module
is included
}
```

2. **Utilizing Shared Code in Android:** In your **androidMain** source set, import the shared business logic, and utilize it within your Android components. This might occur within **ViewModels**, **Activities**, or **Fragments**.

```
class PricingViewModel : ViewModel() {
   fun getDiscountedProductPrice(originalPrice: Double): Double {
      return calculateDiscountedPrice(originalPrice, 0.15)
   }
}
```

3. **Debugging Interaction:** As you integrate the shared code, use Android Studio's debugging tools to monitor how shared functionalities behave within the Android context, ensuring compatibility and performance.

4. **Handling Platform-Specific Cases:** If you need to handle differences in behavior due to platform requirements, consider using the expect/actual mechanism in Kotlin to define platform-specific implementations of a shared interface.

```
expect class Platform() {
   fun platformName(): String
}

actual class Platform {
   actual fun platformName(): String = "Android"
}
```

5. **Synchronizing Updates in Shared Code:** Regularly update your shared code to reflect any changes or enhancements. Sync your project to ensure that the Android code recognizes updated functionality.

By mastering the integration of shared code in Android projects using Kotlin Multiplatform, you enhance your ability to develop robust, scalable applications that maintain shared logic across multiple platforms. This integration enables you to leverage the strengths of Kotlin Multiplatform, while optimizing development workflows, and maintaining code consistency.

Using Android-Specific APIs and Libraries

To take full advantage of the Android platform, while developing with Kotlin Multiplatform, it is necessary to effectively utilize Android-specific APIs and libraries. This section will dive into how to integrate Android SDK features and popular Jetpack libraries within your Kotlin Multiplatform applications.

Android SDK Integration

Integrating the Android SDK into your Kotlin Multiplatform projects is essential for harnessing the full capabilities of Android devices. This integration allows developers to interact with various device functionalities, such as location services, camera access, and more, while still maintaining the benefits of shared code. In the following sections, we will delve into the fundamentals of the Android SDK, how to access its features, manage permissions effectively, and implement lifecycle-aware components to create responsive applications. By understanding these aspects, you will be better equipped to develop high-performance applications that fully utilize the Android ecosystem.

1. **Understanding the Android SDK:** The Android SDK provides a comprehensive set of APIs that allow developers to interact with device functionalities. Kotlin Multiplatform allows you to blend these platform-specific APIs with shared code seamlessly.

2. **Accessing Android SDK Features:** In your **androidMain** source set, you can write Kotlin code that directly utilizes Android SDK features such as GPS, camera access, or databases.

   For example, to access location services, you can use the following code:

```
fun getLastKnownLocation(context: Context): String {

    val locationManager = context.getSystemService(Context.
LOCATION_SERVICE) as LocationManager
    val provider = LocationManager.GPS_PROVIDER
    val location: Location? = locationManager.getLastKnown
Location(provider)

    return "Latitude: ${location?.latitude},
Longitude: ${location?.longitude}"

}
```

3. **Managing Permissions:** Accessing certain features of the Android SDK requires appropriate permissions. Ensure that you handle permission requests, and checks in your code.

```
if (ContextCompat.checkSelfPermission(
        context,
        Manifest.permission.ACCESS_FINE_LOCATION
    ) != PackageManager.PERMISSION_GRANTED
) {

    ActivityCompat.requestPermissions(
        activity,
        arrayOf(Manifest.permission.ACCESS_FINE_LOCATION),
        REQUEST_LOCATION_PERMISSION
    )
}
```

4. **Implementing Android Lifecycle Awareness:** Utilize components such as Lifecycle and LiveData or ViewModel to ensure that your app responds appropriately to lifecycle events.

```
class LocationViewModel : ViewModel() {

    private val _location = MutableLiveData<Location>()
    val location: LiveData<Location> get() = _location

    fun updateLocation(location: Location) {
        _location.value = location
    }
}
```

Utilizing Jetpack Libraries

Utilizing Jetpack libraries is a fundamental practice in modern Android development, aimed at simplifying the development process, and enhancing the functionality of applications. Jetpack provides a collection of libraries and components that promote efficient development, offering backward compatibility, and reducing the need for boilerplate code. In the following sections, we will explore the introductory concepts of Jetpack libraries, how to set them up in your project, the advantages of using Jetpack Compose for UI development, and the management of navigation within your application. By mastering these tools, you will be well-equipped to build high-quality, responsive applications that utilize the full potential of the Android ecosystem, while benefiting from shared code in Kotlin Multiplatform.

1. **Introduction to Jetpack Libraries:** Jetpack is a suite of libraries and

components that help build Android applications more effectively, providing backward compatibility, and reducing boilerplate code.

2. **Setting Up Jetpack Libraries:** Include necessary Jetpack libraries in your build.gradle.kts file. Popular libraries include LiveData, ViewModel, Room for database management, and Navigation for handling navigation within your application.

```
dependencies {
   implementation("androidx.lifecycle:lifecycle-viewmodel-ktx
:2.3.1")
   implementation("androidx.lifecycle:lifecycle-livedata-ktx
:2.3.1")
   implementation("androidx.room:room-runtime:2.3.0")
   kapt("androidx.room:room-compiler:2.3.0")
}
```

3. **Using Jetpack Compose:** Jetpack Compose is Android's modern toolkit for building native UIs. It offers a declarative way to build interactive UIs. You will work with composable functions to build UI elements that can be easily reused and tested.

```
@Composable
fun Greeting(name: String) {
   Text(text = "Hello, $name!")
}

@Composable
fun GreetingScreen() {
   Column {
      Greeting("Android Developer")

      Button(onClick = { /* Handle button click */ }) {
         Text("Click Me")
      }
   }
}
```

4. **Managing Navigation with Jetpack:** Use Jetpack Navigation for handling navigation between different screens in your application. Define navigational graphs, and safely transition between destinations.

```
NavHost(navController, startDestination = "home") {
   composable("home") { HomeScreen(navController) }
   composable("details/{itemId}") { backStackEntry ->
```

```
            val itemId = backStackEntry.arguments?.getString("itemId")
            DetailScreen(itemId)
        }
    }
```

Thus, by effectively integrating Android-specific APIs, and utilizing Jetpack libraries, you can develop powerful Android applications that leverage the strengths of the Android platform, while maintaining the benefits of shared code in Kotlin Multiplatform. These integrations significantly enhance your app's functionality and user experience, allowing for more robust and scalable projects.

Handling UI with Jetpack Compose

Jetpack Compose is a modern toolkit for building native Android UIs. It simplifies UI development through a declarative approach, allowing developers to describe the UI components, and how they should update based on state changes. This section covers the basics of Jetpack Compose, and guides you in creating reusable UI components.

Basics of Jetpack Compose

Jetpack Compose is a modern toolkit for building user interfaces in Android applications, making UI development faster and more intuitive. By embracing a declarative approach, developers can create dynamic and responsive interfaces that seamlessly adapt to changes in state. In the following sections, we will explore the fundamental concepts of Jetpack Compose, including how to declare UI elements, leverage composable functions, manage state effectively, utilize Material Design components, and implement themes and styles for a cohesive user experience.

- **Declarative UI:** Jetpack Compose allows developers to declare what the UI should look like based on the current state. You define your UI using composable functions, which render the UI elements in response to changes in state.
- **Composable Functions:** The main building block of Jetpack Compose is the @Composable function. These functions define UI elements that can be combined to construct complex layouts.

```
@Composable
fun Greeting(name: String) {
    Text(text = "Hello, $name!")
}
```

- **State Management:** Compose integrates seamlessly with state management through built-in features such as MutableState. When the state changes, the composables recompose, reflecting the new values in the UI.

```
@Composable
fun Counter() {
   var count by remember { mutableStateOf(0) }
   Button(onClick = { count++ }) {
      Text(text = "Count: $count")
   }
}
```

- **Material Design Components:** Jetpack Compose includes a rich set of Material Design components that can be easily customized to fit your application needs. Components such as Button, Card, Column, and Row help create a cohesive user interface.
- **Themes and Styles:** Theming in Jetpack Compose enhances user experience by maintaining visual consistency. Use **`MaterialTheme`** to define colors, typography, and shapes.

```
MaterialTheme {
   // Define the UI components here
}
```

Creating UI Components

Designing intuitive and reusable user interfaces is a key aspect of modern Android development, especially when working within a Kotlin Multiplatform project. Jetpack Compose offers a powerful, declarative approach to building UIs that are both flexible and maintainable. In this section, you will learn how to create composable UI components, handle user interactions, structure complex layouts, and preview designs—all while seamlessly integrating the shared logic. These practices not only improve development efficiency but also ensure a cohesive and responsive user experience across your application.

1. **Building Reusable Components:** One of the best practices in UI development using Jetpack Compose is to create reusable components. This keeps your code organized, and promotes reusability.

```
@Composable
fun ProfileCard(name: String, age: Int) {

   Card(
       modifier = Modifier.padding(8.dp),
       elevation = 4.dp
   ) {
       Column(modifier = Modifier.padding(16.dp)) {
           Text(text = "Name: $name", style = MaterialTheme.
typography.h6)
           Text(text = "Age: $age", style = MaterialTheme.
typography.body1)
```

```
        }
    }
}
```

2. **Handling User Interactions:** Compose supports various ways to handle user interactions. Use clicks, gestures, or animations to create interactive UI elements.

```
@Composable
fun InteractiveButton() {
    Button(onClick = { /* Handle button click */ }) {
        Text("Click Me")
    }
}
```

3. **Complex Layouts:** Compose makes it easy to create complex layouts by nesting composable functions, and utilizing Row, Column, and Box for arranging UI elements.

```
@Composable
fun UserList(users: List<User>) {
    LazyColumn {
        items(users) { user ->
            ProfileCard(name = user.name, age = user.age)
        }
    }
}
```

4. **Previewing Composables:** Compose allows you to preview your UI components, without running the app. This feature speeds up the UI development process.

```
@Preview(showBackground = true)
@Composable
fun PreviewGreeting() {
    Greeting(name = "Kotlin Developer")
}
```

5. **Integrating Shared Logic in UI:** You can access shared business logic, such as view models or data classes, within your composables. This allows your UI to stay synced with the underlying application logic efficiently.

```
@Composable
fun MainScreen(viewModel: MainViewModel) {
    val user = viewModel.user.collectAsState()
    ProfileCard(name = user.value.name, age = user.value.age)
}
```

By mastering the basics of Jetpack Compose, and creating reusable UI components, you can build powerful and flexible user interfaces for your Android applications.

This approach saves time, enhances maintainability, and leverages the strengths of Kotlin Multiplatform, allowing code to remain clean and efficient, while delivering an engaging user experience.

Managing Platform-Specific Code

While Kotlin Multiplatform allows for code sharing among different platforms, certain functionalities require platform-specific implementations. This section discusses how to manage platform-specific code effectively, including implementing interfaces, and handling features unique to Android.

Implementing Platform Interfaces

To build truly cross-platform Kotlin Multiplatform applications, it is crucial to abstract platform-specific behavior in a clean and scalable way. This is where shared interfaces and Kotlin's expect/actual mechanism come into play. By defining common interfaces in the shared code, and implementing them separately for each platform, you can decouple business logic from platform-specific APIs. This section guides you through the process of creating and implementing these interfaces, ensuring that your codebase remains modular, testable, and easy to extend across Android, iOS, and beyond.

1. **Defining Shared Interfaces:** Start by creating interfaces in the **`commonMain`** source set that define the expected behaviors or functionalities for various platforms.

   ```
   interface DataProvider {
      fun getData(): List<String>
   }
   ```

2. **Implementing Android-Specific Logic**: In the **`androidMain`** source set, provide actual implementations for the shared interfaces defined earlier, using Android-specific resources and APIs.

   ```
   actual class AndroidDataProvider : DataProvider {
      actual override fun getData(): List<String> {
          // Implement logic to fetch data, e.g., from a database or
   API
          return listOf("Item 1", "Item 2", "Item 3")
      }
   }
   ```

3. **Using Expect/Actual Mechanism:** Use the expect keyword in **`commonMain`** to declare the platform-specific details that need implementation. The actual keyword in the Android source set provides the concrete implementation.

```
expect class PlatformLogger {
    fun log(message: String)
}
```

The Android implementation might look like this:

```
actual class PlatformLogger {
    actual fun log(message: String) {
        Log.d("PlatformLogger", message)
    }
}
```

4. **Decoupling Business Logic:** By using interfaces and the **`expect/actual`** mechanism, you ensure that your shared business logic can remain agnostic to the implementation details, leading to cleaner and more maintainable code.

Handling Android-Specific Features

While Kotlin Multiplatform promotes code sharing across platforms, certain functionalities–such as accessing device hardware, managing permissions, or using Android SDK libraries–must be handled natively. This section focuses on how to implement and integrate Android-specific features within your Multiplatform project. From working with Android APIs and libraries to managing UI with activities as well as handling runtime permissions, you will learn how to seamlessly bridge the gap between shared logic and platform-specific capabilities, ensuring a fully functional and optimized Android experience.

1. **Accessing Android APIs:** Use Android SDK features directly within the **`androidMain`** source set. This includes accessing services such as location, camera, and notifications.

```
fun startLocationUpdates(context: Context) {
    val locationManager = context.getSystemService(Context.
LOCATION_SERVICE) as LocationManager
    // Assume necessary permissions are checked

    locationManager.requestLocationUpdates(LocationManager.GPS_
PROVIDER, 2000, 1f, locationListener)
}
```

2. **Using Android-Specific Libraries:** Integrate libraries that are specific to the Android platform to enhance functionality. For instance, you can use Retrofit for network requests or Room for local database management.

```
dependencies {
    implementation("com.squareup.retrofit2:retrofit:2.9.0")
    implementation("androidx.room:room-runtime:2.3.0")
    kapt("androidx.room:room-compiler:2.3.0")
}
```

3. **Managing UI with Activity/Fragment:** When developing Android-specific features, continue to use Activities and Fragments alongside Jetpack Compose for the UI layer. The UI components can call into shared logic, while managing platform-specific operations gracefully.

```
class MainActivity : AppCompatActivity() {
   override fun onCreate(savedInstanceState: Bundle?) {
      super.onCreate(savedInstanceState)
      setContent {
         MyApp {
            // Application layout, possibly including Jetpack
Compose UI
         }
      }
   }
}
```

4. **Handling Platform-Specific Permissions:** Ensure that proper permissions are declared in the **`AndroidManifest.xml`**, and handle permission requests within your activities or fragments.

```
<uses-permission android:name="android.permission.ACCESS_FINE_
LOCATION" />

if (ContextCompat.checkSelfPermission(
      this,
      Manifest.permission.ACCESS_FINE_LOCATION
   ) != PackageManager.PERMISSION_GRANTED
) {

   ActivityCompat.requestPermissions(
      this,
      arrayOf(Manifest.permission.ACCESS_FINE_LOCATION),
      LOCATION_PERMISSION_REQUEST_CODE
   )

}
```

5. **Testing and Debugging:** Utilize Android Studio's powerful debugging tools to test platform-specific code. Thus, make sure to verify that shared logic integrates correctly with the Android-specific implementations.

Hence, by effectively managing platform-specific code, and implementing necessary interfaces, you will optimize how your Android application operates, while maintaining the benefits of Kotlin Multiplatform. This strategy aids in code reuse, and helps to leverage platform-specific features, creating a robust application experience.

Building a Sample Android App

Creating a sample Android application is an effective way to solidify your understanding of Kotlin Multiplatform development. This section provides a step-by-step guide to build a sample app, along with common pitfalls and solutions to ensure a smooth development experience.

Step-by-Step Guide

Building a Kotlin Multiplatform application becomes significantly easier, when you follow a structured, hands-on approach. This step-by-step guide walks you through the entire development process–from setting up your environment, and organizing your project structure to writing shared business logic, creating Android UIs with Jetpack Compose, and implementing testing strategies. Therefore, whether you are targeting Android alone or planning to scale to multiple platforms, these steps provide a practical roadmap to bring your Kotlin Multiplatform project to life with clarity and confidence.

1. **Set Up Your Development Environment:**
   - Ensure that you have Android Studio installed with the Kotlin plugin, and Multiplatform support configured.
   - Create a new Kotlin Multiplatform project using the "**`Kotlin Multiplatform Mobile`**" template.
2. **Define Project Structure:** Create separate modules for **`shared`**, **`androidApp`**, and any other platforms you wish to target (such as iOS). The shared module will contain business logic and common code.
3. **Implement Shared Logic:** In the shared module, define your business logic such as data models and utility functions. Use **`commonMain`** for shared code.

```
// Define a simple data model

data class User(val name: String, val age: Int)

// A function to get user data

fun getUserData(): List<User> {
    return listOf(User("Alice", 30), User("Bob", 25))
}
```

4. **Create Android UI:** In the **androidApp** module, use Jetpack Compose to build the user interface. Create composable functions for UI components.

```
@Composable
fun UserListScreen() {
    val users = getUserData() // Call function from shared module
    LazyColumn {
        items(users) { user ->
            Text(text = "${user.name}, Age: ${user.age}")
        }
    }
}
```

5. **Control Navigation:** Use Jetpack Navigation or a simple **Composable** setup to handle the navigation between different screens (if applicable).

```
@Composable
fun MainScreen() {
    Scaffold {
        Column {
            Button(onClick = { /* Navigate to User List Screen */
}) {
                Text("See Users")
            }
        }
    }
}
```

6. **Set Up Dependency Injection:** If necessary, incorporate Dependency Injection with libraries such as Koin or Dagger to manage cross-cutting concerns, and allow for easier testing.

7. **Test Your Application:** Create unit tests for your shared logic in the shared module, and UI tests for your Android module, using the Android testing framework.

8. **Run the Application:** Build and run your application on an Android emulator or physical device. Ensure to set the necessary permissions in the AndroidManifest.xml file, if accessing specific device features.

Common Pitfalls and Solutions

Even with a solid understanding of Kotlin Multiplatform development, developers can encounter challenges that hinder progress or impact application quality. Recognizing common pitfalls–and knowing how to address them–can save valuable time, and prevent frustration. This section highlights typical issues that arise during development, such as Gradle sync errors, state mismanagement in Jetpack Compose, and platform-specific conflicts. Alongside each pitfall, you will find practical solutions to help you navigate these obstacles, and maintain a smooth, efficient development workflow.

- **Pitfall: Gradle Sync Issues**

  Solution: If you encounter issues during Gradle sync, check that all dependencies are correctly declared in your `build.gradle.kts` files, and ensure that your internet connection is stable, while syncing.

- **Pitfall: Incorrect State Management**

  Solution: Ensure that state management in Jetpack Compose is handled properly. Use remember and mutableStateOf to manage state, ensuring that recomposition occurs correctly.

- **Pitfall: Platform-Specific Code Conflicts**

  Solution: Use the expect/actual mechanism to handle platform-specific functionality without conflict. Keep clear distinctions between shared and platform-specific code.

- **Pitfall: UI Not Reflecting State Changes**

  Solution: When adding or removing items from the state, ensure that they are wrapped in state variables so that Compose can respond to changes appropriately.

- **Pitfall: Permissions Not Granted**

  Solution: Make sure to handle permissions at runtime for features that require user consent (for example, location access). Test on devices to ensure that services are accessible, if needed.

- **Pitfall: Performance Issues with Jetpack Compose:**

  Solution: Profile your app performance using Android Studio's built-in tools. Optimize composable calls, and ensure that heavy computation is done outside UI rendering, maintaining a responsive user interface.

Thus, by following this step-by-step guide, and being aware of common pitfalls, you will successfully create a working Android app using Kotlin Multiplatform. This experience will enhance your understanding of the workflow needed for effective application development across platforms, utilizing shared code for maximum efficiency.

Debugging and Testing on Android

Effective debugging and testing are necessary for ensuring the reliability and performance of your Android application. In the context of Kotlin Multiplatform, you will need to adopt strategies that accommodate both shared and platform-specific code. This section outlines the debugging tools available, and provides guidance in writing unit and instrumentation tests to verify your applications.

Debugging Tools

Efficient debugging is vital for identifying and resolving issues quickly during Kotlin Multiplatform development. Hence, whether you are working on shared business logic or platform-specific features, having the right tools can significantly streamline the troubleshooting process. This section introduces a range of powerful debugging utilities–from Android Studio's built-in debugger and Logcat to performance profilers and remote debugging options. You will also learn how to incorporate unit testing into your workflow to catch issues early, and ensure that your code behaves as expected across all platforms.

- **Android Studio Debugger:**
  - Android Studio comes with a powerful debugger that allows you to set breakpoints, inspect variables, and evaluate expressions at runtime.
  - You can pause execution at specific points, and inspect the call stack to understand how the app's state changes over time.

  ```
  fun exampleFunction() {
     val data = fetchData()
     Log.d("DebugData", data.toString()) // Set a breakpoint
  here
  }
  ```
- **Logcat:**
  - Logcat is an essential tool for logging runtime information and debugging output.
  - Use Log functions available in Android to log messages, which can be viewed in the Logcat window:

  ```
  Log.d("TAG", "This is a debug message")
  Log.e("TAG", "This is an error message")
  ```
- **Performance Profiler:**
  - Use Android Studio's built-in performance profilers (CPU, Memory, Network, and Energy) to analyze your application's resource consumption.
  - This is crucial for identifying performance bottlenecks, particularly when dealing with shared code that is executed across platforms.
- **Remote Debugging:** For more complex scenarios, Android Studio supports remote debugging, allowing you to debug an app running on a physical device.
- **Unit Testing:** Ensure that unit tests are correctly set up in the `commonTest`

source set for shared logic, and utilize Android's testing tools for Android-specific components.

Writing Unit and Instrumentation Tests

Testing is a fundamental part of developing reliable and maintainable Kotlin Multiplatform applications. By validating your code through unit and instrumentation tests, you can ensure consistent behavior across platforms and catch issues early in the development cycle. This section walks you through writing platform-independent unit tests using the commonTest source set, implementing Android-specific instrumentation tests, and integrating automated testing into your CI pipeline. These practices help maintain code quality, and build confidence in every release.

1. **Writing Unit Tests:** Unit tests are used to check the functionality of individual components or functions. Write these tests in the commonTest source set for shared logic to ensure that it works correctly across all platforms.

```
class ExampleTest {

   @Test
   fun testCalculateDiscountedPrice() {
        val result = calculateDiscountedPrice(100.0, 0.10)
        assertEquals(90.0, result, 0.01)
   }
}
```

2. **Setting Up Instrumentation Tests:**

   - Instrumentation tests are used to test Android-specific components, and ensure that your UI behaves correctly. These tests reside in the **`androidTest`** source set.
   - Use libraries such as Espresso for UI testing, and JUnit for structuring tests.

```
@RunWith(AndroidJUnit4::class)
class MainActivityTest {

   @get:Rule
   val activityRule = ActivityScenarioRule(MainActivity::class.
java)

   @Test
   fun testUserNameDisplayed() {
        onView(withId(R.id.userNameTextView)).check(matches
(withText("Alice")))
   }
}
```

3. **Running Tests:**
   - You can run your tests directly from Android Studio by right-clicking on the **`test`** class or method, and selecting "**`Run`**". Alternatively, use Gradle commands from the terminal to execute all tests.
   - For unit tests:
     ```
     ./gradlew test
     ```
   - For instrumentation tests:
     ```
     ./gradlew connectedAndroidTest
     ```
4. **Continuous Integration for Testing:** Integrate a Continuous Integration (CI) system such as GitHub Actions, CircleCI, or Jenkins to automate running your tests whenever code changes are made. This ensures that any introduced bugs are caught early in the development process.

Summary

Thus, by utilizing the various debugging tools available in Android Studio, and writing comprehensive unit as well as instrumentation tests, you can significantly improve the quality of your Android applications developed with Kotlin Multiplatform. Continuous testing and debugging will ensure that your app is both robust and responsive, delivering a seamless user experience across platforms.

Best Practices for Android Development

Adopting best practices is crucial in developing high-quality Android applications using Kotlin Multiplatform. This section discusses the key aspects of code organization and performance optimization, which help create maintainable, efficient, and scalable applications.

Code Organization

Effective code organization is necessary for building scalable and maintainable Kotlin Multiplatform applications. By structuring your project with clear boundaries between shared and platform-specific logic, adopting proven architectural patterns, and maintaining consistent practices, you lay the foundation for efficient development and collaboration. The following best practices outline the key strategies–from modular architecture and resource management to MVVM adoption and documentation–that help ensure your codebase remains clean, understandable, and adaptable across platforms.

- **Modular Architecture:**
  - Organize your application into modules–such as one for shared code and

separate modules for platform-specific code—to enhance maintainability and clarity.

  - This modular approach facilitates code reuse, allowing shared business logic to be used across different platforms seamlessly.

- **`UseCommonRV` (Common Resource Vocabulary):** Define common resources in a universal manner. Utilize **`commonMain`** for shared functionality, ensuring that any platform-specific logic resides in **`androidMain`**, **`iosMain`**, and so on.
- **Separation of Concerns:** Follow the principle of Separation of Concerns (SoC) to keep your code organized. This means separating business logic, UI code, and data handling facilitates easier testing and maintenance.
- **Adopt MVVM Pattern:** Utilize the Model-View-ViewModel (MVVM) architecture, a proven pattern in Android development for organizing UI code effectively. This separation allows better handling of UI states, and promotes code reusability.
- **Consistent Naming Conventions:** Use consistent naming conventions for your classes, functions, and variables across your codebase. This practice enhances code readability, and makes it easier for others (or you in the future) to understand the code.
- **Documentation:** Document your code adequately using KDoc (Kotlin documentation) to explain complex logic, and to guide future developers on how to use shared modules.

Performance Optimization

Performance is a critical factor in delivering smooth, responsive, and reliable applications—especially in mobile and multiplatform environments where resource constraints and user expectations are high. This section outlines the essential strategies for optimizing your Kotlin Multiplatform code, from managing resource usage and leveraging asynchronous programming to profiling and continuous improvement. Thus, by applying these practices, developers can enhance application speed, reduce latency, and ensure consistent performance across all supported platforms.

- **Efficient Use of Resources:** Minimize resource usage by optimizing images, using vector graphics, and limiting memory consumption where possible. This is especially important for mobile applications where resources are constrained.
- **Asynchronous Programming:** Utilize coroutines and asynchronous programming to prevent blocking the UI thread. This ensures a responsive user experience, particularly during network calls or database queries.

```
fun fetchData() {
   viewModelScope.launch {
      val data = withContext(Dispatchers.IO) {
         // Simulate network operation
      }
      // Update UI with the fetched data
   }
}
```

- **Reduce Layout Overdraw:** In Jetpack Compose, ensure that your layouts are efficiently structured to minimize overdraw, which occurs when a pixel is drawn multiple times. This impacts rendering performance.
- **Lazy Loading:** Use lazy loading techniques for collections or heavy resource objects. Jetpack Compose provides LazyColumn for efficient rendering of lists, without blocking the UI.
- **Profile Application Performance:** Regularly, profile your application using Android Studio's profiling tools. Monitor CPU, memory, and network usage to identify bottlenecks, and optimize your application accordingly.
- **Testing and Continuous Improvement:** Invest time in writing tests for performance comparisons. Use tools such as Java Microbenchmark Harness (JMH) to benchmark your code, ensuring that improvements do not regress performance.

So, by following these best practices in code organization and performance optimization, you can significantly enhance the quality and maintainability of your Android applications developed using Kotlin Multiplatform. These practices enable a more efficient development process, leading to robust applications that provide an excellent user experience across platforms.

Conclusion

In this chapter, you have taken a significant step toward mastering Android development using Kotlin Multiplatform. We explored how to set up Android Studio for a multiplatform environment, integrate shared business logic, leverage Android-specific APIs and Jetpack libraries, and build responsive UIs using Jetpack Compose. You also learned how to debug, test, and manage platform-specific code, while maintaining consistency with shared modules—enabling faster, cleaner, and more maintainable Android apps.

Kotlin Multiplatform not only streamlines code reuse but also enhances collaboration across platform teams, reducing effort duplication, and minimizing bugs. With the ability to harness both shared and native Android capabilities, you are now well-equipped to build scalable Android applications that fit seamlessly into a broader multiplatform architecture.

But Android is just one side of the multiplatform coin.

In the next chapter, we shift our focus to iOS Development with Kotlin Multiplatform, where you will learn how to configure Xcode with shared Kotlin modules, integrate Kotlin frameworks into SwiftUI, and manage interoperability with native iOS components. Therefore, get ready to unlock the full potential of cross-platform development–on Apple devices!

Chapter 8

iOS Development with Kotlin Multiplatform

Introduction

In this chapter, we delve into the specifics of developing iOS applications using Kotlin Multiplatform. You will learn how to set up Xcode to support Kotlin Multiplatform, integrate shared code seamlessly, and leverage iOS-specific APIs and frameworks. We will guide you through building a sample iOS app, emphasizing practical implementation, efficient code reuse, and adherence to best practices. Topics include handling UI with SwiftUI, managing platform-specific code, and strategies for debugging and testing on iOS devices. By the end of this chapter, you will be proficient in developing robust iOS applications with Kotlin Multiplatform, ensuring a smooth development process and high-quality end products.

Structure

In this chapter, we will cover the following topics:

- Setting Up Xcode for Multiplatform
- Integrating Shared Code in iOS Projects
- Using iOS-Specific APIs and Frameworks
- Handling UI with SwiftUI
- Managing Platform-Specific Code
- Building a Sample iOS App
- Debugging and Testing on iOS
- Best Practices for iOS Development

Setting Up Xcode for Multiplatform

Setting up Xcode for Kotlin Multiplatform development is essential to ensure that you can successfully integrate and utilize the shared code created in your Kotlin modules within your iOS application. This section covers the installation of the necessary plugins and the configuration of build settings.

Installing Necessary Plugins

Installing necessary plugins is a fundamental step in preparing your development environment for Kotlin Multiplatform projects, specifically when working with iOS applications. This process ensures that all required tools and dependencies are in place for a smooth development experience. In this section, we will cover the essential steps to install and configure Xcode, check for Command Line Tools, integrate Cocoapods for dependency management, and consider the Kotlin Multiplatform Mobile plugin for optimal framework generation. Additionally, we will discuss setting up your Podfile to include the Kotlin shared module, which is crucial for effectively linking shared code within your iOS application. By following these steps, you will establish a robust foundation for developing, building, and managing your Kotlin-based iOS projects.

1. **Installing Xcode**: Begin by ensuring that you have the latest stable version of Xcode installed on your macOS machine. You can download or update Xcode through the Mac App Store.

2. **Checking for Command Line Tools**: Ensure that the Xcode Command Line Tools are installed. Open a terminal and run the following command:

   ```
   xcode-select --install
   ```

   This installs the necessary tools required for development with Xcode.

3. **Cocoapods Integration**: To manage dependencies within your iOS application, you will need to install Cocoapods, which is commonly used for managing external libraries in iOS projects.

   ```
   sudo gem install cocoapods
   ```

4. **Kotlin Multiplatform Mobile Plugin for Xcode**: Although Xcode itself does not require any additional plugins to utilize Kotlin Multiplatform, ensure that you are aware of the Kotlin Multiplatform Mobile (KMM) plugin available for Android Studio IDEs, as this will assist in generating the necessary framework to be used in your Xcode projects.

5. **Setting Up Your Podfile**: Create a **Podfile** in the iOS project directory if it does not already exist. Configure it to include the Kotlin shared module, specifying the path to your generated framework.

   ```
   platform :ios, '13.0'

   use_frameworks!
   ```

```
target 'Your_iOS_App' do

   pod 'YourKotlinSharedModule', :path => '../path_to_your_
shared_code'

end
```

Configuring Build Settings

Configuring build settings is a crucial step in integrating Kotlin Multiplatform with your Xcode project, enabling you to leverage shared code effectively, while still utilizing platform-specific features in your iOS applications. This process involves setting up a new Xcode project, adding the Kotlin framework as a dependency, and adjusting various build settings to ensure seamless interaction between Kotlin and Swift code. In this section, we will outline the necessary steps to create your Xcode project, include the Kotlin shared module, properly configure build settings such as linker flags and header visibility, and conduct tests to verify that your integration is functioning as intended. By following these guidelines, you will lay a solid foundation for developing robust applications that benefit from shared logic across multiple platforms.

1. **Creating an Xcode Project**: Open Xcode and create a new project. Choose `App` under the iOS section and select **`Swift`** as the interface option for the UI.

2. **Adding Kotlin Framework as a Dependency**: After you have set up your Xcode project, you need to include the Kotlin shared module as a dependency. Run the following command in your terminal from the iOS project directory to install the pods.

   ```
   pod install
   ```

   After running this command, open the generated **`.xcworkspace`** file instead of the **`.xcodeproj`** file.

3. **Adjusting Build Settings**: In your Xcode project, navigate to the project settings, and ensure that the following settings are configured:

   a. **Build Phases:** Ensure that the built Kotlin framework is linked under the "*Link Binary with Libraries*" section.

   b. **Other Linker Flags:** In the "**`Build Settings`**", add **`-lc++`** to the **`Other Linker Flags`** section to prevent potential linker errors related to C++ code used by Kotlin.

4. **Verifying Header Visibility**: Make sure that the generated Kotlin framework's headers are visible to your Swift code. This often requires adjusting the module map or ensuring that the correct import syntax is used when accessing Kotlin classes and functions from Swift.

5. **Testing Your Setup**: After setting up the xcode project and the Kotlin framework, create a simple Swift integration to confirm that the integration is working appropriately. This can involve calling a simple function from your Kotlin shared code.

```
import SharedCode

class ViewController: UIViewController {
   override func viewDidLoad() {
      super.viewDidLoad()
      let greeting = Greeting().greeting(name: "iOS Developer")
      print(greeting) // This should print the greeting message
from Kotlin
   }
}
```

By completing these steps, you will successfully configure Xcode to work with Kotlin Multiplatform. This setup allows you to harness the power of shared code across platforms, while maintaining the ability to develop and utilize platform-specific features in your iOS applications.

Integrating Shared Code in iOS Projects

Integrating shared code into your iOS applications allows you to maximize code reuse across platforms, which is one of Kotlin Multiplatform's primary advantages. This section outlines the process of sharing and accessing business logic within your iOS projects.

Sharing Business Logic

Sharing business logic is a fundamental aspect of Kotlin Multiplatform that enables developers to write code once and use it across multiple platforms, thereby reducing redundancy and improving maintainability. By defining shared logic in a dedicated Kotlin module, you can encapsulate core functionalities such as data models, utility functions, and algorithms that are independent of platform specifics. In this section, we will discuss the steps to define shared logic within the shared module, generate a Kotlin/Native framework compatible with iOS, compile the framework for use in Xcode, and discuss the importance of documenting your shared code for clarity and collaboration among development teams. By effectively sharing business logic, you can enhance the efficiency and consistency of your application development across different platforms.

1. **Defining Shared Logic in the Shared Module**: In your Kotlin **`shared`** module,

define business logic that does not depend on the platform. This can include data models, utility functions, and algorithms.

```
package com.example.shared

data class User(val name: String, val age: Int)

fun getUserGreeting(user: User): String {
   return "Hello, ${user.name}, you are ${user.age} years old!"
}
```

2. **Kotlin/Native Framework Generation**: Ensure that your shared module is configured to generate a framework compatible with iOS. This is typically specified in your **build.gradle.kts** file under the Kotlin targets.

```
kotlin {
   ios {
      binaries {
         framework {
            baseName = "SharedCode"
         }
      }
   }
}
```

3. **Building the Framework**: Run the **Gradle** command to build the Kotlin framework for iOS:

```
./gradlew build
```

After building, this generates a framework file that can be integrated into your Xcode project.

4. **Documenting Business Logic**: As you define shared logic, document your functions and classes to provide clarity for iOS developers utilizing that code. This promotes better collaboration and understanding across teams.

Accessing Shared Modules

Accessing shared modules is a vital aspect of leveraging Kotlin Multiplatform in your iOS applications, allowing you to utilize common business logic across platforms. By integrating your Kotlin code into your Xcode project, you can enhance code consistency and maintain efficiency throughout your development process. In this section, we will explore the steps necessary to import the generated Kotlin framework into your Xcode project, manage dependencies using Cocoapods, access shared code within Swift, handle nullable types appropriately, and test the integration to ensure everything works as expected. Additionally, we will cover debugging strategies for optimizing your shared code interactions. By effectively implementing these practices, you can create robust iOS applications that harness the power of shared modules while adhering to the specificities of the iOS platform.

1. **Importing the Generated Framework into Xcode**: Open your iOS Xcode project, navigate to the project settings, and ensure that the generated Kotlin framework (**`SharedCode.framework`**) is included under the "*Frameworks, Libraries, and Embedded Content*" section.

2. **Using Cocoapods for Dependency Management**: If using Cocoapods, ensure that the **`Podfile`** points to the correct path of the generated framework.

```
target 'Your_iOS_App' do
    pod 'SharedCode', :path => '../path_to_your_shared_code'
end
```

3. **Accessing Shared Code in Swift**: Once the framework is accessible, you can import it and utilize its functionalities in your Swift files.

```
import SharedCode

class ViewController: UIViewController {
    override func viewDidLoad() {
        super.viewDidLoad()
        let user = User(name: "Jane Doe", age: 30)
        let greeting = getUserGreeting(user: user)
        print(greeting) // Output: Hello, Jane Doe, you are 30
years old!
    }
}
```

4. **Handling Nullable Types**: Keep in mind Kotlin's handling of nullability when calling shared code from Swift. Kotlin's non-null types may require you to ensure safe unwrapping in Swift.

5. **Testing the Integration**: Run the application to test if the shared logic integrates correctly. Ensure that functions from the shared module operate as expected without runtime issues.

6. **Debugging Shared Code**: Utilize Xcode's debugging tools to step through the Swift code and observe interactions with the Kotlin shared logic. You may need to set breakpoints in both Swift and Kotlin source files for effective debugging.

By effectively sharing business logic and accessing shared modules in your iOS projects, you leverage the full potential of Kotlin Multiplatform. This integration enhances code consistency across both iOS and Android platforms, making your development process more efficient and streamlined. With these techniques, you can create robust iOS applications that benefit from shared code while still adhering to platform-specific guidelines and best practices.

Using iOS-Specific APIs and Frameworks

Kotlin Multiplatform allows developers to share code across platforms while leveraging platform-specific APIs and frameworks where necessary. This section covers how to integrate iOS SDK features into your Kotlin Multiplatform applications, focusing on iOS SDK integration, as well as utilizing Core Data and UIKit.

iOS SDK Integration

iOS SDK integration is essential for harnessing the full power of device functionalities while building applications with Kotlin Multiplatform. By understanding how to effectively use the iOS SDK, developers can create richer user experiences and access advanced capabilities such as networking, multimedia, and device sensors. In this section, we will cover the fundamentals of the iOS SDK, including setting up your Xcode project correctly, utilizing specific iOS frameworks within your app, calling iOS-specific APIs through custom wrappers, and handling necessary permissions for accessing sensitive functionalities. By integrating the iOS SDK thoughtfully, you can elevate your Kotlin Multiplatform applications to deliver seamless and engaging experiences for users on the iOS platform.

1. **Understanding the iOS SDK**: The iOS SDK provides a large range of APIs for accessing device functionalities such as networking, multimedia, sensors, and user interactions. Kotlin Multiplatform enables you to access these features from your shared code, and build unique platform-specific functionalities.

2. **Setting Up Your Xcode Project**:

    a. Ensure that your Xcode project is appropriately set up with the Kotlin framework included as a dependency, as described in previous sections.

    b. In the context of using the iOS SDK, make sure your project is set to the appropriate iOS deployment target to access the desired features.

3. **Using iOS Frameworks**: Incorporate iOS frameworks within your Swift files to utilize specific functionalities provided by those frameworks.

```
import UIKit

class ViewController: UIViewController {

    override func viewDidLoad() {
        super.viewDidLoad()
        // Example of accessing UIKit functionality
        let helloLabel = UILabel()
        helloLabel.text = "Hello, Kotlin!"
```

```
        self.view.addSubview(helloLabel)
    }
}
```

4. **Calling iOS-Specific APIs**: When needing to interact with platform-specific services, you can create custom Swift functions or classes that wrap up iOS SDK calls, enabling only necessary functions to be exposed to Kotlin code.

5. **Handling Permissions**: Use the appropriate APIs for accessing sensitive functions (such as camera or location services) to ensure that you request permissions at runtime.

```
func requestLocationAccess() {
    let locationManager = CLLocationManager()
    locationManager.requestWhenInUseAuthorization()
}
```

Utilizing CoreData and UIKit

Utilizing CoreData and UIKit allows developers to tap into the full potential of iOS's robust frameworks while working within the Kotlin Multiplatform ecosystem. Core Data serves as a powerful model layer for managing application data efficiently, while UIKit remains a key player in building traditional user interfaces. In this section, we will cover how to seamlessly integrate Core Data within your Kotlin Multiplatform applications, including creating a Core Data model and interfacing with it from your shared code. Additionally, we will explore the use of UIKit components, demonstrating how to incorporate UIKit alongside SwiftUI or as the primary framework for your app's interface. By mastering these integrations, you will be equipped to build comprehensive applications that leverage both Kotlin's strengths and the rich features of iOS.

Core Data Integration

Core Data is a powerful framework for managing the model layer objects in your application. To use Core Data with Kotlin Multiplatform, you will maintain entity definitions and data access patterns in your Kotlin shared code, but the Core Data integration will occur on the iOS side.

1. **Creating a Core Data Model:** Open your Xcode project and create a Core Data model. Define your entities and attributes within the **`.xcdatamodeld`** file.

2. **Interfacing with Core Data:** Create a Core Data stack inside your iOS code that integrates with your shared code:

```
lazy var persistentContainer: NSPersistentContainer = {
    let container = NSPersistentContainer(name: "YourModelName")
    container.loadPersistentStores(completionHandler: { (store
Description, error) in
```

```
            if let error = error {
                fatalError("Unresolved error \(error)")
            }
        })
        return container
    }()

    func saveContext() {
        let context = persistentContainer.viewContext

        if context.hasChanges {
            do {
                try context.save()
            } catch {
                let nserror = error as NSError
                fatalError("Unresolved error \(nserror), \(nserror.
userInfo)")
            }
        }
    }
```

Using UIKit

While SwiftUI is a modern way to build UI in iOS applications, UIKit remains a robust framework used for more traditional UI development. In your Kotlin Multiplatform applications, you can still utilize UIKit alongside SwiftUI or solely, depending on your project requirements.

Use UIKit components by accessing them directly in your Swift code, setting up view controllers, and constructing your app's overall layout.

```
class CustomViewController: UIViewController {

    override func viewDidLoad() {
        super.viewDidLoad()
        view.backgroundColor = .white
        let button = UIButton(type: .system)
        button.setTitle("Press Me", for: .normal)
        button.addTarget(self, action: #selector(buttonTapped),
for: .touchUpInside)
        view.addSubview(button)
        // Add constraints or frames for layout
    }

    @objc func buttonTapped() {
```

```
            print("Button was tapped!")
        }
    }
```

By leveraging iOS-specific APIs and frameworks, you can create powerful applications that fully utilize the capabilities of the iOS ecosystem while still managing shared code efficiently with Kotlin Multiplatform. This approach not only enhances the functionality of your app but also ensures that you maintain the advantages of code reuse and modularity provided by Kotlin.

Handling UI with SwiftUI

SwiftUI is Apple's modern framework for building user interfaces across all Apple platforms. It provides a declarative syntax for constructing UIs, enabling developers to create complex views with less code and real-time previews that can significantly enhance the development workflow. This section covers the basics of SwiftUI, and guides you in creating reusable UI components.

Basics of SwiftUI

Understanding the basics of SwiftUI is essential for building modern, responsive user interfaces in your applications. SwiftUI's declarative syntax and reactive data model simplify the development process, allowing developers to focus on what the user interface should represent rather than the intricate details of how to construct it. In this section, we will explore key concepts of SwiftUI, including the use of declarative syntax for clear code, the composition of views and the application of modifiers for customization, effective state management techniques to ensure dynamic UI updates, and the powerful preview functionality that allows for real-time design testing. Mastering these fundamentals will lay a strong foundation for creating engaging applications with Kotlin Multiplatform and SwiftUI.

- **Declarative Syntax**: SwiftUI allows developers to declare the user interface in a straightforward manner, emphasizing the desired outcome, rather than the steps to achieve it. This leads to cleaner and more understandable code.

```
struct ContentView: View {

    var body: some View {
        Text("Hello, Kotlin Multiplatform!")
            .padding()
            .font(.largeTitle)
    }
}
```

- **Views and Modifiers**: In SwiftUI, everything is a view, which can be composed using various view elements such as **Text**, **Image**, **Button**, **List**, and more. You can customize these views using modifiers that adjust how they appear and behave.

```
struct WelcomeView: View {
    var body: some View {
        VStack {
            Text("Welcome to the Sample App")
                .font(.title)
                .foregroundColor(.blue)

            Image(systemName: "star.fill")
                .resizable()
                .frame(width: 100, height: 100)
        }
        .padding()
    }
}
```

- **State Management**: SwiftUI uses a reactive data model, and provides powerful tools for managing state. You can use properties marked with **`@State`**, **`@Binding`**, or `@ObservedObject` to reflect data changes in the UI.

```
struct CounterView: View {
   @State private var count: Int = 0
   var body: some View {
        VStack {
            Text("Count: \(count)")
            Button("Increase Count") {
                count += 1
            }
        }
    }
}
```

- **Previews**: SwiftUI enables you to see a real-time preview of your UI as you design it. Using the **`@PreviewProvider`** annotation, you can provide different views for testing various states.

```
struct CounterView_Previews: PreviewProvider {
   static var previews: some View {
       CounterView()
   }
}
```

Creating UI Components

Creating UI components is a fundamental aspect of developing engaging and dynamic applications using SwiftUI. By mastering the art of building reusable and interactive components, developers can create a cohesive user experience that promotes design consistency and enhances maintainability. In this section, we will explore several key techniques for crafting UI components, including building reusable views, combining smaller components into compound views, handling user interactivity with intuitive controls, and establishing theme and design consistency throughout the application. By following these guidelines, you will be well-equipped to create sophisticated and user-friendly interfaces for your Kotlin Multiplatform applications.

1. **Building Reusable Components**: One of the powerful features of SwiftUI is the ability to create reusable components through reusable view structures. This promotes code reuse and simplifies maintenance.

```
struct ProfileCard: View {
   var user: User
   var body: some View {
        VStack(alignment: .leading) {
             Text(user.name)
                  .font(.headline)
             Text("Age: \(user.age)")
                  .font(.subheadline)
        }
        .padding()
        .background(Color.gray.opacity(0.1))
        .cornerRadius(8)
        .shadow(radius: 2)
   }
}
```

2. **Combining Components**: You can create compound views by combining multiple smaller views into a larger one, enhancing organization and readability.

```
struct UserListView: View {
   let users: [User]
   var body: some View {
        List(users) { user in
             ProfileCard(user: user) // Use the custom ProfileCard
view
        }
   }
}
```

3. **Handling User Interactivity**: SwiftUI provides straightforward ways to handle user interactions with buttons and gestures. Use **onTapGesture**, **Button**, and other controls to create interactive experiences.

```
struct InteractiveCard: View {
   var user: User
   var body: some View {
        HStack {
```

```
                ProfileCard(user: user)
                Button(action: {
                    // Handle action, such as navigating or displaying
more info
                }) {
                    Text("View Details")
                }
            }
        }
}
```

4. **Theme and Design Consistency**: SwiftUI allows you to define a consistent look and feel across your application using the SwiftUI `Material` and `Theme` systems. Create a custom style to apply it throughout your components.

   ```
   struct MyAppTheme {
       static let primaryColor = Color.blue
       static let secondaryColor = Color.green
   }
   ```

By mastering the basics of SwiftUI and the creation of reusable UI components, you can leverage the power of this framework for developing sophisticated iOS applications with Kotlin Multiplatform. This approach not only maximizes code reuse but also enhances overall application maintainability and performance, ensuring a high-quality user experience.

Managing Platform-Specific Code

Managing platform-specific code is essential when developing iOS applications with Kotlin Multiplatform, as it allows you to utilize the unique capabilities of the iOS environment while still leveraging shared functionalities. This section covers implementing platform interfaces and handling iOS-specific features effectively.

Implementing Platform Interfaces

Implementing platform interfaces is a crucial step in leveraging the unique capabilities of different environments while maintaining a unified codebase in Kotlin Multiplatform development. By defining common interfaces in shared code, developers can create a flexible architecture that allows for platform-specific implementations to thrive without coupling the shared logic. In this section, we will discuss how to define common interfaces in the shared code, provide iOS-specific implementations, utilize the expect/actual mechanism in Kotlin to handle platform differences, and encapsulate platform-specific functionality for better maintainability. By mastering these techniques, you will enhance the functionality of your applications, while preserving a clean and efficient architecture.

1. **Defining Common Interfaces in Shared Code**: To ensure that your shared code can leverage platform-specific functionality, start by defining interfaces in the **commonMain** source set. These interfaces outline the methods that the platform-specific implementations will provide.

```
interface AnalyticsService {
   fun logEvent(eventName: String)
}
```

2. **Providing iOS-Specific Implementations**: In the **iosMain** source set, implement the interfaces defined in the shared code. This allows your iOS application to perform specific actions that leverage iOS APIs.

```
actual class iOSAnalyticsService : AnalyticsService {
   actual override fun logEvent(eventName: String) {
       // Use iOS-specific analytics SDK to log events
       print("Event logged: $eventName")
   }
}
```

3. **Using Expect/Actual in Kotlin**: Use the `expect` keyword to define a class or function in your shared code and the `actual` keyword in the iOS implementation to fulfill that contract.

```
expect class PlatformSpecificAnalytics {
   fun trackEvent(event: String)
}
```

Implementing it in iOS:

```
actual class PlatformSpecificAnalytics {
   actual fun trackEvent(event: String) {
       // Perform iOS-specific tracking event logic here
   }
}
```

4. **Encapsulating Platform-Specific Functionality**: Encapsulating platform-specific code behind interfaces maintains clean code architecture and ensures that your shared code remains platform-agnostic.

Handling iOS-Specific Features

Handling iOS-specific features is essential for creating applications that fully leverage the power of the iOS platform while utilizing Kotlin Multiplatform. By integrating native features, developers can deliver a richer user experience that takes advantage of the unique functionalities available in the iOS ecosystem. In this section, we will explore how to access iOS frameworks, implement notifications, utilize SwiftUI for modern

UI development, manage the iOS app lifecycle, and test iOS-specific functionalities. By effectively handling these aspects, you will be better equipped to build high-performance applications that resonate with iOS users, ensuring a seamless and engaging experience.

1. **Accessing iOS Frameworks**: Leverage iOS frameworks such as **`CoreLocation`**, **`UIKit`**, or **`AVFoundation`** directly from your Swift code in the iOS project, enabling access to native features and functionalities.

```
import CoreLocation

class LocationManager: NSObject, CLLocationManagerDelegate {
   var locationManager: CLLocationManager?
   override init() {
       super.init()
       locationManager = CLLocationManager()
       locationManager?.delegate = self
       locationManager?.requestWhenInUseAuthorization()
   }

   func startUpdatingLocation() {
       locationManager?.startUpdatingLocation()
   }

   func locationManager(_ manager: CLLocationManager,
didUpdateLocations locations: [CLLocation]) {
       // Handle location updates
   }
}
```

2. **Using Notifications**: Implement iOS notifications using the **`UNNotification`** framework. Set up local notifications to alert users about important events or reminders in your app.

```
import UserNotifications

func scheduleNotification() {

   let content = UNMutableNotificationContent()
   content.title = "Hello!"
   content.body = "Don't forget to check the app."

   let trigger = UNTimeIntervalNotificationTrigger(timeInterval:
60, repeats: false)
   let request = UNNotificationRequest(identifier: UUID().uuid-
String, content: content, trigger: trigger)
```

```
    UNUserNotificationCenter.current().add(request, withCompletion-
Handler: nil)
    }
```

3. **Using SwiftUI for UI Development**: While developing the user interface in iOS, SwiftUI can be used to create modern and flexible UI components that respond to state changes efficiently.

```
struct ContentView: View {

    @State private var greeting: String = "Welcome to Kotlin
Multiplatform!"
    var body: some View {
        Text(greeting)
            .padding()
    }
}
```

4. **Handling iOS App Lifecycle**: Understand how to manage the app lifecycle specific to iOS. Use **AppDelegate** or SwiftUI's app struct to handle application state transitions and manage resources effectively.

```
@main
struct MyApp: App {
    var body: some Scene {
        WindowGroup {
            ContentView()
        }
    }
}
```

5. **Testing iOS-Specific Features**: Test platform-specific functionalities on iOS devices or simulators. Make use of XCTest for unit and UI tests to ensure that your app behaves as expected on all supported iOS versions and devices.

By establishing robust implementations of platform interfaces and properly handling iOS-specific features, you can enhance the performance and user experience of your Kotlin Multiplatform applications. This approach enables developers to leverage the strengths of both Kotlin and iOS, resulting in applications that provide seamless functionality and an engaging user interface.

Building a Sample iOS App

Creating a sample iOS application using Kotlin Multiplatform is an excellent way to apply the skills you have learned and understand the integration of shared code with iOS-specific features. This section provides a comprehensive step-by-step guide to building a sample app for iOS, along with insights into common pitfalls you may encounter.

Step-by-Step Guide

This step-by-step guide provides a comprehensive approach to integrating Kotlin Multiplatform into your iOS application, allowing developers to take advantage of shared business logic while creating a native user interface using SwiftUI. Throughout the guide, you will learn how to set up your iOS app project in Xcode, configure CocoaPods for dependency management, build and implement shared Kotlin code, and create a user-friendly interface. Additionally, we will cover optional navigation setup for multi-screen functionality and how to run and test your application effectively. By following these steps, you will gain the skills necessary to develop a robust iOS app that leverages the benefits of both Kotlin and Swift.

1. Setting Up the iOS App Project:

    a. Open Xcode and create a new project. Choose the "**`App`**" template under the iOS section.

    b. Specify the project name, organization identifier, and interface setup (choose SwiftUI for this guide).

2. **Configuring Podfile for CocoaPods**: Navigate to the project directory in your terminal and create a `Podfile` if it does not already exist. Inside the Podfile, add the Kotlin framework as follows:

    ```
    platform :ios, '13.0'

    use_frameworks!
            target 'MySampleApp' do
    pod 'SharedCode', :path => '../path_to_your_shared_code'

    end
    ```

    Install the pods by running:

    ```
    pod install
    ```

    Always use the **`.xcworkspace`** file for your project moving forward.

3. **Building the Shared Kotlin Code**: In your Kotlin shared module, create a simple business logic implementation. For example, you can define a **`User`** data model and a function to retrieve user greetings.

    ```
    data class User(val name: String)

    fun greetUser(user: User): String {
       return "Hello, ${user.name}!"
    }
    ```

4. **Implementing the UI in SwiftUI**: In Xcode, navigate to the main SwiftUI view (for example, **`ContentView.swift`**) and integrate the shared logic. Access your Kotlin code directly from Swift.

```
import SwiftUI

import SharedCode

struct ContentView: View {
    var body: some View {
        let user = User(name: "Kotlin Developer")
        Text(greetUser(user: user)) // Calls Kotlin's greetUser
function
            .padding()
    }
}
```

5. **Setting Up Navigation (Optional)**: If your app requires multiple screens, set up navigation using SwiftUI's **`NavigationView`** and **`NavigationLink`**.

```
struct UserListView: View {
    var body: some View {
        NavigationView {
            List {
                NavigationLink(destination: DetailView()) {
                    Text("User Profile")
                }
            }
        }
    }
}
```

6. **Running and Testing the Application**:

    a. With the code in place, build and run your app on an iOS simulator or device to test its functionality.

    b. Verify interactions, the ability to access shared Kotlin code, and the overall smoothness of the UI.

Common Pitfalls and Solutions

Navigating the challenges of Kotlin Multiplatform development is crucial for building successful iOS applications. Understanding common pitfalls can help you avoid issues that might impede progress and ensure a smoother development experience. In this section, we will discuss several frequent obstacles developers encounter, such as frameworks not being found, recognition issues with Kotlin functions, compatibility challenges, state management in SwiftUI, compilation errors, and UI performance issues. For each pitfall, we will provide practical solutions to help you troubleshoot effectively. By gaining insights into these common issues and their remedies, you will enhance your ability to integrate shared logic in iOS applications, and greatly improve your overall productivity as a developer.

- **Pitfall**: Framework Not Found

  Solution: Ensure that the generated Kotlin framework (**`SharedCode.framework`**) is correctly added to the Xcode project under "*Frameworks, Libraries, and Embedded Content*." Also, verify that the Podfile is correct and that you have run **`pod install`**.

- **Pitfall**: Kotlin Function Not Recognized

  Solution: Ensure that the Kotlin function or class you are trying to access is public and properly declared in the shared code. Also, check that you are using the correct import statements in Swift.

- **Pitfall**: Compatibility Issues

  Solution: Keep an eye on iOS deployment targets in both your Podfile and your Xcode project. Ensure they are compatible with the features you are implementing in your shared code.

- **Pitfall**: State Management in SwiftUI

  Solution: Make sure to manage the state using **`@State`**, **`@Binding`**, or **`@ObservedObject`** properly to ensure UI updates when the underlying data changes.

- **Pitfall**: Compilation Errors

  Solution: If you encounter compilation errors, check for issues in the Kotlin code, ensuring that all dependencies are intact and that there are no missing imports or mismatches in data types.

- **Pitfall**: UI Performance Issues

  Solution: Profile your app's performance using Xcode's Instruments to find bottlenecks, and avoid unnecessary recomposition in SwiftUI by structuring your views carefully.

By following this step-by-step guide and being cognizant of common pitfalls, you will successfully build a sample iOS application using Kotlin Multiplatform. This experience will enhance your skills and deepen your understanding of integrating shared logic in iOS apps, while maximizing productivity.

Debugging and Testing on iOS

Debugging and testing are critical aspects of iOS application development. When using Kotlin Multiplatform, it is essential to understand how to effectively debug and test both shared and platform-specific code. This section outlines the tools available for debugging, and provides guidelines for writing unit and UI tests to ensure that your application performs as expected.

Debugging Tools

Debugging tools play a pivotal role in developing reliable applications by allowing developers to identify and resolve issues effectively. Utilizing the right debugging strategies can dramatically improve the efficiency of your development process and enhance the overall quality of your applications. In this section, we will explore various debugging tools available for iOS development, including the Xcode debugger for setting breakpoints and inspecting code, methods for debugging Kotlin code within SwiftUI or UIKit components, leveraging console logging, utilizing Xcode Instruments for performance tracking, and exploring real-time debugging capabilities in SwiftUI. By effectively using these tools, you can streamline your debugging process and ensure a smoother, more reliable application development experience.

- **Xcode Debugger:**
  - Xcode comes equipped with a powerful debugger that allows developers to set breakpoints, inspect variables, and step through code. The debugger can be used for both Swift and Kotlin code when the application runs in Xcode.
  - To set a breakpoint, click on the line number in your code, which halts execution at that point when running in debug mode. This allows you to inspect the state of your application, including the values of variables and objects.
- **Debugging Kotlin Code**: While debugging SwiftUI or UIKit components, you can still set breakpoints in the Kotlin shared code. This allows you to ensure that the shared logic interacts appropriately with the iOS UI.

```
fun greetUser(user: User): String {
    // Set a breakpoint here
    return "Hello, ${user.name}!"
}
```

- **Console Logging**: Make use of `print` statements in Swift and **`Log`** functions in Kotlin/Native to output messages to the console, helping to trace execution and spot issues.

```
actual class PlatformLogger {
    actual fun log(message: String) {
        print("Log from Kotlin: $message")
    }
}
```

- **Instruments**: Use Xcode Instruments to track performance and memory usage. Instruments help to identify performance bottlenecks, memory leaks, or other runtime issues that can affect app behavior.
- **Real-time Debugging with SwiftUI**: SwiftUI provides a live preview feature in Xcode, which can significantly help in visualizing layout changes without running the application multiple times.

Writing Unit and UI Tests

Writing unit and UI tests is a vital practice in software development that ensures the reliability and stability of your applications. Effective testing allows developers to confirm that business logic works as intended and that user interfaces respond correctly to interactions, ultimately leading to a better user experience. In this section, we will explore the importance of writing unit tests using XCTest in your iOS project, utilizing XCTest for UI testing, running tests effectively within Xcode, and setting up Continuous Integration (CI) systems to automate test execution. Additionally, we will discuss best practices for testing to enhance the clarity and effectiveness of your test cases. By adopting these testing strategies, you will be well-equipped to maintain high standards for quality in your Kotlin Multiplatform applications.

- Writing Unit Tests:
    a. Unit tests are essential for verifying the correctness of your business logic within the shared module. Use XCTest in the iOS project to test this logic.

    b. Create a test target for your iOS project. Write tests that invoke functions in your shared Kotlin code, validating the expected outputs.

    ```
    import XCTest

    @testable import Your_iOS_App

    import SharedCode

    class UserTests: XCTestCase {
       func testUserGreeting() {
            let user = User(name: "Kotlin Developer")
            let greeting = greetUser(user: user)
            XCTAssertEqual(greeting, "Hello, Kotlin Developer!")
       }
    }
    ```
- **Using XCTest for UI Testing**: For UI tests, XCTest allows you to simulate user interactions and verify that the UI responds correctly. UI tests are placed in the `UITests` target of your Xcode project.

```
class MyAppUITests: XCTestCase {

    func testLoginButton() {
        let app = XCUIApplication()
        app.launch()
        // Simulate a button tap
        app.buttons["Login"].tap()
        XCTAssert(app.staticTexts["Welcome!"].exists)
    }
}
```

- **Running Tests**: You can execute your tests from Xcode by selecting **Product > Test** or using the keyboard shortcut ⌘U. This will run all unit and UI tests, reporting any failures directly in the editor.
- **Continuous Integration**: Set up a Continuous Integration (CI) system (such as GitHub Actions, CircleCI, or Jenkins) to automate test execution. Running unit and UI tests automatically whenever changes are made helps catch issues early.
- Best Practices for Testing:
    - Write clear and concise test cases. Group related tests logically to maintain organization.
    - Use mock objects for any external dependencies (for example, network calls) to isolate tests from side effects.

By effectively utilizing debugging tools and writing comprehensive tests for your iOS application developed with Kotlin Multiplatform, you can ensure a high-quality user experience. This focus on debugging and testing will help you identify and resolve issues promptly, ultimately leading to a more stable and robust application.

Best Practices for iOS Development

Adhering to best practices in iOS development helps maintain high-quality code, enhances performance, and ensures code maintainability. In this section, we will explore effective strategies for code organization and performance optimization in iOS applications built with Kotlin Multiplatform.

Code Organization

Code organization is a fundamental aspect of software development that significantly impacts the maintainability, scalability, and clarity of your applications. Properly structuring your code allows for easier collaboration among team members, enhances code reuse, and simplifies the process of implementing changes or adding new features. In this section, we will explore several key strategies for effective code organization, including adopting a modular architecture, adhering to the separation of concerns principle, maintaining consistent naming conventions, documenting your code thoroughly, and leveraging design patterns and best practices. By implementing these strategies, you will create a well-organized codebase that is easier to manage and evolve over time.

- **Modular Architecture**: Organize your project into separate modules for shared code and platform-specific code. This modular approach allows for better maintainability and encourages the reuse of shared logic across different platforms.
- **Separation of Concerns**: Follow the principle of separating business logic, UI components, and service data. This ensures that your codebase is organized in a way that is easy to understand and manage.
- **Utilizing MVVM Pattern**: Adopt the Model-View-ViewModel (MVVM) architecture to structure your app effectively. This pattern separates the user interface from the business logic, facilitating better testing and maintenance.

```
class UserViewModel: ObservableObject {

   @Published var user: User
   init(user: User) {
       self.user = user
   }

   func updateUser(with newName: String) {
       user.name = newName
   }
}
```

- **Consistent Naming Conventions**: Use consistent naming conventions for files, classes, and methods to enhance code readability. For example, follow **`camelCase`** for properties and methods, and **`PascalCase`** for classes.
- **Documentation and Comments**: Document your code as you write it. Use comments and KDoc for Kotlin and appropriate Swift documentation methods to explain complex logic. This helps in onboarding new developers and maintaining the code in the long run.
- **Design Patterns and Best Practices**: Utilize design patterns such as Singleton, Factory, and Observer appropriately throughout your codebase. Familiarize yourself with commonly used patterns in iOS development, and follow the best practices laid out by Apple.

Performance Optimization

Performance optimization is crucial in developing high-quality applications, as it directly affects the user experience and resource management. By implementing effective optimization techniques, you can ensure that your applications run smoothly and efficiently, even under heavy loads. This section will discuss several key strategies for optimizing performance, including efficient resource usage, leveraging asynchronous programming with Kotlin coroutines, reducing app launch times, utilizing SwiftUI for efficient UI changes, and the importance of profiling and instrumentation. Additionally, we will explore testing performance and managing background tasks effectively. By adopting these best practices, you can develop responsive and efficient iOS applications using Kotlin Multiplatform, ultimately leading to a more enjoyable experience for your users.

- **Efficient Resource Usage**: Minimize the use of resources by optimizing images, using vector graphics, and avoiding excessive memory consumption. Be mindful of any large assets your app may use, and ensure that they are appropriately managed.
- **Asynchronous Programming**: Leverage Kotlin coroutines for performing asynchronous tasks, such as network calls or data processing, to avoid blocking the main UI thread. This ensures that your app remains responsive even during heavy operations.

```
fun fetchData() {
    viewModelScope.launch {
        val data = withContext(Dispatchers.IO) {
            // Perform network request
        }
        // Update UI with the received data
    }
}
```

- **Reducing App Launch Time**: Optimize your app's startup time by deferring non-essential tasks and using lazy loading for resources. This enhances user experience by allowing users to access functionality quickly.
- **Using SwiftUI for Efficient UI Changes**: SwiftUI is designed for efficient UI updates. When a state change occurs, SwiftUI only redraws the necessary parts of the UI, improving rendering performance. Use state properties effectively to ensure responsive updates.
- **Profiling and Instrumentation**: Regularly profile your application using Xcode Instruments to identify performance bottlenecks. Monitor CPU, memory, and network usage to continuously improve the application's performance.
- **Testing Performance**: Write performance tests to track your app's responsiveness and resource consumption. This can help identify regressions in performance and ensure that optimizations are effective over time.
- **Handling Background Tasks**: Use background tasks appropriately in your app to manage tasks that need to continue running after the app goes into the background. Consider using `BeginBackgroundTask` when lengthy tasks need to be completed.

By following these best practices in code organization and performance optimization, you can develop high-quality iOS applications with Kotlin Multiplatform. These strategies not only improve maintainability but also enhance the overall user experience, ensuring that your applications meet the performance and usability standards expected in modern iOS development.

Conclusion

In this chapter, we explored the complete process of integrating Kotlin Multiplatform with iOS development. From configuring Xcode and integrating shared code to utilizing SwiftUI and iOS-specific APIs, you learned how to bridge Kotlin's shared logic with Apple's native ecosystem. We covered best practices for handling platform-specific code, accessing shared business logic, and maintaining seamless interoperability between Kotlin and Swift.

By building a sample iOS application, managing dependencies with Cocoapods, and implementing real-world use cases, you have gained practical experience that demonstrates Kotlin Multiplatform's ability to streamline iOS development while maintaining full access to native capabilities.

With this foundation, you are now equipped to develop iOS apps that benefit from a shared codebase—ensuring consistency and accelerating development across platforms.

In the next chapter, we shift our focus from mobile to the web. You will learn how to build performant and interactive web applications using Kotlin/JS and compose for Web. We will explore how to configure your project for web targets, integrate shared business logic, and implement dynamic UIs with modern web technologies. Thus, whether you are building internal tools or full-scale web apps, Kotlin Multiplatform has the tools to help you do it efficiently—all from a unified codebase.

So, let us take Kotlin to the browser!

CHAPTER 9
Web Development with Kotlin Multiplatform

Introduction

This chapter explores the exciting possibilities of web development using Kotlin Multiplatform. You will learn how to set up a web project with Kotlin/JS, integrate shared code, and utilize web-specific libraries to build dynamic and interactive web applications. We will walk you through creating a sample web app, focusing on practical implementation, efficient code reuse, and best practices. You will gain insights into handling UI with Kotlin/React, managing platform-specific code, and debugging as well as testing your web applications. By the end of this chapter, you will be equipped to develop robust and scalable web applications using Kotlin Multiplatform.

Structure

In this chapter, we will cover the following topics:

- Setting Up a Web Project with Kotlin/JS
- Integrating Shared Code in Web Projects
- Using Web-Specific Libraries and Frameworks
- Handling UI with Kotlin/React
- Managing Platform-Specific Code
- Building a Sample Web App
- Debugging and Testing Web Applications
- Best Practices for Web Development

Setting Up a Web Project with Kotlin/JS

To develop web applications using Kotlin/JS, you need to ensure that your development environment is correctly set up. This involves installing necessary tools, configuring your build settings, and preparing your project structure. This section provides a comprehensive guide on how to get started with web development using Kotlin/JS.

Installing Necessary Tools

Installing the necessary tools is a crucial first step in setting up a robust development environment for Kotlin/JS applications. These tools will facilitate an efficient workflow and streamline the development process. In this section, we will guide you through the installation of essential software, starting with IntelliJ IDEA, which provides excellent support for Kotlin development. We will also cover the installation of Node.js, a requirement for building and running Kotlin/JS web applications. Additionally, we will discuss the importance of the Kotlin plugin for IntelliJ IDEA and the optional Yarn package manager for managing dependencies. Finally, we will provide instructions on how to verify that all installations were successful, ensuring that your development environment is ready for Kotlin/JS projects. With these tools in place, you will be well-equipped to embark on your Kotlin/JS development journey.

1. **Installing IntelliJ IDEA**: Begin by downloading and installing IntelliJ IDEA (Community Edition or Ultimate) from the official JetBrains website (https://www.jetbrains.com/idea/download/?section=windows). IntelliJ IDEA has excellent support for Kotlin development.

2. **Installing Node.js**: Since Kotlin/JS relies on Node.js for building and running web applications, make sure that you have it installed on your system. Download and install Node.js from the official Node.js website (https://nodejs.org/en).

3. **Installing the Kotlin Plugin (if necessary)**: If you are using IntelliJ IDEA, the Kotlin plugin should already be integrated. If not, check for updates to install the Kotlin plugin via `File` > `Settings` > `Plugins`.

4. **Installing Yarn (optional)**: Yarn is a package manager for `Node.js` projects that can help manage dependencies efficiently. You can install it globally by running:

   ```
   npm install --global yarn
   ```

5. **Verifying Your Installation**: Open your terminal, and verify the installations by running:

```
node -v    # Check Node.js installation
npm -v     # Check npm installation
yarn -v    # Check Yarn installation (if installed)
```

Configuring Build Settings

Configuring build settings is essential for establishing a well-structured and efficient Kotlin/JS project. By following a systematic approach, developers can set up their development environment to facilitate the creation of modern web applications that harness the power of Kotlin Multiplatform. In this section, we will guide you through the process of creating a new Kotlin/JS project, ensuring that the project structure is organized for optimal development. We will cover configuring Gradle to specify the Kotlin/JS target, adding necessary dependencies, and setting up the HTML and CSS files required for your application. Additionally, we will discuss defining build configurations to streamline the building and running of your application. By the end of this section, you will have a fully configured web project ready to leverage Kotlin's capabilities for building engaging web experiences.

1. **Creating a New Kotlin/JS Project**: In IntelliJ IDEA, select **`File`** > **`New`** > **`Project`**. Choose **`Kotlin`** from the list and then select **`Kotlin/JS for Frontend Development`**. Follow the wizard to set up the project details such as name, location, and module type.

2. **Project Structure**: Ensure that your project structure is organized with the following primary directories:
   - **`src/main/kotlin`**: Housing your Kotlin source files.
   - **`src/main/resources`**: To include any static resources (HTML, CSS, and JavaScript files).
   - **`build.gradle.kts`**: The Gradle configuration file.

3. **Configuring Gradle for Kotlin/JS**: In your **`build.gradle.kts`**, apply the Kotlin plugin for JS and configure the Kotlin/JS target. This allows you to specify the target JavaScript environments (for instance, "browser").

   Here is an example **`build.gradle.kts`** configuration:

```
plugins {
    kotlin("js") version "1.6.10" // Ensure you are using the latest version
}

kotlin {
    js(IR) { // Use new IR backend
        browser {
            testTask {
```

```
                useKarma {
                    useFirefox()
                }
            }
        }
    }
}
```

4. **Adding Dependencies**: Include necessary dependencies, such as for Kotlin/React or any other libraries you plan to use.

```
dependencies {
    implementation("org.jetbrains.kotlin-wrappers:kotlin-
react:17.0.2-pre.236-kotlin-1.6.10")
    implementation("org.jetbrains.kotlin-wrappers:kotlin-
react-dom:17.0.2-pre.236-kotlin-1.6.10")
}
```

5. **Setting Up HTML and CSS**: Create an HTML file (**`index.html`**) in the **`src/main/resources`** directory to serve as your entry point. This HTML file will be what users navigate to when accessing your web application.

```
<!DOCTYPE html>
<html lang="en">
<head>
    <meta charset="UTF-8">
    <meta name="viewport" content="width=device-width, ini-
tial-scale=1.0">
    <title>Kotlin/JS Sample App</title>
    <script src="output.js"></script>
</head>
<body>
<div id="root"></div>
</body>
</html>
```

6. **Build Configuration**: Define the build configurations within Gradle to facilitate building the compiled JavaScript code. You may configure the output directory if desired.

```
tasks {
    val webpackDev = named("jsWebpackDevelopment") {
        dependsOn("jsBrowserDevelopmentRun")
    }
}
```

7. **Running Your Application**: To build and run your application, use Gradle commands. You can run:

```
./gradlew jsBrowserDevelopmentRun
```

This command compiles your Kotlin code and starts a local server to preview your web application.

By completing these steps, you will have successfully set up a web project using Kotlin/JS. This environment will allow you to leverage Kotlin Multiplatform's capabilities to create interactive and dynamic web applications, paving the way for efficient code reuse across platforms.

Integrating Shared Code in Web Projects

Integrating shared code into web projects allows developers to leverage the benefits of Kotlin Multiplatform, enabling code reuse across different platforms such as iOS, Android, and the web. This section outlines how to effectively share business logic and access shared modules within your web applications.

Sharing Business Logic

Sharing business logic across platforms is a core benefit of using Kotlin Multiplatform, enabling developers to create a unified codebase that drives the application's essential functionality regardless of the target platform. In this section, we will discuss how to define shared logic within the shared module, focusing on crafting data models and functions that are independent of platform specifics. This shared code should reside in the commonMain source set, allowing seamless access from all platforms, including web applications. We will also cover best practices for writing unit tests for shared logic to ensure reliable functionality across different environments. Additionally, the expect/actual mechanism will be introduced, showcasing how to handle platform-specific implementations while maintaining a clean separation of concerns. By effectively sharing business logic, you can create robust, maintainable applications that benefit from a single source of truth for core functionalities.

1. **Defining Shared Logic in the Shared Module**: In your shared module, create data models and functions that are independent of platform specifics. This logic should encompass your application's core functionalities, such as business rules, calculations, and data processing.

```
package com.example.shared

data class Product(val id: Int, val name: String, val price:
Double)

fun calculateTotalPrice(products: List<Product>): Double {
   return products.sumOf { it.price }
}
```

2. **Common Code Structure**: This shared code should reside in the **`commonMain`** source set of your Kotlin Multiplatform project, ensuring that it can be accessed by all target platforms, including the web.
3. **Testing Shared Logic**: Write unit tests for your shared code in the **`commonTest`** source set to verify functionality independently of the platforms that consume it.

```
class ProductTests {

   @Test
   fun testCalculateTotalPrice() {
       val products = listOf(Product(1, "Widget", 19.99),
Product(2, "Gadget", 29.99))
       val total = calculateTotalPrice(products)

       assertEquals(49.98, total, 0.01)
   }
}
```

4. **Using Expect/Actual Mechanism**: If you require platform-specific functionality (for example, file access, network requests), use the **`expect/actual`** mechanism to define the interfaces in the shared module, implementing platform-specific details separately.

```
expect class NetworkClient {
   fun fetchData(url: String): String
}
```

In the web module, you can implement the `actual` function using JavaScript:

```
actual class NetworkClient {
   actual fun fetchData(url: String): String {
       // Implement JavaScript-specific network fetching logic
       return fetch(url).then { response -> response.text() }
   }
}
```

Accessing Shared Modules

Accessing shared modules is a fundamental aspect of leveraging Kotlin Multiplatform, allowing developers to efficiently share business logic between different platforms, such as web and mobile. This practice not only promotes code reuse but also ensures consistency across your applications. In this section, we will explore how to integrate shared modules into your web project by adding them as dependencies in the build configuration. We will demonstrate how to import and utilize shared code within your Kotlin/JS files, making shared functionality readily accessible in your application.

Furthermore, we will discuss how to seamlessly integrate shared logic with Kotlin/React components while maintaining a clear separation between UI and business logic. We will also cover the importance of implementing web-specific features separately and highlight the value of regular testing to ensure that your shared code works flawlessly in the web environment. By mastering these techniques, you can maximize the advantages of Kotlin Multiplatform, and enhance the efficiency and maintainability of your development process.

1. **Adding the Shared Module to Your Web Project**: In the **build.gradle.kts** file of your web project, make sure to include the shared module as a dependency. This will allow you to access functionality defined in the shared code from your web application.

```
dependencies {
    implementation(project(":shared"))
}
```

2. **Importing Shared Code in Kotlin/JS**: Once the shared module is added, you can import it into your Kotlin/JS files and utilize its functionalities directly.

```
import com.example.shared.*

fun main() {
    val products = listOf(Product(1, "Widget", 19.99), Product(2,
"Gadget", 29.99))
    val totalPrice = calculateTotalPrice(products)
    println("Total Price: $$totalPrice")
}
```

3. **Using Kotlin/React for UI**: You can directly call shared functions from your Kotlin/React components. This integration helps maintain a clean separation of UI and business logic.

```
import react.*
import react.dom.*

val App = functionalComponent<RProps> {
    val products = listOf(Product(1, "Widget", 19.99), Product(2,
"Gadget", 29.99))
    val total = calculateTotalPrice(products)
    div {
        h1 { +"Total Price: $$total" }
    }
}

fun main() {
    render(document.getElementById("root")!!) {
```

```
        App {}
    }
}
```

4. **Handling Web-Specific Features**: For any web-specific functionality, make sure to implement this logic separately in your Kotlin/JS files. You can utilize the extensive JavaScript ecosystem alongside Kotlin/JS to enhance your web application.

5. **Testing Integration**: Regularly test your integrated shared code to ensure it functions correctly within the web context. Utilize Jest or another JavaScript testing library suitable for testing Kotlin/JS code to automate this with ease.

By effectively sharing business logic and accessing shared modules in your web projects, you maximize the benefits of Kotlin Multiplatform, allowing your web applications to utilize a single codebase while still being able to leverage platform-specific advantages. This integration enables efficient and maintainable code management across various platforms, fostering a streamlined development process.

Using Web-Specific Libraries and Frameworks

Integrating web-specific libraries and frameworks in your Kotlin/JS project enhances the functionality and interactivity of your web applications. This section covers how to incorporate popular JavaScript libraries into your Kotlin Multiplatform projects and how to effectively use Kotlin/React for building user interfaces.

Integration with Popular JS Libraries

Integration with popular JavaScript libraries is a vital capability of Kotlin/JS that enhances the functionality and flexibility of your applications. By leveraging existing JavaScript libraries, developers can tap into a vast ecosystem of tools while maintaining the elegant syntax and features of Kotlin. In this section, we will explore the principles of JavaScript interoperability with Kotlin, discuss how to add JavaScript libraries to your project through dependency declarations, and delve into the benefits of using Kotlin wrappers for improved integration and type safety. Additionally, we will guide you on how to effectively use the imported libraries in your Kotlin code, offering practical examples. Finally, we will address potential library conflicts and discuss best practices for encapsulating JavaScript usage to ensure smooth operation within your projects. By mastering these integration techniques, you can significantly enhance your Kotlin applications, and streamline the development process.

1. **Understanding JS Interoperability**: Kotlin/JS provides excellent

interoperability with JavaScript code. You can easily use existing JavaScript libraries in your Kotlin code, allowing you to leverage a broad ecosystem of tools and libraries.

2. **Adding JS Libraries to Your Project**: Include the desired JavaScript libraries in your Kotlin project's **build.gradle.kts** file using the **npm** or **yarn** dependency declaration. For example, to add **axios** for HTTP requests:

```
dependencies {
    implementation("axios:0.21.1") // Using npm
}
```

3. **Using the Kotlin Wrapper for JS Libraries**: Some popular JS libraries have Kotlin wrappers that provide better integration and type safety. For example, you can use **kotlinx.serialization** for JSON conversion, or **kotlin-wrappers** for popular libraries such as React or Axios.

```
dependencies {
    implementation("org.jetbrains.kotlin-wrappers:kotlin-
react:17.0.2-pre.236-kotlin-1.5.30")
    implementation("org.jetbrains.kotlin-wrappers:kotlin-
react-dom:17.0.2-pre.236-kotlin-1.5.30")
}
```

4. **Using Imported Libraries**: Once you have added a JavaScript library, you can use it in your Kotlin code by importing the relevant packages. For instance, integrating Axios for API requests can look like this:

```
import axios

fun fetchData(url: String) {
    axios.get(url).then { response ->
        console.log(response.data)
    }.catch { error ->
        console.error("Error fetching data: $error")
    }
}
```

5. **Avoiding Library Conflicts**: When using multiple libraries, be cautious of potential conflicts, especially with global variables. It is a good practice to encapsulate JavaScript library usage within Kotlin wrapper functions to prevent unintended interference.

Utilizing Kotlin/React

Utilizing Kotlin/React provides a robust framework for developers to create interactive web applications with the expressive power of Kotlin. By merging Kotlin's strong typing and null safety with React's dynamic component architecture, this approach enhances productivity while maintaining code quality. In this section, we will explore the foundational aspects of Kotlin/React, beginning with an overview of its capabilities and setup instructions to integrate it within your project. We will then showcase how to create React components using Kotlin syntax, manage component states effectively with **useState**, and handle side effects through the **useEffect** hook for lifecycle management. Additionally, we will emphasize the importance of building responsive user interfaces by leveraging reusable components. Through these techniques, you will be well-equipped to develop high-quality, dynamic web applications that take full advantage of Kotlin Multiplatform features.

1. **Introduction to Kotlin/React**: Kotlin/React is a powerful tool that allows developers to build React applications using Kotlin. It simplifies the process of creating interactive UIs without sacrificing Kotlin's advantages, such as type safety and nullability.

2. **Setting Up Kotlin/React**: Ensure that you have added the Kotlin/React dependencies in your **build.gradle.kts** file as shown earlier. This setup enables you to build React components using Kotlin syntax.

3. **Creating React Components**: Define composable components using Kotlin syntax. The following example illustrates how to create a simple functional component:

```
import react.*
import react.dom.*

val GreetingComponent = functionalComponent<RProps> { props ->
   h1 { +"Hello, Kotlin/React!" }
}
```

4. **State Management in Kotlin/React**: Use **useState** for managing component state, similar to React's **useState** hook. This allows you to manage interactive elements effectively.

```
val CounterComponent = functionalComponent<RProps> {
   val (count, setCount) = useState(0)
   button {
        attrs.onClick = {
            setCount(count + 1)
        }
        +"Count: $count"
   }
}
```

5. Handling Effects with **useEffect**: Use **useEffect** for side effects, such as data fetching or subscriptions. This hook mirrors the behavior of React's **useEffect**, providing lifecycle management for your components.

```
val DataFetchingComponent = functionalComponent<RProps> {
    val (data, setData) = useState<String?>(null)
    useEffect(listOf()) {
        fetchData("https://api.example.com/data").then { response ->
            setData(response)
        }
    }

    data?.let {
        p { +"Data fetched: $it" }
    }
}
```

6. **Building Responsive UI**: Take advantage of React's component-based architecture to build responsive and adaptive UI. Compose your UI from multiple components that can be reused across your application.

Thus, by effectively integrating web-specific libraries and utilizing Kotlin/React, you can create dynamic web applications that are both efficient and robust. This approach maximizes your productivity, and enables you to leverage both Kotlin and established JavaScript libraries, ensuring that you can build high-quality web applications using Kotlin Multiplatform.

Handling UI with Kotlin/React

Kotlin/React allows developers to write React applications using Kotlin, leveraging both the power of Kotlin's type safety and React's component-based architecture. This section covers the basics of Kotlin/React and provides guidance on creating interactive components.

Basics of Kotlin/React

Understanding the basics of Kotlin/React is necessary for developers looking to create modern web applications with Kotlin's expressive syntax while leveraging the powerful React library. Kotlin/React provides seamless bindings to React, facilitating component creation and maintaining compatibility with existing JavaScript libraries and frameworks. In this section, we will cover the fundamental aspects of Kotlin/React, starting with an overview of its features and advantages. We will then guide you through setting up the necessary dependencies in your project, defining basic components, and rendering them to the DOM. Additionally, we will explore the concept of props to enable data passing into components, enhancing reusability and configurability. By mastering these basics, you will lay a strong foundation for developing dynamic web applications with Kotlin/React.

- **Overview of Kotlin/React**: Kotlin/React provides bindings to the React library, enabling developers to create React components with Kotlin syntax. This enhances developer productivity while maintaining the ability to take advantage of existing JavaScript libraries and frameworks.

- **Setting Up Kotlin/React**: Ensure you have the necessary dependencies in your **`build.gradle.kts`** file:

```
dependencies {
   implementation("org.jetbrains.kotlin-wrappers:kotlin-
react:17.0.2-pre.236-kotlin-1.5.30")
   implementation("org.jetbrains.kotlin-wrappers:kotlin-
react-dom:17.0.2-pre.236-kotlin-1.5.30")
}
```

- **Creating a Basic Component**: Define a simple React component using Kotlin syntax. The following example shows how to create a functional component that displays a welcome message.

```
import react.*
import react.dom.*

val WelcomeMessage: FC<RProps> = functionalComponent {
   h1 { +"Welcome to Kotlin/React!" }
}
```

- **Rendering Components**: Use the `main` function to render your component into the HTML. This ties your Kotlin/React application to a specific DOM node.

```
import react.dom.render

fun main() {
   render(document.getElementById("root")!!) {
       WelcomeMessage {}
   }
}
```

- **Using Props**: Props allow you to pass data into components, promoting reusability and making components more configurable.

```
external interface GreetingProps : RProps {
   var name: String
}

val GreetingComponent = functionalComponent<GreetingProps> {
props ->
   h1 { +"Hello, ${props.name}!" }
}
```

Usage:

```
render(document.getElementById("root")!!) {
    GreetingComponent {
        attrs.name = "Kotlin Developer"
    }
}
```

Creating Interactive Components

Creating interactive components is a vital aspect of building engaging user interfaces in web applications utilizing Kotlin/React. By effectively managing the state and responding to user events, developers can create dynamic experiences that enhance user interaction. In this section, we will delve into key techniques for developing interactive components, including managing state with **useState** to enable real-time updates, handling events through event listeners, and implementing consistent styling methods for a polished appearance. Additionally, we will discuss the importance of designing reusable components for streamlined code management and the benefits of using React's Context API for more complex state management scenarios. Emphasizing these practices will facilitate the development of scalable, maintainable applications that fully leverage Kotlin Multiplatform's capabilities for code reuse and interoperability across platforms.

1. **Managing State**: React components can manage their state using **useState**. This allows you to build interactive components that update the UI dynamically.

```
val CounterComponent = functionalComponent<RProps> {
    val (count, setCount) = useState(0) // State for counting
    button {
        attrs.onClick = {
            setCount(count + 1) // Update state on button click
        }
        +"Count: $count"
    }
}
```

2. **Handling Events**: Use event handlers to respond to user interactions. Attach event listeners directly to components using relevant props.

```
import react.dom.*

val InteractiveButton = functionalComponent<RProps> {
    button {
        attrs.onClick = {
            println("Button was clicked!")
        }
```

```
        +"Click me"
    }
}
```

3. **Styling Components**: You can style your components directly using inline styles, CSS imports, or styled-components libraries. Keep designs consistent with CSS-in-JS solutions or by importing global stylesheets.

```
val StyledComponent = functionalComponent<RProps> {
    val style = jsObject<CSSProperties> {
        background = "lightblue"
        padding = "10px"
    }

    div {
        attrs.style = style
        +"This is a styled component!"
    }
}
```

4. **Creating Reusable Components**: Design your components to be reusable across different parts of your application. For example, create a reusable card component that accepts content as props.

```
external interface CardProps : RProps {
    var title: String
    var content: String
}

val CardComponent = functionalComponent<CardProps> { props ->
    div {
        h2 { +props.title }
        p { +props.content }
    }
}
```

5. **Using Context for State Management**: For more complex applications, you may use React's Context API to manage the global state across your components efficiently.

```
val AppContext = createContext()

// Using context in a component

val ConsumerComponent = functionalComponent<RProps> {
    AppContext.Consumer { value ->
        +"Current value: $value"
    }
}
```

Incorporating Kotlin/React into your web applications allows you to create dynamic, interactive UIs using the advantages of Kotlin's type system. Handling state, events, and props effectively will lead to scalable, maintainable, and high-quality web applications that leverage Kotlin Multiplatform's capabilities for maximum code reuse and collaboration across different platforms.

Managing Platform-Specific Code

Managing platform-specific code in your Kotlin Multiplatform web projects is essential to leverage the unique functionalities of the web environment while maintaining the advantages of shared logical code. This section discusses how to implement platform interfaces and handle web-specific features effectively.

Implementing Platform Interfaces

Implementing platform interfaces is a key practice in Kotlin Multiplatform development, allowing for seamless integration of shared code with platform-specific functionality. By defining interfaces in shared code, developers can create a clean separation between core logic and implementation details tailored for particular platforms. In this section, we will explore the process of defining common interfaces within the shared codebase, implementing these interfaces in a web-specific environment, and utilizing Kotlin's expect/actual mechanism to manage platform-specific variations. Additionally, we will discuss how to encapsulate web-specific logic, ensuring that your shared code remains agnostic to the underlying JavaScript implementations. Through this approach, you can achieve greater code reuse and maintainability while effectively leveraging the unique capabilities of each platform.

1. **Defining Common Interfaces in Shared Code**: Start by defining interfaces in the `commonMain` source set that expose the functionality you need on the web. This allows for a clean separation of shared logic and platform-specific implementations.

```
interface HttpClient {
    suspend fun get(url: String): String
}
```

2. **Implementing the Interface for Web**: In the `jsMain` source set, implement the defined interface using JavaScript libraries such as `fetch` for making HTTP requests.

```
actual class JsHttpClient : HttpClient {
    actual override suspend fun get(url: String): String {
        return kotlinx.coroutines.await(CoroutinesScope()) {
            // Use fetch API to get data from the provided URL
```

```
                val response = kotlinx.browser.window.fetch(url)
                return@await response.text()
            }
        }
    }
```

3. **`Expect/Actual` Mechanism**: Use the **`expect`** and **`actual`** keywords to declare the interface in shared code and provide the platform-specific implementation in the JavaScript context.

```
expect class PlatformHttpClient {
    suspend fun fetchData(url: String): String
}
```

In **`jsMain`**, implement:

```
actual class PlatformHttpClient {
    actual suspend fun fetchData(url: String): String {
        val response = /* fetch logic here */
            return response
    }
}
```

4. **Encapsulating Web-Specific Logic**: Use the newly implemented **`JsHttpClient`** to manage web-specific HTTP requests from anywhere in your shared logic, thereby keeping your shared logic agnostic of the JavaScript-specific implementations.

Handling Web-Specific Features

Handling web-specific features is essential for creating engaging and dynamic applications using Kotlin Multiplatform. By effectively leveraging the capabilities offered by the browser and integrating external libraries, developers can enhance the functionality and user experience of their web applications. In this section, we will discuss accessing the Browser API to manage data storage and interact with the DOM, utilizing popular JavaScript libraries to enrich application features, and handling various browser events to improve interactivity. We will also explore how to create Single Page Applications (SPAs) with routing functionality using Kotlin/React, manage application state efficiently, and ensure accessibility and responsive design principles are adhered to. By mastering these web-specific strategies, you can build robust applications that provide a seamless user experience while optimizing the reuse of shared code across platforms.

1. **Accessing the Browser API**: Kotlin/JS allows you to directly access the Browser API, enabling features such as local storage, session storage, and the DOM. Use these capabilities to enhance web applications seamlessly.

```
fun saveToLocalStorage(key: String, value: String) {
   window.localStorage.setItem(key, value)
}

fun getFromLocalStorage(key: String): String? {
   return window.localStorage.getItem(key)
}
```

2. **Utilizing JavaScript Libraries**: You can easily integrate JavaScript libraries to enrich functionalities in your web application. For example, you can include popular libraries such as Lodash or Axios.

   Add the libraries in **package.json** or **build.gradle.kts** if they have Kotlin wrappers.

3. **Handling Events**: Use Kotlin's event-handling capabilities to respond to browser events such as clicks, inputs, and key presses. This can be done using the provided event types in Kotlin/JS.

```
document.getElementById("myButton")?.addEventListener("click", {
   println("Button clicked!")
})
```

4. **Creating Single Page Applications (SPAs)**: Utilize frameworks such as React (with Kotlin/React) to create SPAs with routing. Handle navigation using the Kotlin wrapper for React Router.

```
import react.router.*

val App = functionalComponent<RProps> {
   BrowserRouter {
      Route(path = "/", exact = true) {
         HomePage()
      }

      Route(path = "/about") {
         AboutPage()
      }
   }
}
```

5. Managing State in Web Applications: Leverage tools such as Redux or Kotlin's **MutableState** for effective state management in your web applications. This will maintain a clear separation between UI and application state.

```
val (count, incrementCount) = useState(0)
```

6. Accessibility and Responsive Design: Ensure that your web applications are accessible to all users. Follow web accessibility standards (WCAG) and implement responsive design principles using CSS Flexbox or Grid.

By effectively managing platform-specific code and leveraging web-specific features, you can enhance your Kotlin Multiplatform web applications. This approach enables developers to create seamless, dynamic, and robust web applications, while maintaining the reusability of shared code across various platforms.

Building a Sample Web App

Creating a sample web application using Kotlin/JS allows you to put into practice the principles of Kotlin Multiplatform development. The following sections provide a step-by-step guide to building a sample web app, along with common pitfalls and solutions you may encounter during the process.

Step-by-Step Guide

A step-by-step guide serves as a comprehensive roadmap for successfully setting up and developing a web application using Kotlin Multiplatform. This structured approach helps developers navigate through each phase of project creation, ensuring clarity and efficiency. In this section, we will outline the essential steps, starting from setting up your Kotlin/JS project and creating the appropriate project structure, to implementing shared code logic and developing React components. Additionally, we will discuss how to establish an HTML entry point for your application, render the app using Kotlin/React, and run your application locally. By following this guide, you will gain the necessary skills to build robust web applications that seamlessly integrate Kotlin code and leverage the strengths of modern web technologies.

1. **Setting Up Your Kotlin/JS Project**: Begin by creating a new Kotlin/JS project in your IDE (for example, IntelliJ IDEA). Choose the option for Kotlin/JS for Web Development and set up the project structure.

```
plugins {
   kotlin("js") version "1.6.10" // Replace with the Latest
version
}

kotlin {
   js(IR) {
      browser {
         testTask {
            useKarma {
               useChrome() // Use Chrome for testing
            }
         }
      }
   }
}
```

2. **Creating Project Structure**: Define your project structure with the following directories:
   - **src/main/kotlin**: For Kotlin source files.
   - **src/main/resources**: For static resource files (HTML, CSS).
   - **build.gradle.kts**: The Gradle configuration.
3. **Setting Up HTML Entry Point**: Create an **index.html** file in the **src/main/resources** directory. This file serves as the entry point for your web application.

```
<!DOCTYPE html>
<html lang="en">

<head>
    <meta charset="UTF-8">
    <meta name="viewport" content="width=device-width, ini-
tial-scale=1.0">
    <title>Kotlin Multiplatform Sample App</title>
    <script src="output.js"></script>
</head>

<body>
<div id="root"></div>
</body>

</html>
```

4. **Implementing Shared Code Logic**: In the shared Kotlin module, create business logic that can be reused across your project. For example, define a model and a function to manipulate data.

```
data class Task(val title: String, var completed: Boolean)

fun fetchTasks(): List<Task> {
    return listOf(Task("Learn Kotlin Multiplatform", false),
Task("Build a Web App", false))
}
```

5. **Creating React Components**:
   a. Use Kotlin/React to create the UI components of your application. Ensure that you include Kotlin/React dependencies in your **build.gradle.kts**.

```
dependencies {
    implementation("org.jetbrains.kotlin-wrappers:kotlin-
react:17.0.2-pre.236-kotlin-1.5.30")
    implementation("org.jetbrains.kotlin-wrappers:kotlin-
react-dom:17.0.2-pre.236-kotlin-1.5.30")
}
```

b. Define a main **App** component that retrieves and displays tasks:

```
import react.*
import react.dom.*

val App = functionalComponent<RProps> {
    val tasks = fetchTasks()
    div {
        h1 { +"Task List" }
        ul {
            tasks.forEach { task ->
                li { +task.title }
            }
        }
    }
}
```

6. Rendering the Application: Render your application into HTML using the **main** function:

```
import react.dom.render

fun main() {
    render(document.getElementById("root")!!) {
        App {}
    }
}
```

7. **Building and Running Your Application**: Execute the following Gradle command in your terminal to build and run your web application:

```
./gradlew jsBrowserDevelopmentRun
```

This command compiles your Kotlin code and starts a local development server. Open your web browser and navigate to **http://localhost:8080** to view your application.

Common Pitfalls and Solutions

Understanding common pitfalls and their solutions is crucial for developers working with Kotlin Multiplatform to build web applications. Navigating challenges effectively can save time and enhance the overall development experience. In this section, we will identify typical mistakes encountered during the development process and provide practical solutions to overcome them. We will cover a range of issues, from compilation errors and state management complications to runtime exceptions and dependency conflicts. By being proactive in recognizing these pitfalls, and implementing the suggested resolutions, you can foster a smoother development process, leading to more robust and efficient applications. This knowledge will empower you to anticipate potential challenges and mitigate them effectively as you build your projects.

- **Pitfall**: Compilation Errors

  Solution: Check for incorrect imports or missing dependencies in your **`build.gradle.kts`**. Ensure all necessary libraries are included and properly spelled.

- **Pitfall**: HTTP Requests Not Working

  Solution: If you are making HTTP requests, ensure that the endpoints are reachable and that you are handling CORS issues properly. Investigate using a Proxy or configuring CORS on the server side if needed.

- **Pitfall**: State Management Issues

  Solution: Ensure that you are using **`useState`** or **`useEffect`** properly. Be aware of how state updates trigger re-renders in React. Debugging state management can often resolve rendering issues.

- **Pitfall**: UI Not Updating

  Solution: If UI components are not reflecting state changes, confirm that the state variables are being updated with Kotlin/React's hooks (**`useState`**, **`useEffect`**). Ensure that your state updates are inside the appropriate event handlers.

- **Pitfall**: Runtime Exceptions

  Solution: Use console logging to identify any exceptions that may arise at runtime. It is beneficial to surround potentially throwing code with try-catch blocks to gracefully handle errors and provide feedback.

- **Pitfall**: Dependency Conflicts:

  Solution: If you encounter version conflicts or dependency issues, review your **`package.json`** and **`build.gradle.kts`** files to ensure consistency amongst various library versions.

By following this step-by-step guide and being aware of common pitfalls, you will successfully build a sample web application using Kotlin Multiplatform. This experience will help you grasp the core concepts involved in developing dynamic web applications while maximizing the reuse of shared code across platforms, ultimately improving your coding efficiency and workflow.

Debugging and Testing Web Applications

Debugging and testing are crucial practices in web development that ensure your application runs smoothly, functions correctly, and provides a great user experience. This section discusses the tools available for debugging and presents methodologies for writing unit and integration tests in Kotlin/JS.

Debugging Tools

Debugging tools play a crucial role in identifying and resolving issues within web applications built with Kotlin Multiplatform. Effective debugging can significantly enhance the development workflow by providing insights into application behavior and performance. In this section, we will explore essential debugging tools and techniques, including the powerful built-in developer tools available in modern web browsers for inspecting and logging application output, how to set breakpoints in your Kotlin code to pause execution and examine variable states, the importance of source maps for tracking down issues in the original Kotlin source code, and the use of linting and static analysis tools to maintain code quality. Additionally, we will discuss how to leverage the console and network panels for monitoring API calls and executing JavaScript expressions. By employing these debugging strategies, you can streamline the development process and ensure that your application functions as intended.

- **Browser Developer Tools:**
  - Modern web browsers, such as Chrome and Firefox, come with built-in developer tools that can be invaluable for debugging web applications. Access these tools by right-clicking on the webpage and selecting "**`Inspect`**."
  - Use the **`Console`** tab to view logs, debug messages, and errors from your application. Here is how to log messages in Kotlin:

    ```
    console.log("This is a debug message from Kotlin!")
    ```
- **Setting Breakpoints**: You can set breakpoints in your Kotlin code when compiling for development. Use the Debugger tab in the browser's developer tools to pause on the lines you want to inspect. This allows you to step through code execution and examine variable states.
- **Source Maps**: Ensure that source maps are generated when building your application. Source maps allow you to view the original Kotlin source code even after it has been compiled into JavaScript, making debugging much easier.

  To include source maps, ensure your **`build.gradle.kts`** contains the appropriate configuration:

  ```
  kotlin {
     js {
          browser {
              binaries.executable()
              sourceMaps = true
          }
     }
  }
  ```
- **Linting and Static Analysis**: Implement tools such as ESLint for static analysis

of JavaScript code to catch potential errors and enforce coding standards. Integrate linters into your development workflow for continuous quality checks.

- Testing with Console and Network Panel: The console allows you to execute JavaScript expressions directly, while the network panel gives your insight into all network requests made by your application. Use it to track API calls and ensure responses are handled correctly.

Writing Unit and Integration Tests

Writing unit and integration tests is a vital practice in software development, particularly for ensuring the functionality and reliability of applications built with Kotlin Multiplatform. These testing methodologies help verify individual components and their interactions, ultimately leading to more robust applications. In this section, we will explore the process of writing unit tests using the **kotlin-test** library to validate individual functions, setting up integration tests to assess how different modules work together using tools such as Jest and configuring a testing environment suitable for Kotlin-generated JavaScript. Additionally, we will discuss how to run your tests using npm scripts and the benefits of utilizing Kvision for testing web components. By incorporating these testing strategies, you can enhance the quality of your code and ensure that your applications meet the highest standards of performance and reliability.

1. **Writing Unit Tests**: Unit tests are essential for ensuring that individual functions in your Kotlin code work as expected. Use the **kotlin-test** library to write your tests in the **commonTest** source set.

   Set up your **build.gradle.kts**:

   ```
   dependencies {
       testImplementation("org.jetbrains.kotlin:kotlin-test-js")
   }
   ```

   Here is an example of a simple unit test:

   ```
   import kotlin.test.Test
   import kotlin.test.assertEquals

   class ExampleTests {

       @Test
       fun testGreeting() {
           val user = User("John")
           assertEquals("Hello, John!", greetUser(user))
       }
   }
   ```

2. **Setting Up Integration Tests**: Integration tests check how different modules work together and can be particularly useful in detecting issues when combining shared and platform-specific code. For web projects, you can utilize tools such as Jest for front-end testing.

   Define Jest as a testing dependency in your **`build.gradle.kts`**:

```
dependencies {
   testImplementation("jest:latest")
}
```

3. **Creating a Testing Environment**: Configure your testing environment using appropriate Jest settings, ensuring that it is set up to run with Kotlin-generated JavaScript.

   For a simple Jest configuration, you can create a **`jest.config.js`** in the project root:

```
module.exports = {
   testEnvironment: "jsdom",
   transform: {
       "^.+\\.kotlin$": "kotlin-jest-transformer",
   },
};
```

4. **Running Tests**: You can run your unit or integration tests using npm scripts or directly from the command line:

```
npm test  # Runs the Jest tests
```

5. **Using `Kvision` for Web Testing**: If you are using **`Kvision`** (a Kotlin-React wrapper), it provides convenient methods to test components in isolation.

```
class MyComponent : KComponent() {
   override fun RBuilder.render() {
       button {
           +"Press Me"
           attrs.onClickFunction = {
               console.log("Button Clicked")
           }
       }
   }
}

class MyComponentTests : KvisionTest() {
   @Test
   fun testButtonClick() {
       val component = MyComponent()
       val button = component.getElementById("button")
```

```
            button.click() // Simulate click

            // Verify expected change or action
        }
    }
```

Hence, by leveraging effective debugging tools and comprehensive testing methodologies, you can ensure that your web applications developed with Kotlin Multiplatform perform reliably, meet user expectations, and maintain high code quality. This meticulous approach to debugging and testing will empower you to deliver robust, scalable applications to your users.

Best Practices for Web Development

Adhering to best practices in web development is essential for creating high-quality, maintainable, and performant applications. This section discusses effective strategies for organizing your code and optimizing performance in your Kotlin Multiplatform web applications.

Code Organization

Code organization is an essential aspect of software development that promotes maintainability, readability, and scalability within your projects. A well-structured codebase allows developers to efficiently navigate through their applications, reduces complexity, and fosters collaboration among team members. In this section, we will discuss key strategies for effective code organization, including adopting a modular structure to separate shared code from platform-specific implementations, maintaining a clear separation of concerns between business logic and UI code, adhering to consistent naming conventions, leveraging Kotlin's data classes for clarity, documenting code using KDoc, and creating reusable components to minimize duplication. By implementing these organizational practices, you will improve the overall quality of your codebase, making it easier to manage and extend as your application evolves.

Modular Structure

Organize your project into distinct modules for shared code and platform-specific implementations. This modular approach allows you to create clear boundaries between components and promote code reuse.

```
my-web-app/

├── shared/

│   └── src/
```

```
|       └── main/
|           └── kotlin/     // Shared Kotlin code
├── web/
|   └── src/
|       └── main/
|           └── kotlin/     // Web-specific Kotlin/JS code
└── resources/
    └── index.html          // HTML entry point
```

- **Separation of Concerns**: Keep your business logic separate from UI code. Implementation of business rules should reside in the shared module, while UI components and routing should be defined within the web module.
- **Consistent Naming Conventions**: Use clear and consistent naming conventions for components, functions, and variables. This enhances the readability and maintainability of your codebase.
- **Use of Data Classes**: Define data models in your shared code using Kotlin's data classes. By using data classes, you reduce boilerplate code and maintain clarity across your application's data representations.

```
data class Task(val id: Int, val title: String, val completed:
Boolean)
```

- **Document Your Code**: Utilize KDoc in Kotlin to document your shared code. This makes it easier for other developers (or your future self) to understand the purpose and usage of classes and functions.
- **Create Reusable Components**: Break down your UI into small, reusable components that can be used in multiple places throughout your application. This reduces duplication and eases maintenance.

```
val TaskCard = functionalComponent<TaskProps> { task ->
    div {
        className = "task-card"
        h3 { +task.title }
        checkbox {
            attrs.checked = task.completed
            attrs.onChange = { /* Handle completion change */ }
        }
    }
}
```

Performance Optimization

Performance optimization is crucial for developing high-quality web applications using Kotlin Multiplatform, as it directly affects user experience and application efficiency. By focusing on various optimization strategies, developers can ensure that their applications run smoothly and respond quickly to user interactions. In this section, we will explore key techniques for enhancing performance, including optimizing resource usage through image management and lazy loading, employing efficient state management practices, leveraging asynchronous programming with Kotlin coroutines, minimizing direct DOM manipulation, implementing code splitting for faster load times, and utilizing performance profiling tools for ongoing assessment. Additionally, we will discuss the importance of setting up Continuous Integration/Continuous Deployment (CI/CD) to maintain performance standards throughout your development cycle. By applying these best practices, you will be better equipped to build robust and scalable web applications that provide an excellent user experience.

- **Optimize Resource Usage**: Be mindful of resource usage; optimize images and use lazy loading for large resources to minimize initial load times. Tools such as WebP for images can help reduce file sizes without compromising quality.
- **Use Efficient State Management**: For better performance, utilize state management libraries or tools, such as Zustand or Redux, with your Kotlin components when needing to manage complex application states across components.
- **Asynchronous Programming**: Make use of Kotlin coroutines and asynchronous programming patterns to prevent blocking the UI thread. This allows for non-blocking calls, enhancing the user experience.

```
suspend fun fetchTasks() {
    val response = fetchApiCall()  // Hypothetical function invok-
ing network call
    // Handle response
}
```

- **Minimize DOM Manipulation**: Excessive direct DOM manipulation can slow down your application. Use Kotlin/React's declarative nature to update the UI in response to state changes efficiently, reducing manual DOM updates.
- **Code Splitting**: Implement code splitting to load only the necessary code for the parts of your application that users are accessing. This can help reduce the initial load time of your web app.
- **Performance Profiling**: Regularly profile your web application using performance profiling tools in the browser's developer tools. Look for bottlenecks, render times, and unnecessary re-renders that could slow down user interaction.

- **Set Up CI/CD for Automated Testing**: Use Continuous Integration/Continuous Deployment (CI/CD) tools to automate your testing and deployment processes. This ensures that performance optimizations are integrated and tested continuously.

By adhering to these best practices for code organization and performance optimization, you can create robust, high-performing web applications using Kotlin Multiplatform. This approach will not only enhance the user experience but also ensure that your codebase remains clean, maintainable, and scalable as your application grows.

Conclusion

This chapter concludes by demonstrating how Kotlin Multiplatform, combined with Kotlin/JS, empowers developers to build efficient, scalable, and maintainable web applications by sharing core business logic across platforms. It covered setting up a Kotlin/JS project, integrating shared code via the `commonMain` module, building reactive UIs with Kotlin/React, using JavaScript libraries through Kotlin wrappers, and handling platform-specific features and network interactions, all while applying best practices for maintainability and testing. Mastering these techniques enables the unification of backend, mobile, and web logic, resulting in responsive and flexible web applications. The next chapter will focus on ensuring reliability in Kotlin Multiplatform projects through unit testing in shared modules, platform-specific testing, debugging techniques, and tools such as JUnit, Ktor test client, native test runners, and CI workflows–all essential for maintaining code quality and confidence across platforms.

CHAPTER 10
Testing and Debugging Multiplatform Code

Introduction

This chapter focuses on the critical aspects of testing and debugging Kotlin Multiplatform code. You will learn effective strategies for ensuring the quality and reliability of your multiplatform applications through comprehensive testing and efficient debugging practices. We will cover unit testing, integration testing, and the use of powerful debugging tools to identify and resolve issues. Additionally, you will gain insights into handling platform-specific testing and best practices for maintaining high code quality. Thus, by the end of this chapter, you will be well-equipped with the knowledge and skills to implement robust testing and debugging processes in your Kotlin Multiplatform projects.

Structure

In this chapter, we will cover the following topics:

- Importance of Testing in Multiplatform Development
  - Benefits of Comprehensive Testing
  - Challenges in Testing Multiplatform Code
- Writing Unit Tests for Shared Code
  - Test Frameworks (JUnit, TestNG)
  - Best Practices for Unit Testing
- Integration Testing Strategies
  - Tools and Frameworks
  - Writing Effective Integration Tests

- Using Debugging Tools
  - Debugging in IntelliJ IDEA
  - Platform-Specific Debugging Tools
- Handling Platform-Specific Testing
  - Differences in Testing Across Platforms
  - Strategies for Managing Platform-Specific Tests
- Best Practices for Testing and Debugging
  - Creating a Robust Testing Strategy
  - Common Debugging Techniques
  - Practical Examples and `ExercisesSample` Test Cases
  - Debugging Scenarios

Importance of Testing in Multiplatform Development

Testing is a crucial aspect of software development that significantly impacts the quality and reliability of applications built using Kotlin Multiplatform. As developers work to ensure that the code functions correctly across various platforms, understanding the importance of testing becomes paramount. This section explores the benefits of comprehensive testing and the inherent challenges that arise in a multiplatform context.

Benefits of Comprehensive Testing

Comprehensive testing provides numerous advantages for Kotlin Multiplatform applications. Here are the key benefits:

- **Ensures Code Quality:** Comprehensive testing helps identify bugs and issues early in the development process, ensuring that the code meets quality standards before being deployed to production. This emphasis on quality is critical for user satisfaction.
- **Increases Reliability:** Thorough testing guarantees that applications function consistently across various platforms, which builds user trust. Users expect a seamless experience, no matter what device or operating system they use to access the application.
- **Facilitates Refactoring:** With a robust test suite in place, developers can confidently refactor code, as tests help verify that existing functionality remains intact during changes. This leads to improved code quality over time.

- **Supports Continuous Integration (CI):** Automated tests are integral to a CI pipeline, enabling rapid feedback every time changes are made. This allows for quick identification and resolution of issues, maintaining stability in the codebase.
- **Enhances Collaboration:** Well-defined tests serve as documentation of expected behavior, improving communication among team members. This clarity ensures that everyone understands how components should interact and what functionality is required.
- **Early Detection of Issues:** Testing can catch potential issues before they reach production, preventing critical failures that could affect users. This proactive approach improves software reliability, and reduces the cost of post-release fixes.
- **Reduces Maintenance Costs:** By identifying bugs during development, comprehensive testing helps reduce the time and cost associated with fixing issues after deployment, contributing to a more maintainable codebase.

Challenges in Testing Multiplatform Code

Despite the significant benefits of comprehensive testing, there are several challenges associated with testing in a multiplatform environment:

- **Platform-Specific Variability:** Different platforms can exhibit unique behaviors, functionalities, and APIs that complicate the implementation of a unified testing strategy. A solution that works on one platform may not be appropriate for another.
- **Complex Testing Environments:** Setting up and maintaining testing environments tailored to each platform can be complex and often requires significant effort and expertise from the development team.
- **Integration Testing Complexity:** Validating interactions between various components across different platforms can be more intricate than unit testing. Developers must be diligent in ensuring that all integrations function correctly and consistently.
- **Limited Tooling Support:** The evolving nature of Kotlin Multiplatform means that testing tools may not yet be fully comprehensive or well-supported across all platforms, which can hinder the effectiveness of testing strategies.
- **Maintaining Consistency:** Ensuring that shared logic behaves consistently across all supported platforms is both crucial and challenging, requiring extensive validation through various tests to capture discrepancies.

Therefore by recognizing the importance of testing and understanding both the benefits and challenges of testing in a multiplatform environment, developers can adopt effective strategies to implement comprehensive testing in their Kotlin Multiplatform projects. This proactive approach not only enhances software quality but also promotes a smoother development process.

Writing Unit Tests for Shared Code

Unit testing is a fundamental practice aimed at verifying the functionality of individual components within your Kotlin Multiplatform applications. Writing effective unit tests for shared code ensures that your implementation behaves as expected across multiple platforms. This section provides an overview of the test frameworks you can utilize for writing unit tests and outlines best practices for effective unit testing.

Test Frameworks (Junit and TestNG)

JUnit

- **Overview:** JUnit is one of the most widely used testing frameworks in the Java ecosystem, making it an ideal choice for Kotlin applications. It provides a straightforward, organized approach to writing and executing tests.
- **Setup:** To include JUnit in your Kotlin Multiplatform project, add the following dependency in your **build.gradle.kts** file:

```
dependencies {
   testImplementation("org.jetbrains.kotlin:kotlin-test")
// Enables Kotlin testing support
}
```

- **Example of a JUnit Test:** Here is a simple example demonstrating how to write a unit test using JUnit.

```
import kotlin.test.Test
import kotlin.test.assertEquals

class ArithmeticTests {
   @Test
   fun testAddition() {
        // Arrange
        val a = 5
        val b = 3

        // Act
        val sum = a + b
```

```
        // Assert
        assertEquals(8, sum, "5 + 3 should equal 8")
    }
}
```

TestNG

- **Overview:** TestNG is an advanced testing framework that enhances JUnit by offering additional features such as data-driven testing, grouping of test cases, and parallel execution, making it suitable for more complex testing scenarios.
- **Setup:** To utilize TestNG in your Kotlin project, include the following dependency in your **`build.gradle.kts`**:

```
dependencies {
   testImplementation("org.testng:testng:7.3.0") // Specify the
desired TestNG version
}
```

- **Example of a TestNG Test:** The following is an example of a basic TestNG test case.

```
import org.testng.Assert.assertEquals
import org.testng.annotations.Test

class CalculatorTests {

    @Test
    fun testSubtraction() {
        val result = 10 - 5

        assertEquals(5, result, "10 - 5 should equal 5")
    }
}
```

Best Practices for Unit Testing

- **Descriptive Test Names:** Use clear and descriptive names for your test methods to convey the purpose of the test. This clarity helps team members (and your future self) understand the intent of each test at a glance.

```
@Test
fun `calculates total with valid prices`() {
    // Test implementation
}
```

- **Keep Tests Isolated:** Ensure that tests are independent of each other. This practice means that the success or failure of one test does not impact the outcomes of others, which is essential for maintaining reliable test suites.

- **Test Edge Cases:** Always include tests that cover edge cases and potential erroneous input conditions. This helps ensure that your code functions correctly under various scenarios.

```
@Test
fun testCalculateTotalPriceHandlesEmptyList() {
   val total = calculateTotalPrice(emptyList())

   assertEquals(0.0, total, "Total price for an empty list should
be 0")
}
```

- **Utilize Mocks and Stubs:** Use mocking frameworks such as MockK to simulate dependencies in your tests. This will allow you to isolate the unit of work in the test without relying on the behavior or state of external systems.

```
val mockApiService = mockk<ApiService>()

every { mockApiService.fetchData() } returns listOf(
            Product(1, "Mocked Product", 10.0)
      )
```

- **Automate Test Execution:** Include tests in the CI/CD process to ensure they run automatically with every code change. This practice helps catch regressions early and maintains code quality over time.
- **Regularly Review and Refactor Tests:** Just like production code, your tests should be reviewed and refactored regularly. This helps maintain clarity, reduces duplication, and improves maintainability of the test suite.

By leveraging these test frameworks and adhering to the best practices for unit testing, developers can create effective and meaningful tests for their shared Kotlin code. This approach ensures that your applications remain robust, reliable, and well-tested across all platforms.

Tool	**Purpose**	**Language/Platform**	**Strengths**
Junit	Unit Testing Framework	JVM, Kotlin	Mature, widely supported
MockK	Mocking Framework	Kotlin	Kotlin-first, coroutine support
Mockito	Mocking Framework	Java, Kotlin	Well-documented, powerful
Kotest	Expressive Testing DSL	Kotlin	Rich assertions, test styles
Spek	Specification Framework	Kotlin	BDD-style test structure

Kotlinx. coroutines.test	Coroutine test utilities		Precise control over coroutine dispatchers

Table 10.1: *Testing Tools Comparison Table*

Integration Testing Strategies

Integration testing is a crucial part of the software development lifecycle that focuses on assessing the interactions between different components or modules in your Kotlin Multiplatform applications. This section presents an overview of the tools and frameworks available for conducting integration testing, along with guidelines for writing effective integration tests.

Tools and Frameworks

- **JUnit:**
  - **Overview:** JUnit is a widely used testing framework that supports both unit and integration testing. It provides a simple and effective way to write and manage tests in Kotlin applications.
  - **Setup:** To include JUnit in your Kotlin Multiplatform project, add the following dependency to your build.gradle.kts:

```
dependencies {
    testImplementation("org.jetbrains.kotlin:kotlin-test") //
Test support for Kotlin
}
```

Example of an Integration Test Using JUnit:

```
import kotlin.test.Test
import kotlin.test.assertNotNull

class ApiIntegrationTests {

    @Test
    fun testApiClientIntegration() {
        val apiService = ApiService() // Your API service instance

        val data = apiService.fetchData("https://api.example.com/
resource")

        assertNotNull(data, "Expected data should not be null")
    }
}
```

- **KotlinTest (Kotest):**
  - **Overview:** KotlinTest, now referred to as Kotest, is a flexible testing framework tailored for Kotlin. It offers a rich set of features that allow for expressive and readable tests, making it suitable for integration scenarios.
  - It supports a wide range of test styles, making it suitable for both unit and integration tests, as well as property-based and data-driven testing.

  Example of 'shouldSpec' style:

```
class PriceCalculatorTest : ShouldSpec({
    should("return 0 for empty list") {
        calculateTotalPrice(emptyList()) shouldBe 0.0
    }
})
```

- **Mocking Libraries (MockK and Mockito):** These libraries facilitate the creation of mock instances of external dependencies during integration testing, helping isolate components to test their interactions effectively.

  Example of Using MockK for Mocking:

```
val mockApiService = mockk<ApiService>()

every { mockApiService.fetchData() } returns listOf(Product(1,
"Mock Product", 20.0))
```

- **Ktor Testing Framework:** If you are using Ktor for server-side functionalities, its testing framework provides tools for verifying the correctness of HTTP interactions and simulating backend services during integration tests.
- **TestNG:** TestNG is an advanced testing framework that includes functionalities for grouped testing, parallel execution, and data-driven testing, making it suitable for diverse integration testing needs.

Writing Effective Integration Tests

- **Define Clear Objectives:** Set specific objectives for your integration tests. Clearly articulate what interactions or functionalities you are validating, and what the expected outcomes should be.

  Example test objective:

```
@Test
fun testUserRegistrationFlow() {
    // Validate that the user registration process functions as
expected.
}
```

- **Utilize Realistic Test Data:** Employ meaningful test data that closely mimics actual usage scenarios. This allows for validating the interactions and behaviors of components within the context of how they will be used in production.

  Example with realistic data:

```
@Test
fun testLoginWithValidCredentials() {
   val userCredentials = UserCredentials("validUser", "secure-
Password")

   val loginResult = authService.login(userCredentials)

   assertTrue(loginResult.isSuccessful, "Login should be
successful with valid credentials")
}
```

- **Setup and Teardown Procedures:** Implement setup and teardown methods to prepare and clean up the environment for your tests. This ensures that tests run in a consistent state and helps maintain test integrity.

```
@Before
fun setUp() {
   // Initialize any required resources or mocks
}

@After
fun tearDown() {
   // Clean up resources or reset states
}
```

- **Mock External Dependencies:** For any external services or APIs, utilize mocks in your integration tests to control responses and states, ensuring that your tests remain predictable and free of external factors.
- **Assertions on Multiple Outcomes:** When writing tests, make assertions not only on primary outputs but also on state changes and side effects that occur due to the interaction between components. This provides thorough validation.

  Example assertion:

```
@Test
fun testAddProductUpdatesInventory() {
   val originalCount = inventoryService.getProductCount
("productId")

   inventoryService.addProduct("productId", 5)
```

```
    assertEquals(originalCount + 5, inventoryService.getProduct-
Count("productId"))
}
```

- **Run Tests in Multiple Configurations:** Whenever possible, execute integration tests across different configurations (for example, different databases, network conditions) to thoroughly validate component interactions under various scenarios.

By using the right tools and frameworks for integration testing, coupled with these strategies for writing effective tests, you can ensure that your Kotlin Multiplatform applications perform as intended when all components interact. This focus on integration testing is vital for the application's overall reliability and user satisfaction.

Using Debugging Tools

Debugging tools are essential for identifying and resolving issues within Kotlin Multiplatform applications. They provide developers with the capability to inspect their code, understand application behavior, and track down bugs effectively. This section discusses how to leverage debugging tools found in IntelliJ IDEA and explores various platform-specific debugging tools.

Debugging in IntelliJ IDEA

- **Integrated Debugger Features:** IntelliJ IDEA features a powerful integrated debugger that simplifies the debugging process for Kotlin applications. Key functionalities include:
    - o **Setting Breakpoints:** You can set breakpoints by clicking in the gutter next to the line number. When executing the application in debug mode, the execution will pause at these breakpoints, allowing inspection of variable values and application state.
    - o **Step through Code Execution:** Use "`Step Over`" (F8) to execute the current line of code and move to the next, or "`Step Into`" (F7) to delve into method calls and observe their execution.
    - o **Inspect Variables:** While paused at breakpoints, hover over variables to check their current values, or utilize the "`Variables`" window to view all local variables.
- **Using Watches:** The "`Watches`" panel allows you to add expressions and monitor the values of specific variables or expressions during execution, making it easier to track changes and debug complex logic.
- **Exception Breakpoints:** Configure breakpoints to halt execution when exceptions occur. This helps identify the source of errors quickly, allowing for in-depth inspection of the context when they arise.

- **Call Stack Inspection:** While debugging, you can view the call stack to understand the sequence of function calls that led to the current execution point. This helps trace back errors to their origins and understand the flow of your code.
- **Debugging Kotlin/JS Applications:** When working with Kotlin/JS applications, ensure source maps are enabled in your **build.gradle.kts**. This lets you debug the original Kotlin code in the browser instead of the compiled JavaScript, simplifying the debugging process.

```
kotlin {
    js {
        browser {
            binaries.executable()
            sourceMaps = true // Enable source maps for easier
debugging
        }
    }
}
```

Platform-Specific Debugging Tools

- **Browser Developer Tools:** Modern web browsers include powerful developer tools that are essential for debugging Kotlin/JS applications. Important features include:
    - **Elements Tab:** Inspect and modify HTML elements and CSS styles in real-time, helping you diagnose layout issues and design inconsistencies.
    - **Console Tab:** View console logs, warnings, and errors generated by your application. You can use console.log() to output debugging information, aiding in tracking application behavior.
    - **Network Tab:** Monitor all network requests made by your application, examining headers, responses, and timing to identify issues with API calls.
    - **Sources Tab:** Set breakpoints directly in the JavaScript code (generated from Kotlin) and step through execution to identify errors or issues in the logic.
- **Remote Debugging for Mobile Applications:** For applications accessed via mobile browsers or running on mobile devices, utilize remote debugging capabilities in browsers such as Chrome. This allows you to debug applications as they run on actual devices, providing insights into user interactions and behavior.
- **Profiler Tools:** Utilize profiling tools to monitor application performance. Profilers can help identify bottlenecks and optimize resource usage by

tracking memory consumption, CPU cycles, and execution time, ensuring your application runs efficiently.

By effectively utilizing debugging tools within IntelliJ IDEA and leveraging platform-specific debugging capabilities, developers can isolate and resolve issues in their Kotlin Multiplatform applications more efficiently. This proactive approach to debugging enhances the quality and reliability of applications across all platforms.

Handling Platform-Specific Testing

In Kotlin Multiplatform development, it is crucial to effectively manage testing tailored to the unique characteristics of each platform. This section highlights the differences in testing across platforms and provides strategies for managing platform-specific tests effectively.

Differences in Testing across Platforms

- **Platform-Specific APIs:** Each platform (for example, Android, iOS, Web) has its own set of APIs and functionalities, leading to differences in how code behaves. This variability necessitates distinct testing approaches for each platform, ensuring that all features work as intended.
- **User Interface Variations:** UI components may be designed and implemented differently depending on the platform, often adhering to specific design principles and user expectations. This requires that UI tests be adapted to match the interface standards for each platform while verifying their functionality.
- **Environmental Factors:** The operating environment for each platform differs, which can introduce various constraints. Factors such as resource availability, operating system behaviors, and hardware specifications may impact how an application runs, necessitating specific tests to account for these variations.
- **Testing Frameworks:** Different platforms utilize different testing frameworks. For instance, Android typically uses Espresso for UI tests, iOS developers may use XCTest, and web developers commonly employ Jest. Familiarity with these frameworks is necessary to implementing effective tests.
- **Performance Characteristics:** Performance testing can differ between platforms due to variation in hardware capabilities and resource management strategies. Therefore, it is vital to consider these differences when structuring performance tests.

Strategies for Managing Platform-Specific Tests

- **Utilize the `expect/actual` Mechanism:** Kotlin's expect and actual mechanism allows developers to define common interfaces in shared code and provide platform-specific implementations. This method streamlines testing for shared logic while addressing individual platform needs.

```
// Common Code

expect class LocalizationService {
    fun getLocalizedString(key: String): String
}


// Android Implementation

actual class LocalizationService {
    actual fun getLocalizedString(key: String): String {
        // Android-specific localization logic
    }
}


// iOS Implementation

actual class LocalizationService {
    actual fun getLocalizedString(key: String): String {
        // iOS-specific localization logic
    }
}
```

- **Separate Test Suites:** Organize your tests into separate suites for each platform. This allows for tailored testing strategies and ensures that platform-specific behaviors are covered without confusion.

```
my-project/
│
├── shared/
│   └── src/
│       └── commonTest/         // Shared tests for common logic
├── android/
│   └── src/
│       └── androidTest/        // Android-specific tests
├── ios/
│   └── src/
│       └── iosTest/            // iOS-specific tests
```

```
└── web/
    └── src/
        └── test/                    // Web-specific tests
```

- **Write Shared Tests for Common Logic:** Implement tests for code logic that is common across platforms in the shared test sources. This allows you to validate functionality once while still ensuring it adheres to requirements across all platforms.
- **Mocking and Stubbing:** Use mocking frameworks to create mock versions of dependencies when testing platform-specific functionality. This isolation will help you to focus your tests on specific logic without interference from external systems.
- **Continuous Integration (CI):** Set up CI pipelines that run all platform-specific tests automatically after every change to the codebase. This ensures that regressions or issues are caught early and addressed promptly.
- **Documentation:** Maintain clear documentation that explains the different testing strategies used for each platform. This should include setup instructions, platform-specific behaviors, and the rationale for chosen approaches to provide clarity for the development team.

Thus, by understanding the differences in testing across platforms and employing these effective strategies for managing platform-specific tests, developers can ensure that their Kotlin Multiplatform applications are thoroughly tested. This practice leads to enhanced quality and improved user experiences across all supported platforms.

Best Practices for Testing and Debugging

Implementing best practices for testing and debugging is essential for ensuring the quality and reliability of Kotlin Multiplatform applications. This section outlines effective strategies for creating a robust testing strategy and highlights common debugging techniques that can help streamline the development process.

Creating a Robust Testing Strategy

- **Define Clear Testing Objectives:** Begin by establishing clear goals for your testing. Specify the functionalities and behaviors that need to be validated, and determine the expected outcomes. Clear objectives direct your testing efforts and help prioritize testing scenarios.
- **Adopt Test-Driven Development (TDD):** Embrace Test-Driven Development principles by writing tests before implementing the actual functionality. This practice encourages thoughtful design and leads to better-structured, testable code.
- **Integrate Continuous Integration (CI) Systems:** Incorporate automated

testing into your CI pipelines to run tests automatically anytime changes are made. This ensures that regressions are caught quickly and maintains a consistent code quality throughout the development lifecycle.

- **Prioritize Test Coverage:** Aim for comprehensive test coverage across critical functionalities. Utilize code coverage tools to identify untested areas and address gaps in your testing strategy, focusing on high-risk and vital components.
- **Organize Tests Effectively:** Maintain a well-organized test structure by implementing separate directories for unit tests, integration tests, and platform-specific tests. This organization enhances clarity and simplifies test management.
- **Utilize Mocks and Stubs:** Use mocking frameworks to create fake implementations of external dependencies in your tests. Mocks and stubs help isolate the components being tested, and avoid interference from external factors, resulting in stable and predictable tests.
- **Keep Tests Independent:** Ensure that tests do not depend on the results of other tests. This independence allows tests to run in any order without failure and contributes to consistent testing results.
- **Regularly Review and Refactor Tests:** Treat your test code with the same importance as production code. Regularly review and refactor tests to improve clarity, eliminate duplication, and ensure they remain relevant as the application evolves.
- **Document Your Testing Process:** Maintain documentation outlining your testing strategy, including conventions, processes, and the rationale behind your approaches. This documentation aids collaboration and supports knowledge sharing within your team.

Common Debugging Techniques

- **Effective Logging:** Implement logging throughout your application to capture important runtime information. Logging provides insights into the application's behavior and helps identify issues quickly.

  ```
  console.log("Current user session: ", userSession) // Example log statement
  ```
- **Breakpoints and Step-through Debugging:** Use the debugger available in your IDE (such as IntelliJ IDEA) to set breakpoints and step through the execution of your code. This allows inspection of the values of variables and understanding how the logic flows through the application.
- **Inspect Call Stacks:** While debugging, you can review the call stack to see the sequence of function calls that led to the current execution point. This

insight is valuable for tracing back errors and understanding the context of exceptions.

- **Exception Breakpoints:** Set breakpoints to halt execution when exceptions are thrown. This allows you to catch and analyze exceptions at the point they occur, helping to identify and resolve issues more effectively.
- **Testing in Different Environments:** Regularly test your application in various environments (development, staging, production) to uncover platform-specific issues that might not be apparent during local testing.
- **Profiling Application Performance:** Utilize profiling tools to monitor application metrics, such as memory usage and CPU cycles. Profilers help identify performance bottlenecks and optimize the application's resource utilization.
- **Remote Debugging:** For applications running on mobile devices or remote servers, use remote debugging tools that allow you to debug code directly on the target device. This capability provides real-time insights into application behavior in different environments.

Hence, by following these best practices for testing and debugging, developers can ensure that their Kotlin Multiplatform applications are reliable, maintainable, and of high quality. A structured approach to both testing and debugging not only fosters a collaborative development environment but also results in a robust product that meets user expectations across all platforms.

Practical Examples and Exercises

This section provides practical examples and exercises designed to reinforce your understanding of testing and debugging in Kotlin Multiplatform projects. You will encounter sample test cases that illustrate effective unit and integration testing techniques, along with common debugging scenarios to help you develop problem-solving skills in real application contexts.

Sample Test Cases

- **Unit Test for Business Logic:** This example demonstrates how to create a unit test to validate a function that calculates the total price of a list of products.

```
package com.example.shared

import kotlin.test.Test
import kotlin.test.assertEquals

data class Product(val id: Int, val name: String, val price:
Double)
```

```
fun calculateTotalPrice(products: List<Product>): Double {
    return products.sumOf { it.price }
}

class PriceCalculationTests {

    @Test
    fun testCalculateTotalPrice() {
        // Arrange
        val products = listOf(
            Product(1, "Widget", 19.99),
            Product(2, "Gadget", 29.99)
        )

        // Act
        val totalPrice = calculateTotalPrice(products)

        // Assert
        assertEquals(49.98, totalPrice, 0.01, "Total price should
equal 49.98")
    }
}
```

- **Integration Test for API Client:** This integration test checks that the API client can successfully fetch and process data from a mock API.

```
import kotlin.test.Test
import kotlin.test.assertTrue

class ApiIntegrationTests {

    @Test
    fun testFetchData() {
        // Arrange
        val apiService = ApiService() // Initialize your API
service

        // Act
        val products = apiService.fetchData("https://mockapi.
example.com/products")

        // Assert
        assertTrue(products.isNotEmpty(), "Fetched product list
should not be empty")
    }
}
```

- **Testing Kotlin/React Components**: Below is an example illustrating how to test a React component for displaying a list of products.

```
import react.*
import react.dom.*
import react.testkit.*

class ProductListComponentTest : kotlin.test.Test() {
   @Test
   fun testProductRendering() {
       // Arrange
       val products = listOf(
          Product(1, "Widget", 19.99),
          Product(2, "Gadget", 29.99)
       )

       // Act
       val renderedComponent = render(<ProductListComponent
products={products} />)
       val listItems = renderedComponent.findAllByRole("listitem")
// Assuming each item has a listitem role

       // Assert
       assertEquals(2, listItems.size, "The product list should
render two items")
   }
}
```

Debugging Scenarios

Scenario 1: API Call Fails

When an integration test fails due to an incorrect API call, you can generally inspect the network request using the browser's developer tools to check the headers, URL, and the response returned by the server.

```
// Example API call that might fail

axios.get("https://mockapi.example.com/products")
   .then { response ->
       // Handle successful responses
   }
   .catch { error ->
       console.error("Error fetching data:", error) // Log any
errors for further examination
   }
```

Scenario 2: Unexpected State Changes in UI

If a component does not update as expected when the state changes, use breakpoints in your IDE to inspect the state values before and after the update. Ensure the state setter function is being called correctly to verify the value.

```
val (count, setCount) = useState(0)

button {
   attrs.onClick = {
         setCount(count + 1) // Set a breakpoint here to inspect
count value
         console.log("Count incremented to: ", count + 1)
   }
   +"Increment Count"
}
```

Scenario 3: Component Not Rendering

If a component fails to render, add console logs within the component to verify that the correct props are being received. Check the component lifecycle to ensure that it mounts correctly.

```
val MyComponent = functionalComponent<MyProps> { props ->
   console.log("Props received in MyComponent: ", props)
   h1 { +"Hello, ${props.name}!" }
}
```

Scenario 4: Memory Leaks

In the event of performance issues related to memory usage, utilize the profiling tools available in browser developer tools to identify any memory leaks. Verify that all resources, such as event listeners and subscriptions, are cleaned up properly.

```
val CleanupComponent = functionalComponent<RProps> {
   useEffect {
         // Set up any necessary resources
         onCleanup {
               // Clean up resources to prevent memory leaks
         }
   }
}
```

Engaging with these sample test cases and debugging scenarios will help you gain hands-on experience crucial for mastering testing and debugging in Kotlin Multiplatform projects. These practical exercises will enhance your skills and prepare you to develop robust, high-quality applications across multiple platforms.

Conclusion

In this chapter, we explored the essential practices for testing and debugging Kotlin Multiplatform applications. From crafting unit and integration tests for shared and platform-specific code to leveraging powerful debugging tools across different environments, you have learned how to ensure your application is both reliable and maintainable. By embracing the best practices and testing strategies, you are better equipped to catch issues early, enhance development efficiency, and deliver consistent user experiences across platforms.

As your projects grow, ensuring quality through testing becomes just one part of a larger workflow. In the next chapter, we will shift our focus to Continuous Integration and Deployment (CI/CD)—where you will learn how to automate testing, building, and releasing Kotlin Multiplatform apps using tools such as GitHub Actions and Jenkins. This automation will help streamline your development pipeline, reduce manual effort, and maintain high delivery standards with every code change.

CHAPTER 11
Continuous Integration and Deployment

Introduction

In this chapter, we delve into continuous integration (CI) and deployment (CD) practices tailored for Kotlin Multiplatform projects. You will learn how to set up CI/CD pipelines that automate the build, test, and deployment processes, ensuring a streamlined and efficient development workflow. We will cover popular CI/CD tools and services, such as Jenkins and GitHub Actions, and discuss deployment strategies for different platforms. Therefore, by the end of this chapter, you will be able to implement robust CI/CD pipelines for your multiplatform projects, enhancing productivity and maintaining code quality.

Structure

In this chapter, we will cover the following topics:

- Introduction to CI/CD
    - Benefits of CI/CD
    - Overview of CI/CD Pipelines
- Setting Up CI Pipelines
- Using GitHub Actions
- Automating Builds for Multiplatform Projects
- Deployment Strategies for Different Platforms
- Monitoring and Maintaining CI/CD Pipelines

- Best Practices for CI/CD
- Practical Implementation: Setting Up a CI/CD Pipeline

Introduction to CI/CD

Continuous Integration (CI) and Continuous Deployment (CD) are vital practices in modern software development, especially in Kotlin Multiplatform projects. These methodologies focus on automating the process of integrating code changes and deploying applications, allowing teams to deliver high-quality software more efficiently. In this section, we will explore the benefits of CI/CD as well as provide an overview of what a typical CI/CD pipeline entails.

Benefits of CI/CD

Implementing CI/CD practices provides numerous advantages, which can significantly enhance the development workflow:

- **Faster Feedback Loops:** CI/CD allows developers to receive immediate feedback on their code changes. Automated tests are run with each integration, enabling quick detection of any issues introduced by recent changes.
- **Improved Code Quality:** By automating the build and testing processes, CI/CD helps maintain code quality. Regular testing ensures that bugs and vulnerabilities are addressed before deployment, minimizing risks associated with new releases.
- **Increased Development Speed:** Automation of repetitive tasks such as building, testing, and deploying frees developers to focus more on writing code and improving features. This efficiency leads to faster feature delivery and enhanced productivity.
- **Reduced Integration Problems:** CI practices encourage frequent integration of code changes, which reduces the extent of integration issues typically encountered in larger software projects. This practice leads to a more fluid development process.
- **Consistent Deployments:** CI/CD pipelines ensure that deployments are consistent and repeatable. Automating deployment eliminates human error and provides a standardized process for releasing new versions of the software.
- **Enhanced Collaboration:** CI/CD fosters collaboration among team members by providing clear visibility into code changes, build statuses, and test results. This transparency assists in aligning team efforts and expectations.
- **Continuous Delivery:** With CI/CD, teams can implement continuous delivery practices, allowing for frequent releases to production. This continuous flow ensures that users receive updates and features promptly.

Overview of CI/CD Pipelines

A CI/CD pipeline is a series of steps that enable the automation of processes involved in building, testing, and deploying software. The following outlines the typical stages involved in a CI/CD pipeline:

- **Source Code Management:** The pipeline begins with a source code repository where developers commit their code changes. Version control systems such as Git are commonly used for managing source code.
- **Build Stage:** During the build stage, the application code is compiled, and dependencies are resolved. This ensures that the code can be built into a functional executable artifact.
- **Test Stage:** Automated tests, including unit tests and integration tests, are executed to validate that the application behaves as expected. This helps catch and fix errors early in the development process.
- **Deploy Stage:** If the tests pass, the application is deployed to the target environment (for example, staging or production). This can include uploading binaries, refreshing services, and managing configurations.
- **Monitoring and Feedback:** After deployment, monitoring tools track the performance and behavior of the application in the production environment. This feedback loop is critical for making timely improvements and adjustments.

Popular CI/CD tools and services suitable for Kotlin Multiplatform projects include **Jenkins**, **GitHub Actions**, **GitLab CI**, and **CircleCI**. Each tool has its unique features, providing flexibility for teams to choose the best fit for their development workflows.

By understanding the principles of CI/CD and recognizing its benefits, you will be well-prepared to implement robust CI/CD pipelines in your Kotlin Multiplatform projects. This will ultimately enhance productivity, maintain code quality, and streamline your development process.

Setting Up CI Pipelines

Establishing continuous integration (CI) pipelines is a pivotal step in automating the integration, testing, and deployment processes within your Kotlin Multiplatform projects. In this section, we will explore how to configure CI pipelines using two popular tools: Jenkins and GitHub Actions. These tools will help streamline your development workflow and enhance collaboration among team members.

Configuring Jenkins

- **Overview:** Jenkins is a widely used open-source automation server that supports building and deploying software projects. It allows for highly customizable CI pipelines through its extensive plugin ecosystem.

- **Installing Jenkins:** To get started, install Jenkins on your local machine or a dedicated server. Follow the official Jenkins installation documentation available at the Jenkins website (https://www.jenkins.io/doc/book/installing/) for detailed instructions.
- **Setting Up a New Job:** After installing Jenkins, create a new job (pipeline) by selecting "**`New Item`**" on the dashboard. Choose "**`Pipeline`**" as the job type.
- **Configuring the Pipeline Script:** In the pipeline configuration, define the build steps using a Jenkinsfile that outlines the CI process. A sample Jenkins pipeline configuration for a Kotlin Multiplatform project may look like this:

```
pipeline {
    agent any
    stages {
        stage('Build') {
            steps {
                script {
                    // Compile the application
                    sh './gradlew build'
                }
            }
        }

        stage('Test') {
            steps {
                script {
                    // Run the unit and integration tests
                    sh './gradlew test'
                }
            }
        }

        stage('Deploy') {
            steps {
                script {
                    // Deploy the application to the target envi-
ronment
                    sh './gradlew deploy'
                }
            }
        }
    }

    post {
```

```
        always {
            // Archive the test results
            junit 'build/test-results/**/*.xml'
        }
    }
}
```

- **Integrating with Version Control:** Configure your Jenkins job to connect to your version control system (for example, Git) by specifying the repository URL and the branch to monitor. This allows Jenkins to trigger the pipeline whenever new commits are made.
- **Running the Pipeline:** Once your pipeline is configured, you can manually trigger it or set it to run automatically with each commit. Monitor the console output in Jenkins to review the status of the build and test execution.

Using GitHub Actions

1. **Overview:** GitHub Actions is a CI/CD tool integrated within GitHub that allows you to automate workflows directly from your repository. It uses workflows defined in YAML files to handle building, testing, and deployment processes.
2. **Creating a GitHub Action Workflow:** To set up a CI pipeline with GitHub Actions, create a directory called **`.github/workflows`** in the root of your repository. Inside this directory, create a YAML file (for example, **`ci-cd-pipeline.yaml`**) that defines your workflow.
3. **Defining Trigger Events:** Specify which GitHub events should trigger your pipeline. Common options include **`push`** and **`pull_request`** events on branches such as **`main`** or **`develop`**.

```
name: CI/CD Pipeline
on:
 push:
   branches:
     - main
 pull_request:
   branches:
     - main
```

4. **Configuring Build and Test Steps:** Add jobs to your workflow to define the steps for building and testing your application. Make sure to set up the required environment (like the Java version for Kotlin) and include commands to build and test the application.

```
jobs:
 build:
```

```
        runs-on: ubuntu-latest
        steps:
          - name: Checkout code
            uses: actions/checkout@v2

          - name: Set up JDK
            uses: actions/setup-java@v2
            with:
              java-version: '11' // Specify your Java version

          - name: Build with Gradle
            run: ./gradlew build

          - name: Run Tests
            run: ./gradlew test

          - name: Deploy
            run: ./gradlew deploy
```

5. **Monitoring Build Results**: After the workflow file is committed to your repository, GitHub Actions will automatically trigger the pipeline based on the defined events. You can monitor the build status and logs directly in the "`Actions`" tab of your GitHub repository.
6. **Optimize and Iterate:** Continuously monitor the performance of your CI/CD pipeline. Use metrics to assess build times and success rates, and make adjustments as necessary to optimize the process.

Thus, by following these guidelines for setting up CI pipelines with Jenkins and GitHub Actions, you can automate the build, test, and deployment processes for your Kotlin Multiplatform projects. This automation not only improves workflow efficiency but also enhances collaboration within your development team, ultimately leading to high-quality software delivery.

Automating Builds for Multiplatform Projects

Automating the build process is crucial for enhancing efficiency and consistency in Kotlin Multiplatform development. Proper build automation allows teams to streamline artifact creation, manage dependencies, and ensure that the build process remains reproducible across different environments. In this section, we will explore build automation tools, and discuss managing build configurations effectively.

Build Automation Tools

Modern software projects rely on build automation tools to manage complex tasks such as compiling source code, managing dependencies, running tests, and packaging deliverables. In the Kotlin ecosystem, several build systems like **Gradle**, **Maven**, and **Ant** can be used to streamline these processes. Among them, **Gradle** has become the preferred choice for Kotlin Multiplatform projects due to its flexibility, speed, and deep integration with JetBrains and Android development environments. Gradle's support for Kotlin DSL, incremental builds, and multiplatform configurations makes it the most efficient and developer-friendly option for building, testing, and deploying cross-platform applications – which is why this book focuses exclusively on using Gradle for project automation and configuration.

Gradle:

Overview: Gradle is the most widely used build automation tool in Kotlin Multiplatform projects. It is powerful and flexible, allowing developers to define build logic in a straightforward and declarative manner.

Features:

- **Dependency Management:** Gradle facilitates the management of project dependencies, automatically resolving version conflicts and ensuring the correct libraries are included for each platform.
- **Incremental Builds:** By optimizing builds to compile only modified parts of the application, Gradle helps to save time and resources during the build process.
- **Build Scripts:** Developers can create build scripts (usually written in Kotlin or Groovy) that define various tasks, including compiling code, running tests, and packaging applications for different platforms.

  Example of a simple Gradle build script for a Kotlin Multiplatform project:

```
kotlin {
   jvm() // Targeting JVM
   js() // Targeting JavaScript
   ios() // Targeting iOS platforms

   sourceSets {
       val commonMain by getting {
           dependencies {
               implementation("org.jetbrains.kotlin:kotlin-
stdlib-common")
           }
       }
```

```
        val jvmMain by getting {}

        val jsMain by getting {}

        val iosMain by getting {}
    }
}
```

Managing Build Configurations

Managing build configurations effectively is essential for ensuring that your application builds correctly across all platforms. Here are some strategies to help with this:

- **Platform-Specific Configurations:** Define separate configurations for each platform within your Gradle build scripts. This allows you to tailor settings, dependencies, and tasks to the specific needs of each platform.

  Example of configuring platform-specific dependencies in Gradle:

```
kotlin {
   sourceSets {
       val androidMain by getting {
           dependencies {
               implementation("com.android.support:appcom-
pat-v7:1.0.0")
           }
       }

       val iosMain by getting {
           dependencies {
               implementation("org.jetbrains.kotlinx:kotlinx-
coroutines-core:1.3.9")
           }
       }
   }
}
```

- **Environment-Specific Builds:** Utilize build profiles or environment variables to differentiate between development, testing, and production builds. This is especially useful for managing configurations that change depending on the deployment context (for example, API URLs, logging levels).

  Example of adjusting configurations in Gradle:

```
android {
   buildTypes {
       getByName("debug") {
```

```
            buildConfigField("String", "API_URL", "https://dev.api.
example.com")
        }

        getByName("release") {
            buildConfigField("String", "API_URL", "https://api.
example.com")
        }
    }
}
```

- **Consistent Versioning:** Keep the versions of dependencies in sync across platforms to avoid compatibility issues. Centralize version management to streamline updating and maintaining consistent environments.

  Example of managing versions in Gradle:

```
val kotlinVersion = "1.5.31"

dependencies {
    implementation("org.jetbrains.kotlin:kotlin-stdlib:"+kotlin-
Version)
}
```

- **Automated Builds and Testing:** Incorporate CI/CD practices to automate the building and testing processes. Ensure that your CI system is set up to trigger builds and tests based on changes in the repository.

By utilizing effective build automation tools and managing build configurations wisely, developers can streamline the build process for Kotlin Multiplatform projects. This approach not only enhances efficiency but also ensures consistency across different environments, leading to higher-quality applications.

Deployment Strategies for Different Platforms

Successfully deploying applications built with Kotlin Multiplatform requires tailored strategies for each target platform. This section discusses effective deployment techniques for Android and iOS, as well as web and desktop applications, ensuring that developers can efficiently deliver their projects to users across various environments.

Deploying to Android

For Android applications, the deployment process can be accomplished through several methods, including direct deployment to devices or distribution via the Google Play Store.

- **Direct Deployment:** You can deploy your app directly to an Android device connected via USB or through an emulator. Use Android Studio's built-in tools to select a target device, and run your application seamlessly.
- **Google Play Store Deployment:** To publish an Android app to the Google Play Store, follow these steps:
  i. **Generate a Signed APK or AAB:** Use Gradle to create a signed APK (Android Package) or AAB (Android App Bundle) for distribution:

     ```
     ./gradlew assembleRelease
     ```

  ii. **Log into Google Play Console:** Create a new release by accessing the Google Play Console, upload the generated APK/AAB, and fill in the required app information, such as descriptions and screenshots.
  iii. **Submit for Review:** After completing the app's metadata and visuals, submit the app for Google's review before it goes live.

Deploying to iOS

The deployment of iOS applications involves compiling the app and submitting it to the App Store or deploying it to devices for testing.

- **Direct Deployment:** Use Xcode to deploy the application directly to an iOS device. Connect your device, open the project in Xcode, select your device as the target, and click the "`Run`" button to deploy the app.
- **App Store Deployment:** For publishing to the App Store, follow these steps:
  a. **Create an Archive:** Use Xcode to create an archive of your application by selecting `Product > Archive`.
  b. **Distribute the App:** In the Organizer window that appears, click "`Distribute App`" and select "`App Store Connect`".
  c. **Upload Build:** Follow the prompts to upload your build to `App Store Connect`.
  d. **Create a New App Listing:** Log in to App Store Connect, create a new app listing, and provide required information, such as metadata and screenshots.
  e. **Submit for Review:** Finally, submit your application for review to make it available on the App Store.

Web and Desktop Deployment Techniques

After developing and testing your Kotlin Multiplatform applications, the final step is delivering them to end users. Deployment is where your code meets the real world – whether it is a responsive web app running in browsers or a desktop application running natively on Windows, macOS, or Linux. Kotlin Multiplatform simplifies this process by allowing you to reuse shared logic while generating platform-specific outputs suited for each target. In this section, we will explore the essential techniques for deploying Kotlin/JS web applications and Kotlin/Native desktop applications, including hosting options, packaging strategies, and practical steps to publish and distribute your builds efficiently across different environments.

Web Deployment

Deploying a Kotlin/JS application typically involves hosting the generated JavaScript files on a web server. Common deployment methods include:

- **Static File Hosting:** Use static file hosting services such as GitHub Pages, Netlify, or Vercel. The deployment process generally involves:

  a. **Build the Project:** Compile the Kotlin/JS project using Gradle:

  ```
  ./gradlew jsBrowserProduction
  ```

  b. **Upload Files:** Upload the contents of the `build/distributions` directory to your chosen hosting platform.

- **Cloud Web Hosting:** Deploy to cloud platforms such as AWS S3 or Azure. For instance, setting up an AWS S3 bucket to host static files can be done by:

  ```
  aws s3 sync build/distributions s3://your-bucket-name
  ```

Desktop Deployment

Deploying Kotlin Multiplatform desktop applications may involve packaging the app for Windows, macOS, and Linux. Common practices include:

- **OS-Specific Packages:** Create platform-specific packages (for example, `.exe` for Windows, `.app` for macOS, or `.deb` for Linux) using Gradle configurations to manage the packaging.
- **Distributing via Package Managers:** For macOS, consider distributing your application through the Homebrew package manager. For Linux, tools such as Snapcraft can be utilized to create and distribute your application package.

By implementing these deployment strategies specific to each platform, Kotlin Multiplatform developers can ensure that their applications are delivered effectively to users. Understanding these methods enhances the overall deployment workflow and contributes to maintaining a high standard of application quality across diverse environments.

Monitoring and Maintaining CI/CD Pipelines

Effective monitoring and maintenance of CI/CD pipelines are essential for ensuring that automated processes run smoothly and efficiently. Continuous improvement of these pipelines not only enhances performance but also helps in quickly identifying and resolving issues. This section will explore tools available for monitoring CI/CD pipelines and outline best practices for maintaining them.

Tools for Monitoring CI/CD

- **Jenkins Monitoring Plugins:** Jenkins offers a range of plugins designed to monitor the health and performance of your CI/CD pipelines. These plugins can enhance visibility into the status of builds and tests.
  - **Build Monitor Plugin:** This plugin provides a visual representation of the status of your builds, allowing you to see which jobs are passing or failing at a glance.
  - **Blue Ocean:** A modern Jenkins interface that allows for better visualization of your pipeline stages, providing insights into the flow and outcomes of your CI/CD processes.
- **GitHub Actions Insights:** GitHub Actions includes built-in insights that track workflow runs. It provides a comprehensive view of the history of runs, helping you analyze the reasons for failures or successes. This feature facilitates quick assessment of pipeline performance, and identifies areas for improvement.
- **CircleCI Insights:** CircleCI provides a detailed dashboard for tracking the performance of your builds. It includes statistics on build times, test results, and overall workflow health, helping teams optimize their CI/CD processes.
- **Slack and ChatOps Integration:** Integrate your CI/CD tools with messaging platforms such as Slack or Microsoft Teams. Setting up notifications allows team members to receive alerts about the status of builds and deployments, fostering timely responses to any issues that arise.
- **Performance Monitoring Tools:** Use performance monitoring tools such as Grafana or Prometheus to collect metrics related to your CI/CD pipeline's performance. These tools can help track build durations, resource usage, and overall system health over time, providing valuable insights into performance optimization.

Best Practices for Maintenance

- **Regularly Review Pipeline Configurations:** Schedule periodic reviews of your CI/CD pipeline configurations to ensure that they reflect best practices and align with current project requirements. This practice allows for proactive optimization of the pipeline.
- **Manage Dependencies:** Regularly update the dependencies used in your build and testing processes. Monitoring for vulnerabilities in dependencies helps maintain security and performance in your CI/CD system.
- **Clean Up Old Builds:** Implement automation that periodically removes old artifacts and build logs to conserve storage space and keep the CI environment organized. Cleaning up unnecessary files improves pipeline performance and simplifies management.
- **Monitor for Failures and Set Alerts:** Configure alerts for pipeline failures, performance issues, or other problems. Ensuring that the team is promptly notified helps address issues quickly and minimize disruptions.
- **Document Pipeline Workflows:** Maintain comprehensive documentation for each pipeline process. This documentation should include descriptions of workflows, important configurations, and the rationale for design decisions. Well-documented processes facilitate easier onboarding of new team members and support collaborative efforts.
- **Test Pipeline Changes:** When making changes to your CI/CD configurations, it is best to test these adjustments in a separate environment to ensure they function correctly without disrupting production pipelines.
- **Gather Feedback:** Regularly solicit feedback from team members regarding the effectiveness of the CI/CD processes. Input from developers and stakeholders can highlight areas for improvement and promote continuous enhancement of the pipelines.

By employing robust monitoring tools and adhering to best practices for maintaining CI/CD pipelines, Kotlin Multiplatform developers can ensure that their automated processes are efficient and reliable. This focus on monitoring and maintenance ultimately leads to improved productivity, better collaboration, and higher-quality software delivery.

Best Practices for CI/CD

Implementing Continuous Integration (CI) and Continuous Deployment (CD) practices in Kotlin Multiplatform projects requires a thoughtful approach to ensure efficiency and reliability. This section discusses best practices for creating efficient CI/CD pipelines and highlights common pitfalls that teams may encounter, along with solutions to address them.

Creating Efficient CI/CD Pipelines

- **Automate Everything:** Strive to automate as many processes as possible, from building and testing to deployment. Automation reduces the risk of human error and speeds up the development workflow.
- **Utilize Parallel Execution:** Configure your CI/CD pipeline to execute tests and other build tasks in parallel where feasible. This approach decreases the overall build time and enhances efficiency by optimizing resource usage.
- **Implement Incremental Builds:** Take advantage of incremental builds in your CI/CD pipeline. This means that only the components that have changed are rebuilt, significantly reducing build times and resource consumption.
- **Ensure Clear Environment Configurations:** Maintain distinct configurations for different environments, such as development, testing, and production. This ensures that the application behaves correctly and consistently in each environment and prevents potential issues during deployment.
- **Use Version Control for Pipeline Configuration:** Store your CI/CD pipeline configuration files (for example, Jenkinsfile, GitHub Actions YAML) in version control alongside your application code. This practice allows you to track changes to your pipeline configurations, and facilitates collaboration among team members.
- **Monitor Pipeline Performance:** Continuously monitor the performance of your CI/CD pipelines using metrics. Track build times, failure rates, and other relevant statistics to identify bottlenecks and opportunities for optimization.
- **Conduct Regular Pipeline Reviews:** Schedule regular reviews of your CI/CD practices and configurations. This allows teams to discuss improvements, update practices based on feedback, and adapt the pipelines to changing project needs.

Common Pitfalls and Solutions

- **Pitfall: Long Feedback Loops**
  - **Issue:** When builds and tests take too long, developers may not receive timely feedback on their code changes, leading to difficulties in identifying the source of issues.
  - **Solution:** Optimize your testing process by running essential tests on every change, while utilizing parallel execution for other tests. Configure incremental builds to speed up the overall process.

- **Pitfall: Flaky Tests**
  - **Issue:** Flaky tests, which intermittently pass or fail, can undermine trust in the test suite, and contribute to confusion among developers.
  - **Solution:** Investigate the underlying causes of flaky tests, such as dependencies on external systems or timing issues. Ensure that tests are well-isolated and reproducible.
- **Pitfall: Inconsistent Environments**
  - **Issue:** Inconsistencies between development and production environments can result in deployment failures.
  - **Solution:** Use containerization (for example, Docker) to standardize the development and production environments. This setup minimizes discrepancies and improves the reliability of deployments.
- **Pitfall: Manual Interventions**
  - **Issue:** Relying too much on manual processes can introduce human error and lead to delays in the deployment cycle.
  - **Solution:** Aim for full automation of your CI/CD processes, eliminating manual steps wherever possible to improve reliability and speed up deployments.
- **Pitfall: Ignoring Security Practices**
  - **Issue:** Failing to integrate security checks into the CI/CD pipeline can leave vulnerabilities in the application.
  - **Solution:** Incorporate security testing tools into the CI/CD pipeline, such as static analysis for security vulnerabilities and vulnerability scanning for third-party dependencies.

Thus, by following these best practices for creating efficient CI/CD pipelines and addressing common pitfalls with proactive solutions, Kotlin Multiplatform developers can significantly improve their development workflows. Effective CI/CD practices enhance productivity, maintain high code quality, and facilitate a robust software delivery process, enabling frequent and reliable releases.

Practical Implementation: Setting Up a CI/CD Pipeline

Setting up Continuous Integration (CI) and Continuous Deployment (CD) pipelines is crucial for automating the processes of building, testing, and deploying Kotlin Multiplatform projects. This section outlines a step-by-step guide to establishing your CI/CD pipeline and provides real-world examples to illustrate the implementation details.

Step-by-Step Guide

1. **Choose Your CI/CD Tool**: Select a CI/CD tool that aligns with your project needs. Popular options include **Jenkins**, **GitHub Actions**, **GitLab CI**, and **CircleCI**. Each tool offers unique features and capabilities that you should evaluate based on your team's familiarity and project requirements.

2. **Set Up Your CI/CD Tool**

   - **For Jenkins:** Install Jenkins on a local server or in the cloud. Follow the installation guide on the Jenkins website (https://www.jenkins.io/doc/book/installing/).
   - **For GitHub Actions:** GitHub Actions is integrated within GitHub, so no additional setup is necessary beyond accessing your existing repository.

3. **Create a Pipeline Definition**

   - **For Jenkins:** Create a new Pipeline job and define your build process using a Jenkinsfile. This file will outline the steps needed for building, testing, and deploying your application.

     Example Jenkinsfile configuration:

```
pipeline {
   agent any
   stages {
       stage('Build') {
           steps {
               sh './gradlew build'
           }
       }

       stage('Test') {
           steps {
               sh './gradlew test'
           }
       }

       stage('Deploy') {
           steps {
               sh './gradlew deploy'
           }
       }
   }

   post {
       always {
```

```
            junit 'build/test-results/**/*.xml' // Archive test
results
        }
    }
}
```

- **For GitHub Actions:** Create a directory named **`.github/workflows`** in your repository, and inside that directory, create a YAML file (for example, **`ci-cd-pipeline.yaml`**) to define your workflow.

  Example GitHub Actions workflow:

```
name: CI/CD Pipeline

on:
  push:
    branches:
      - main

  pull_request:
    branches:
      - main

jobs:
  build:
    runs-on: ubuntu-latest
    steps:
      - name: Checkout code
        uses: actions/checkout@v2

      - name: Set up JDK
        uses: actions/setup-java@v2
        with:
          java-version: '11'

      - name: Build with Gradle
        run: ./gradlew build

      - name: Run Tests
        run: ./gradlew test

      - name: Deploy
        run: ./gradlew deploy
```

4. **Define Trigger Events**: Specify the events that should trigger your pipeline. For CI/CD tools, common triggers include pushes to specific branches or pull requests. Setting these triggers automates the CI/CD process, while ensuring the correct versions of the application are built and tested.

5. **Monitor Builds and Test Results**: After committing the pipeline configuration, trigger the pipeline to run automatically based on the defined events. Monitor the status of builds and results in the respective tool's interface (for example, Jenkins dashboard, GitHub Actions tab) to identify any failures or bottlenecks.

6. **Optimize and Iterate**: Continuously monitor the pipeline performance. Analyze the build times, test results, and error rates to identify opportunities for optimization and improvements in your CI/CD processes. Regularly review and update your pipeline to reflect changes in project requirements or team feedback.

Conclusion

This chapter provided an in-depth exploration of CI/CD practices for Kotlin Multiplatform projects. You learned the importance of automating build, test, and deployment processes, as well as how popular tools such as Jenkins and GitHub Actions can facilitate smooth workflows. By following best practices and understanding deployment strategies, you can enhance productivity and maintain software quality.

As we move forward, the next chapter will dive deeper into debugging techniques specifically tailored for Kotlin Multiplatform, empowering you with the skills to tackle common issues effectively. This will be an essential step in your journey to mastering multiplatform development.

CHAPTER 12
Performance Optimization

Introduction

This chapter is dedicated to optimizing the performance of your Kotlin Multiplatform applications. You will learn various techniques and tools to enhance the efficiency and responsiveness of your apps. We will cover profiling tools, memory management strategies, and code optimization techniques that help you identify and resolve performance bottlenecks. By implementing these practices, you can ensure your applications run smoothly across all platforms, providing a superior user experience. By the end of this chapter, you will have the skills to optimize and maintain high-performance Kotlin Multiplatform applications.

Structure

In this chapter, the following topics will be covered:

- Importance of Performance Optimization
  - Benefits of Optimizing Performance
  - Common Performance Issues
- Using Profiling Tools
- Memory Management Techniques
- Code Optimization Strategies
- Handling Performance Bottlenecks
- Best Practices for Performance Optimization
- Practical Examples and Case Studies

Importance of Performance Optimization

Optimizing the performance of your Kotlin Multiplatform applications is vital for delivering a high-quality user experience. Performance impacts not only user satisfaction but can also affect overall application reliability, scalability, and maintainability. This section discusses the benefits of performance optimization, and highlights common performance issues that developers may encounter in Kotlin Multiplatform projects.

Benefits of Optimizing Performance

In the competitive world of app development, performance is not just a feature–it is a necessity. Whether you are building for mobile, web, or desktop platforms, users expect fast, responsive, and efficient applications. This section explores the key advantages of optimizing performance in your apps, from elevating user experience to improving scalability and lowering operational costs. By focusing on performance optimization, developers can create applications that not only meet functional requirements but also excel in usability, efficiency, and long-term maintainability.

- **Enhanced User Experience:** Applications that perform well and respond promptly lead to higher user satisfaction. Optimizing performance minimizes delays and ensures that users can interact with the app seamlessly, which is crucial for retaining users and driving engagement.
- **Increased Application Responsiveness:** By optimizing performance, applications are able to load faster and provide quicker responses to user inputs. This responsiveness fosters a positive user interaction, which is vital for applications, especially in mobile environments.
- **Reduced Resource Consumption:** Optimized applications use system resources more efficiently, which is particularly important in mobile and embedded systems where battery life and processing power are limited. Reducing unnecessary resource consumption can also lead to increased longevity of devices.
- **Improved Scalability:** Applications designed with performance optimization in mind can handle higher loads more effectively. As user demand grows, optimized applications can scale without sacrificing performance, thus accommodating more users seamlessly.
- **Lower Operational Costs:** Improved performance often leads to reduced operational costs, as efficient use of resources can lower server and infrastructure costs. Applications that consume fewer resources are typically less expensive to operate.

- **Better Search Engine Ranking:** For web applications, fast load times can positively affect search engine optimization (SEO). Websites that load quickly are more likely to rank higher in search engine results, bringing in more traffic and potentially increasing conversions.

Common Performance Issues

Even well-designed applications can suffer from performance bottlenecks that degrade user experience and system reliability. Identifying and addressing common performance issues early in the development cycle is critical to delivering high-quality, responsive apps. This section highlights some of the most frequent pitfalls—ranging from sluggish start-up times to inefficient memory use and network handling—that developers encounter in Kotlin Multiplatform projects. By recognizing these challenges, you can implement targeted optimizations that ensure your application runs smoothly across platforms.

- **Slow Application Start-up:** Applications that take a long time to launch can frustrate users and lead to high abandonment rates. Factors contributing to slow start-up times can include excessive initializations and resource loading during the start-up process.
- **Inefficient Memory Usage:** Poor memory management can lead to excessive consumption of memory resources, which may result in application crashes or degraded performance, especially on devices with limited resources.
- **Unoptimized Network Requests:** Poorly managed network requests can slow down applications and lead to increased latency. Common issues include a lack of request batching, missing caching strategies, and slow server responses.
- **Inefficient Algorithms:** Using unoptimized or inefficient algorithms for data processing can lead to slow performance, especially as data sizes grow. This often requires careful analysis and selection of algorithms with optimal time and space complexity.
- **Complex UI Rendering:** In applications with rich UIs, overly complex layouts or redundant rendering processes can lead to sluggish performance. Optimizing rendering efficiency is crucial for maintaining a smooth user experience.
- **Background Processing Issues:** Background tasks that are not well-managed can lead to slowdowns, particularly if they block the main thread or consume excessive resources. Asynchronous programming techniques should be utilized to handle these tasks.

Thus, by understanding the importance of performance optimization and being aware of common performance issues, developers can take proactive measures to improve the efficiency and responsiveness of their Kotlin Multiplatform applications. This focus on optimization not only enhances user experience but also strengthens the application's overall stability and maintainability.

Using Profiling Tools

Profiling tools are essential for identifying performance bottlenecks and understanding resource utilization in your Kotlin Multiplatform applications. By analyzing how your application performs under various conditions, you can make informed decisions about optimization. This section focuses on how to use profiling tools effectively in both Android Studio and Xcode to enhance your application's performance.

Profiling in Android Studio

Optimizing app performance requires more than intuition–it demands data-driven insights. Android Studio's integrated profiling tools empower developers to monitor and analyze real-time performance metrics, helping to uncover bottlenecks and inefficiencies across CPU, memory, and network usage. This section provides a practical guide to using the Android Profiler, offering step-by-step instructions to help you diagnose and resolve performance issues effectively during Kotlin Multiplatform app development.

- **Overview:** Android Studio includes a built-in Android Profiler that allows developers to analyze various aspects of their applications, including CPU usage, memory consumption, and network activity.
- **Accessing the Android Profiler:** To start profiling your application, follow these steps:
    a. Open your project in Android Studio.
    b. Run your application on a connected device or emulator.
    c. Click on the "`Profiler`" tab at the bottom of the Android Studio window.
- **Analyzing CPU Usage:** The CPU Profiler provides detailed information about how your application utilizes CPU resources:
    a. Start profiling by pressing the "`Record`" button on the CPU Profiler.
    b. Interact with your application to generate the execution data.
    c. Stop recording to view the results, including method call charts where you can identify performance hotspots, and diagnose CPU-intensive operations.
- **Monitoring Memory Usage:** The Memory Profiler helps identify memory leaks and analyze memory allocation:

a. Click on the "`Memory`" panel to monitor real-time memory allocation and deallocation in your app.

b. Use the "`Record Allocations`" feature to track memory usage over time, which can expose inefficient memory practices.

c. Analyze heap dumps to locate leaks and evaluate the overall memory consumption of different object types.

- **Network Profiler:** The Network Profiler lets you inspect network usage in real-time:

  a. Click on the "`Network`" panel to see details about network requests made by your app.

  b. Analyze request and response headers, and understand how long each request takes to complete. This information can help identify slow API calls or suboptimal network usage patterns.

Profiling in Xcode

Performance optimization on iOS requires precise measurement and analysis, and Xcode's Instruments provide just that. With tools tailored for CPU, memory, and network profiling, developers can uncover bottlenecks, detect memory leaks, and evaluate data transfer patterns in their Kotlin Multiplatform iOS applications. This section walks you through the use of Instruments in Xcode, helping you harness these tools to refine your app's performance and ensure a smooth user experience on Apple devices.

- **Overview:** Xcode provides a suite of profiling tools, known as Instruments, which help developers measure performance and resource usage in their iOS applications.
- **Accessing Instruments:** To start profiling your iOS application:

  a. Open your project in Xcode.

  b. Select the target device, then navigate to `Product > Profile` or simply press `Command + I`.

  c. This action launches Instruments, giving you access to various performance analysis templates.

- **Analyzing CPU Performance:** Choose the "`Time Profiler`" template to measure CPU usage:

  a. Start a profiling session by clicking the record button.

  b. Interact with your application to generate performance data.

c. After stopping the recording, you can review the CPU usage graph and call tree, allowing you to identify which functions or methods consume the most processing power.

- **Memory Analysis:** Use the "`Allocations`" template to analyze memory usage:

a. The Allocations tool tracks memory usage in real time and captures data on how memory is allocated.

b. Look for trends in memory consumption and analyze which objects are being retained, helping you identify potential memory leaks.

c. The Leaks instrument can be used to pinpoint specific memory leaks by tracking object allocations over time.

- **Network Profiling:** Use the "`Network`" instrument to monitor HTTP and data transfer requests:

a. Track and analyze the time taken for network calls, along with the amount of data sent and received. This information is crucial for diagnosing inefficiencies in network communication.

By utilizing profiling tools effectively in both Android Studio and Xcode, developers can gain valuable insights into application performance and resource usage. Applying these insights allows for targeted optimizations that enhance the user experience and ensure that Kotlin Multiplatform applications operate efficiently across all platforms.

Memory Management Techniques

Effective memory management is essential for optimizing the performance of your Kotlin Multiplatform applications. Poor memory management can lead to excessive resource consumption, memory leaks, and ultimately application crashes. This section discusses best practices for memory management and highlights tools available for memory analysis, ensuring you can maintain optimal application performance.

Best Practices for Memory Management

Effective memory management is crucial for building performant, stable applications—especially in resource-constrained environments such as mobile devices. Poor memory handling can lead to crashes, sluggish performance, and difficult-to-diagnose bugs. This section outlines proven best practices for managing memory in Kotlin Multiplatform applications, from leveraging immutability and lazy initialization to avoiding memory leaks and minimizing object allocations. By applying these strategies, developers can ensure efficient memory usage and deliver smoother, more reliable user experiences.

1. **Use Immutable Data Structures:** Favor immutable data types whenever possible. Immutability reduces the risk of unintended side effects, making code easier to reason about and minimizing the risk of memory-related issues.

2. **Avoid Memory Leaks:** Be vigilant about preventing memory leaks, which occur when an object is no longer needed but cannot be garbage collected due to lingering references. Common culprits include:

   - Unregistered listeners or observers.
   - Static references to activities or views.
   - Use weak references where appropriate to prevent objects from being retained unnecessarily.

3. **Clean Up Resources:** Regularly dispose of unused resources such as database connections, file handles, and network sockets as soon as they are no longer needed. Proper disposal helps free up memory and reduces the application's memory footprint.

   Example:

   ```
   File("data.txt").bufferedReader().use { reader ->
       val content = reader.readText()
       println(content)
   }
   ```

   In this example, ***use*** automatically closes the **BufferedReader** once the block completes, even if an exception is thrown – ensuring safe resource cleanup.

4. **Minimize Object Allocation:** Reduce the number of objects created, especially in performance-critical code paths or within loops. Consider reusing objects when possible or employing object pools for managing resource-intensive objects.

   Example:

   ```
   // Instead of creating new instances repeatedly, consider reusing
   or using object pools

   val myObject: MyClass = obtainObject() // Reuse or obtain from a
   pool instead of creating new instances
   ```

5. **Profile Memory Usage Regularly:** Continuously profile memory usage during development and testing to identify inefficiencies. Regular profiling helps detect memory leaks and patterns of excessive memory consumption early in the development cycle.

6. **Optimize Data Fetching:** Use efficient data structures and algorithms for data retrieval tasks. When displaying large datasets, consider implementing lazy loading or pagination to minimize memory usage.

7. **Leverage Lazy Initialization:** Utilize lazy initialization for objects that are not immediately required. This approach can help conserve memory and improve the startup performance of your application.

   Example:

```
val heavyResource: Resource by lazy {
    Resource() // Initialized when first accessed
}
```

Tools for Memory Analysis

Detecting and resolving memory-related issues requires the right set of tools to uncover inefficiencies that are not always obvious during development. Whether you are targeting Android, iOS, or both, robust memory analysis tools can help you monitor allocations, identify leaks, and optimize resource usage. This section explores the most effective tools available for Kotlin Multiplatform developers–including Android Profiler, Xcode Instruments, and third-party solutions–to ensure your applications remain performant and stable across platforms.

- **Android Profiler:** Android Studio includes the Android Profiler, which provides real-time insight into your application's memory usage. Use this tool to identify memory allocations and potential leaks by:
  a. Monitoring memory allocation during different app states.
  b. Creating heap dumps that allow you to analyze the memory consumed by various objects.
- **Xcode Instruments:** For iOS applications, Xcode's Instruments tool provides powerful resources for analyzing memory usage. Use the Allocations and Leaks instruments to:
  a. Monitor real-time memory usage and detect memory leaks.
  b. Analyze the retention of objects to identify inefficiencies and improve memory management.
- **Heap Analysis Tools:** Utilize heap analysis tools such as Eclipse MAT (Memory Analyzer Tool) or VisualVM for detailed analysis of memory usage. These tools help identify memory leaks and high memory consumption patterns by:
  a. Visualizing object lifecycles and references.
  b. Allowing deep dives into object allocation history.

- **Third-Party Monitoring Solutions:** Consider integrating third-party solutions such as Firebase Performance Monitoring or Sentry, which can help assess memory usage in production environments and provide insights into performance-related issues as they occur.

By adopting sound memory management practices and utilizing effective tools for memory analysis, developers can ensure that their Kotlin Multiplatform applications run efficiently while providing a smooth user experience. Addressing memory management proactively not only improves application performance but also enhances stability and reliability across all platforms.

Code Optimization Strategies

Optimizing code is crucial for enhancing the performance of your Kotlin Multiplatform applications. Efficient code can greatly improve responsiveness, reduce execution times, and overall provide a smoother user experience. This section outlines various techniques for optimizing code and highlights tools that assist in code analysis and optimization.

Techniques for Optimizing Code

Writing clean code is only part of the equation–ensuring it performs efficiently across platforms is just as critical. In performance-sensitive applications, even minor inefficiencies can scale into major bottlenecks. This section presents practical techniques for optimizing Kotlin Multiplatform code, from minimizing redundant operations and selecting the right data structures to leveraging lazy initialization, asynchronous processing, and effective profiling. By applying these strategies, developers can fine-tune their applications for speed, responsiveness, and resource efficiency.

1. **Minimize Redundant Operations:** Eliminate unnecessary calculations and operations within loops or frequently called functions. By caching results or using variables to store intermediate values, you can prevent needless recalculations.

   Example:

   ```
   // Cache expensive calculations
   val result = expensiveComputation()

   for (i in 0 until 10) {
       process(result) // Use cached result
   }
   ```

2. **Optimize Data Structures:** Select data structures based on the operations required. For example, using a **`HashMap`** for lookups can improve performance compared to using a **`List`** for searching. Analyze the complexities of your operations to choose the most effective data structure.

3. **Leverage Lazy Initialization:** Utilize lazy initialization to defer the creation of heavy objects until they are actually needed. This reduces memory usage, and can enhance the initial load performance of your application.

   Example:

   ```
   val resource: Resource by lazy {
      Resource() // Instantiated only when first accessed
   }
   ```

4. **Use Efficient Algorithms:** Reassess algorithms for efficiency, particularly in loops and recursive functions. Aim for algorithms that have lower time complexity to improve performance.

   Example:

   ```
   // Prefer using a more efficient sorting algorithm
   val sortedList = list.sorted() // Using the built-in optimized
   sort
   ```

5. **Batch Operations:** When performing multiple operations, batch them together to reduce the number of calls and round-trip overhead. This is especially effective for tasks such as network requests or database transactions.

   Example:

   ```
   // Send a batch of updates in one request rather than multiple
   individual requests
   apiService.updateBatch(updatedItems)
   ```

6. **Asynchronous Processing:** Use asynchronous programming techniques to prevent blocking the main thread during resource-intensive operations. In Kotlin, coroutines can be utilized to perform tasks concurrently, allowing for a smooth user experience.

   Example:

   ```
   // Using coroutines for non-blocking network requests
   suspend fun fetchData() {
      withContext(Dispatchers.IO) {
          // Make network call here
      }
   }
   ```

7. **Profile and Refactor Hotspots:** Regularly profile your application to identify performance hotspots. Refactor these areas by optimizing algorithms or simplifying logic to enhance speed.

Tools for Code Analysis

Maintaining high-performance, maintainable code requires more than just good programming practices–it demands continuous analysis and feedback. Fortunately, Kotlin developers have access to a range of powerful tools that automate code inspection, highlight inefficiencies, and enforce best practices. This section explores essential code analysis tools such as IntelliJ IDEA's inspections, Detekt, SonarQube, and others, which help identify potential performance bottlenecks and maintain clean, efficient code in Kotlin Multiplatform projects.

- **IntelliJ IDEA Code Inspections:** IntelliJ IDEA includes static code analysis tools that automatically highlight potential performance issues and suggest code improvements. Use these inspections to refactor code proactively.
- **Kotlin Compiler Warnings:** The Kotlin compiler provides warnings during the build process that can point out potential inefficiencies in your code. Pay attention to these alerts to improve performance.
- **Detekt:** Detekt is a static code analysis tool specifically designed for Kotlin. It helps identify code smells, complexities, and potential bugs, allowing you to refine your code and enhance its performance.
- **SonarQube:** SonarQube is a popular tool that offers static analysis of code quality, focusing on reliability, security vulnerabilities, and potential bugs. It provides insights into code complexity and helps maintain high code quality over time.
- **VisualVM:** VisualVM is a monitoring tool that provides insight into Java application performance. It can be used to analyze CPU and memory usage, allowing you to identify inefficiencies and opportunities for optimization.

Hence, by employing these optimization strategies and utilizing appropriate code analysis tools, developers can significantly enhance the performance of their Kotlin Multiplatform applications. This optimization leads to improved user experience and application reliability, ensuring that software performs well across all platforms.

Handling Performance Bottlenecks

Performance bottlenecks can significantly hinder the efficiency and responsiveness of your Kotlin Multiplatform applications. Identifying and addressing these bottlenecks is crucial for optimizing application performance. This section discusses how to identify performance bottlenecks and outlines effective strategies for resolving them.

Identifying Bottlenecks

Before performance issues can be fixed, they must first be found. Identifying bottlenecks is a crucial step in the optimization process, requiring a combination of tools, metrics, and developer insight. This section outlines effective strategies for diagnosing performance slowdowns in Kotlin Multiplatform applications–from using profiling tools and benchmarking techniques to analyzing metrics, conducting code reviews, and leveraging user feedback. These practices help uncover hidden inefficiencies and guide targeted improvements for a smoother, faster app experience.

- **Profiling Tools:** Utilize profiling tools such as Android Profiler, Xcode Instruments, or other third-party performance monitoring solutions to analyze your application's runtime behavior. These tools provide insights into CPU usage, memory consumption, and network requests, helping to pinpoint areas that require optimization.
- **Performance Monitoring Metrics:** Collect and analyze key performance metrics, such as application load times, response times for user actions, and memory usage patterns. Look for significant spikes or prolonged times in specific areas, which may indicate potential bottlenecks.
- **Benchmarking:** Conduct benchmarking tests to measure the performance of critical functionalities. Establish performance baselines for various components of your application and compare the metrics over time to identify regressions.
- **Code Review:** Perform code reviews with a focus on performance implications. Assess algorithms, data structures, and resource-intensive operations that may introduce inefficiencies during execution.
- **User Feedback:** Gather user feedback regarding application performance. Pay attention to reports of slow responses or lag during interactions, which can help highlight areas that need further investigation.

Strategies for Resolving Bottlenecks

Once performance bottlenecks have been identified, the next step is taking deliberate, targeted action to resolve them. Effective optimization requires more than guesswork–it involves applying proven techniques to enhance efficiency and responsiveness. This section outlines practical strategies for addressing common bottlenecks in Kotlin Multiplatform applications, including algorithm optimization, memory management, network request batching, and asynchronous processing. With these techniques, developers can transform sluggish components into streamlined, high-performing features across all supported platforms.

1. **Optimize Algorithms and Data Structures:** Replace inefficient algorithms with more optimal solutions. Analyze the time and space complexity of your code and select appropriate data structures to ensure that operations are performed efficiently.

   Example:

   ```
   // Instead of using a list for frequent lookups, consider using a set or map
   val efficientLookup = mapOf("key1" to "value1", "key2" to "value2")
   ```

2. **Reduce Memory Footprint:** Identify and eliminate memory leaks by using proper resource management practices. Regularly review object allocations and utilize profiling tools to check for excessive memory usage and find opportunities to refactor or reuse objects.
3. **Batch Network Requests:** When multiple network requests can be batched, combine them into a single request to reduce the volume of data transmitted and the number of API calls required.
4. **Leverage Caching:** Implement caching mechanisms to store frequently accessed data temporarily. This reduces the need for repeated fetches from remote servers or databases, significantly improving response times.
5. **Asynchronous Processing:** Use asynchronous programming techniques to prevent blocking the main thread during resource-intensive operations. In Kotlin, coroutines can be utilized to perform tasks concurrently, allowing for a smooth user experience.

   Example:

   ```
   // Using coroutines for non-blocking network requests

   suspend fun fetchData() {
       withContext(Dispatchers.IO) {
           // Make network call here
       }
   }
   ```

6. **Optimize Rendering Performance:** In UI applications, ensure that rendering performance is optimized by minimizing unnecessary redraws or costly layout operations. Consider offscreen rendering to improve responsiveness during UI transitions.
7. **Test Changes Gradually:** Implement incremental changes and continuously monitor performance. Test each optimization to evaluate its impact on performance to ensure that it effectively addresses the identified bottleneck.

Thus, by systematically identifying and resolving performance bottlenecks, developers can greatly enhance the efficiency and responsiveness of their

Kotlin Multiplatform applications. This focus on performance optimization not only improves user experience but also contributes to the overall stability and maintainability of the software.

Best Practices for Performance Optimization

Establishing best practices for performance optimization is essential for developing high-quality Kotlin Multiplatform applications. By following these guidelines, developers can create efficient code and avoid common pitfalls that may hinder performance. This section outlines best practices for creating efficient code and highlights strategies for avoiding common performance-related issues.

Creating Efficient Code

Writing efficient code is about more than just making things work–it is about making them work well at scale. In performance-sensitive applications, small inefficiencies can compound quickly, especially as data grows or user interactions increase. This section covers key practices for crafting efficient Kotlin Multiplatform code, including algorithm selection, minimizing object allocation, leveraging primitive types, and optimizing rendering and initialization. By applying these principles proactively, developers can build faster, leaner, and more scalable applications across all platforms.

1. **Prioritize Algorithm Efficiency:** Select algorithms that offer optimal time and space complexity for the tasks at hand. Analyze your algorithms and choose the most efficient ones that scale well with increased data sizes.

   Example:

   ```
   // Choosing a search algorithm based on data size
   val result = listOfItems.find { it.id == searchId } // Linear
   search

   // Consider using a hash map for faster lookups if the size is
   large
   ```

2. **Use Primitive Types When Possible:** Leverage primitive types instead of their object counterparts when applicable. Operations on primitives are generally faster and consume less memory.

3. **Reduce Object Allocation:** Minimize the number of objects created, particularly in performance-critical code paths or loops. Consider reusing objects or implementing object pools to limit garbage collection overhead.

Example:

```
// Instead of creating new instances repeatedly, consider reusing
or using object pools
val myObject: MyClass = obtainObject() // Reuse or obtain from a
pool instead of creating new instances
```

4. **Batch Processing:** Process data in batches rather than individually to reduce overhead. This approach is particularly beneficial for tasks such as network requests or database transactions.

   Example:

```
// Send a batch of updates in one request rather than multiple
individual requests
apiService.updateBatch(updatedItems)
```

5. **Lazy Initialization:** Implement lazy initialization for objects that may not be needed immediately. This reduces memory usage and improves application startup performance.

   Example:

```
val heavyResource: Resource by lazy {
    Resource() // Initialized when first accessed
}
```

6. **Optimize Rendering Performance:** In UI-heavy applications, ensure that rendering performance is optimized by minimizing unnecessary redraws or costly layout operations. Simplifying the UI can lead to smoother interactions.

7. **Profile and Refactor Hotspots:** Regularly profile your application to identify performance hotspots. Refactor these areas by optimizing algorithms or simplifying logic to enhance speed.

Avoiding Common Pitfalls

Even with the best intentions, developers can unintentionally introduce performance problems that impact the efficiency and reliability of their applications. Recognizing and avoiding common pitfalls is essential to maintaining high standards in Kotlin Multiplatform development. This section highlights frequent mistakes–such as neglecting memory management, overcomplicating UI layouts, or skipping proper profiling–and offers guidance on how to prevent them. By steering clear of these issues, you can ensure your applications remain performant, maintainable, and responsive across all target platforms.

1. **Ignoring Memory Management:** Failing to manage memory properly can lead to memory leaks and excessive resource consumption. Always release

resources, unregister listeners or observers, and profile memory usage frequently to prevent leaks.

2. **Not Considering Platform Differences:** Different platforms may exhibit varied performance characteristics. Ensure that optimizations account for these differences, and test performance across all targeted platforms.
3. **Overusing Global State:** Using global state can lead to unclear dependencies and unintended side effects that complicate debugging and optimization. Aim to minimize reliance on global state in your application design.
4. **Neglecting Profiling and Testing:** Regularly profile your application and perform performance testing to catch issues early. Avoid making assumptions about code performance without empirical evidence.
5. **Complex UI Layouts:** Overly complex UI layouts can lead to poor rendering performance. Simplify your UI designs and avoid deep view hierarchies or unnecessary compositional layers.
6. **Not Taking Advantage of Caching:** Failure to implement caching can result in frequent, repetitive network calls or computations, negatively impacting performance. Use caching strategies to store frequently accessed data and improve response times.

Therefore, by adhering to these best practices for performance optimization, Kotlin Multiplatform developers can create applications that run efficiently and provide a superior user experience. Focused effort on creating efficient code and avoiding common pitfalls will lead to improved application quality and maintainability, ultimately enhancing user satisfaction.

Practical Examples and Case Studies

In this section, we will explore practical examples and case studies that illustrate how performance optimization techniques can be applied in Kotlin Multiplatform applications. These real-world examples will showcase the impact of optimization on application performance and provide context for the strategies discussed throughout this chapter.

Real-World Examples of Optimization

Example 1: Improving Load Times in a Kotlin/JS Application

A Kotlin/JS application faced slow load times due to large bundle sizes caused by numerous dependencies. The development team implemented the following strategies to optimize performance:

- **Code Splitting:** By configuring Gradle to enable code splitting, the team divided the application into smaller chunks that could be loaded on demand.

This reduced the initial load time as users only loaded the necessary code for their immediate interactions.

- **Tree Shaking:** They applied tree shaking to minimize the size of the final output bundle by removing unused code from the dependencies. This greatly reduced the amount of JavaScript sent to the client, further improving load times.
- **Results:** After implementing these optimizations, the application load times improved significantly, enhancing the user experience and engagement metrics.

Example 2: Enhancing Performance in an Android Application

An Android Kotlin Multiplatform app was encountering performance issues due to long-running network requests blocking the main thread. The development team utilized several approaches to enhance performance:

- **Coroutines:** They replaced synchronous network calls with Kotlin coroutines using `Dispatchers.IO` to perform background operations without blocking the UI thread. This change significantly improved the responsiveness of the application.
- **Caching Mechanisms:** Implementing local caching for frequently accessed data allowed the app to minimize network requests, which enhanced performance during subsequent data retrievals.
- **Results:** Users reported a smoother experience with quicker data retrieval times, and analytics showed reduced bounce rates and higher user satisfaction scores.

Case Studies of Performance Improvements

Case Study 1: Optimizing a Cross-Platform Fitness App

A fitness application developed for Android, iOS, and Web platforms faced user complaints regarding sluggishness during activity tracking. The team undertook a comprehensive performance optimization project that involved:

- **Profiling Tools:** Using Android Profiler and Xcode Instruments, the team identified various bottlenecks, including excessive background processing and inefficient data handling.
- **Memory Management:** They analyzed memory usage patterns to detect and resolve memory leaks in the activity tracking component, which significantly improved stability during prolonged use.
- **Optimization Techniques:** By optimizing algorithms used for calculating metrics and reducing visual complexity in the user interface, the performance of the app improved substantially.

- **Results:** Post-optimization, the application experienced a 40% reduction in processing time for activity tracking, leading to an increase in user engagement and positive feedback in app store reviews.

Case Study 2: Performance Enhancements in a Shopping Application

A multiplatform shopping application showcased performance issues during peak usage times, especially during product searches. The team addressed these issues through a structured optimization approach:

- **Asynchronous Operations:** Implementing asynchronous data fetching reduced loading times during product searches. Users received faster responses while browsing through categories.
- **Backend Optimization:** Collaborating with backend teams to improve API response times through better indexing and optimization of database queries decreased the overall latency.
- **Results:** The optimizations contributed to an improved search experience, with response times decreasing by 50%, leading to higher conversion rates and better customer satisfaction.

Through these practical examples and case studies, it becomes evident that implementing performance optimization techniques in Kotlin Multiplatform applications can yield significant improvements. By understanding and applying these strategies, developers can ensure their applications run efficiently, providing an exceptional user experience across all platforms.

Conclusion

In this chapter, we explored the vital strategies for optimizing the performance of Kotlin Multiplatform applications. From understanding the benefits of performance tuning to identifying common issues and applying practical tools and techniques, you now have a robust foundation for building responsive and efficient apps. With these insights, you are better equipped to diagnose bottlenecks, implement improvements, and deliver a seamless user experience across platforms.

As we continue our journey, the next chapter will build on this foundation by focusing on the best practices for Kotlin Multiplatform development. You will also learn how to structure your codebase for scalability, enhance modularity, manage dependencies effectively, and uphold high standards of code quality and security—ensuring that your applications are not only performant, but also maintainable and production-ready.

CHAPTER 13

Best Practices for Multiplatform Development

Introduction

This chapter outlines the best practices for developing Kotlin Multiplatform applications. You will learn about effective code organization, modularization techniques, and strategies for ensuring code reusability and security. We will also discuss managing dependencies and maintaining high code quality through proper documentation and code comments. By following these best practices, you can create maintainable, scalable, and secure multiplatform applications. This chapter will equip you with the knowledge to adopt industry standards and excel in Kotlin Multiplatform development.

Structure

In this chapter, we will cover the following topics:

- Code Organization and Structure
- Best Practices for Code Structure
- Modularization Techniques
- Ensuring Code Reusability
- Security Best Practices
- Managing Dependencies Effectively
- Documentation and Code Comments
- Practical Tips and Examples

Code Organization and Structure

Organizing code effectively is crucial for the success of Kotlin Multiplatform projects. A well-structured codebase enhances maintainability, scalability, and collaboration among team members. This section outlines how to organize code for multiplatform projects, and provides best practices for code structure.

Organizing Code for Multiplatform Projects

As Kotlin Multiplatform projects scale, the way you organize your code becomes a decisive factor in determining your project's maintainability, clarity, and reusability. A well-structured codebase not only simplifies collaboration across teams but also ensures a smoother development experience across Android, iOS, Web, and Desktop platforms.

This section provides a practical guide to structuring your Kotlin Multiplatform project. We will explore the ideal directory layout, explain how to separate shared and platform-specific logic, and walk through best practices such as using the **`expect/actual`** mechanism and adopting modularization for clean architecture. Whether you are working on a small prototype or a production-grade app, organizing your code thoughtfully is the first step toward building robust and scalable multiplatform applications.

1. **Directory Structure:** Establish a clear directory structure that reflects the shared and platform-specific components of your application. A typical structure for a Kotlin Multiplatform project might look like this:

```
my-multiplatform-project/
├── shared/                       # Shared code across platforms
│   └── src/
│       ├── commonMain/           # Common code
│       ├── commonTest/           # Common tests
│       ├── androidMain/          # Android-specific code
│       ├── androidTest/          # Android-specific tests
│       ├── iosMain/              # iOS-specific code
│       ├── iosTest/              # iOS-specific tests
│       └── jsMain/               # JavaScript-specific code
├── android/                      # Android application module
│   └── src/
│       └── main/                 # Android main code
├── ios/                          # iOS application module
│   └── src/
│       └── main/                 # iOS main code
└── web/                          # Web application module
    └── src/
        └── main/                 # Web main code
```

Figure 13.1: *Project Folder Structure Image*

2. **Common Code:** Place shared code in the **`shared/src/commonMain`** directory. This code should contain logic that is applicable across all platforms, such as business logic, data models, and utility functions.
3. **Platform-Specific Code:** Organize platform-specific code in their respective directories (for example, **`androidMain`**, **`iosMain`**, and **`jsMain`**). This structure allows you to implement functionality that caters to the specific needs and capabilities of each platform.
4. **Test Organization:** Keep tests organized similarly to your codebase. Place common tests in **`shared/src/commonTest`**, and organize platform-specific tests in their respective test directories. This promotes better test coverage and maintainability.
5. **Modularization:** Consider breaking your shared code into smaller modules, if the project grows in size. This modularization promotes reusability and separation of concerns, making it easier to manage dependencies and updates.

Best Practices for Code Structure

Beyond just organizing files and directories, crafting a clean and maintainable Kotlin Multiplatform codebase requires discipline in how code is written, named, and managed. Following best practices for code structure promotes clarity, testability, and long-term maintainability–especially important in cross-platform environments where multiple teams may be involved.

In this section, we will explore essential coding habits that ensure consistency and quality throughout your project. From adopting clear naming conventions and writing focused functions to documenting logic and applying dependency injection, these practices help enforce a professional and scalable architecture. You will also learn how to maintain consistency across projects and leverage version control effectively to streamline collaboration and safeguard your codebase.

- **Follow Naming Conventions:** Adhere to consistent naming conventions for files, classes, and functions. This practice improves code readability and helps developers quickly understand the purpose of various components.

  Example:

```
// Use camelCase for function names and PascalCase for class
names

fun calculateTotalPrice(products: List<Product>) { ... }

class ProductService { ... }
```

- **Keep Functions Small and Focused:** Write small, focused functions that perform a single task. This practice enhances readability and makes it easier to test and maintain code.
- **Use Comments and Documentation Judiciously:**
  - Prefer **self-explanatory function and variable names** over comments. However, use **KDoc** to document **public APIs**, clarify **non-obvious logic**, or explain **design decisions and assumptions** that are not immediately clear from the code alone.
  - Good documentation improves code readability and helps other developers (or your future self) understand the *why* behind the implementation.

  Example:

```
/**
* Calculates the total price of a list of products.
* @param products List of products to calculate the total price
for.
* @return Total price as a Double.
*/

fun calculateTotalPrice(products: List<Product>): Double {
   return products.sumOf { it.price }
}
```

- **Use Consistent Project Structure:** Maintain a consistent project structure across multiple Kotlin Multiplatform projects. This consistency helps developers transition between projects quickly and reduces the learning curve.
- **Leverage Dependency Injection:** Use dependency injection to manage dependencies between classes and modules. This approach helps decouple components, making your codebase more modular and easier to test.
- **Implement Version Control Best Practices:** Use version control systems (for example, Git) to manage your codebase effectively. Follow best practices such as branching strategies, commit messages, and pull request reviews to enhance collaboration and maintain code quality.

Thus, by organizing code effectively and following the best practices for code structure, Kotlin Multiplatform developers can create maintainable, scalable, and secure applications. A well-structured codebase not only enhances collaboration among team members but also facilitates easier updates and improvements in the long run.

Modularization Techniques

Modularization is a key practice in software development that involves breaking down an application into smaller, manageable, and independent modules. This approach is particularly beneficial in Kotlin Multiplatform development, where code is shared across multiple platforms. This section discusses techniques for creating modular code and outlines the benefits of modularization.

Creating Modular Code

Effective modularization starts with thoughtful planning and a clear understanding of your application's structure. In a Kotlin Multiplatform project, creating modular code means isolating functionalities into distinct components that can be shared or customized per platform. This approach not only improves maintainability and testability but also enables parallel development across teams.

In this section, you will learn how to identify logical boundaries within your application, define clean interfaces for inter-module communication, and organize shared and platform-specific modules efficiently. We will also explore how to use Gradle to manage module dependencies and ensure clean separation of concerns, making your codebase more scalable and adaptable as it evolves.

- **Identify Functional Boundaries:** Begin by identifying functional boundaries within your application. Determine which components can be isolated based on their functionality, such as authentication, data management, or user interface elements. This helps in defining clear modules.
- **Define Module Interfaces:** Establish clear interfaces for each module to define how they interact with each other. This encapsulation allows modules to be developed and tested independently, promoting the separation of concerns.

  Example:

  ```
  interface UserRepository {
      fun getUser(id: String): User
      fun saveUser(user: User)
  }
  ```
- **Create Shared and Platform-Specific Modules:** Organize your project structure to include shared modules that contain common code and platform-specific modules that implement functionalities unique to each platform. For example:

```
my-multiplatform-project/
├── shared/                     # Shared module for common code
├── android/                    # Android-specific module
├── ios/                        # iOS-specific module
└── web/                        # Web-specific module
```

Figure 13.2: *Project Module Structure Image*

- **Use Gradle for Module Management:** In your Gradle build scripts, define modules and their dependencies clearly. This allows for better management of dependencies across different platforms and ensures that each module can be built independently.

  Example:

  ```
  kotlin {
      sourceSets {
          val sharedMain by getting {
              dependencies {
                  implementation(project(":shared"))
              }
          }
          val androidMain by getting {
              dependencies {
                  implementation(project(":android"))
              }
          }
      }
  }
  ```

- **Encapsulate Implementation Details:** Keep implementation details hidden within modules and expose only what is necessary through public interfaces. This reduces coupling between modules, and enhances maintainability.
- **Implement Dependency Injection:** Use dependency injection to manage dependencies between modules. This technique allows for greater flexibility in swapping implementations and enhances the reusability of code components.

Benefits of Modularization

Modularization is more than just a structural choice–it is a strategic approach that significantly enhances the development lifecycle of Kotlin Multiplatform applications. By breaking the codebase into smaller, well-defined units, developers gain better control over complexity, collaboration, and scalability.

In this section, we will explore the key advantages of adopting a modular architecture. From improving code reusability and maintainability to enabling parallel development and streamlined testing, modularization lays the groundwork for building robust, scalable, and future-proof applications. So, whether you are working solo or as part of a larger team, understanding these benefits will help you make smarter architectural decisions throughout your project.

- **Improved Code Reusability:** Modularization promotes code reuse across different projects or platforms. By creating independent modules, you can easily share and reuse code without duplicating efforts.
- **Enhanced Maintainability:** Smaller, focused modules are easier to understand, maintain, and update. Changes made within a module can be tested and deployed independently, reducing the risk of introducing bugs in unrelated parts of the codebase.
- **Simplified Collaboration:** Modularization allows multiple developers or teams to work on different modules simultaneously without causing conflicts. This parallel development can speed up the overall development process.
- **Better Testing and Debugging:** Isolated modules can be tested independently, making it easier to identify and fix bugs. Unit tests can be focused on specific functionalities within a module, leading to more reliable and maintainable tests.
- **Scalability:** As the application grows, modularization allows for easier scaling. New features can be added as separate modules, and existing modules can be updated or replaced without affecting the entire application.
- **Clearer Project Structure:** A well-organized modular structure enhances the clarity of the project. Developers can quickly navigate through modules and understand the relationships between different components, leading to improved onboarding for new team members.

Therefore, by implementing effective modularization techniques, Kotlin Multiplatform developers can create maintainable, scalable, and secure applications. This practice not only enhances collaboration and code reusability but also supports long-term project sustainability and quality.

Ensuring Code Reusability

Code reusability is a fundamental principle in software development that allows developers to write code once and use it across different parts of an application or even across multiple applications. In Kotlin Multiplatform development, ensuring code reusability can significantly reduce duplication, streamline maintenance, and enhance collaboration. This section discusses techniques for creating reusable code and outlines best practices for code reuse.

Techniques for Reusable Code

Writing reusable code is essential for maintaining consistency, reducing duplication, and speeding up development across platforms. The following techniques help you design components that can be easily shared, extended, and maintained in Kotlin Multiplatform projects.

- **Create Shared Modules:** Organize common functionalities into shared modules that can be accessed by different platforms. This allows you to write the code once and use it across Android, iOS, and web applications.

  Example:

```
my-multiplatform-project/
├── shared/                   # Shared module for common code
├── android/                  # Android-specific module
├── ios/                      # iOS-specific module
└── web/                      # Web-specific module
```

***Figure 13.3:** Project Module Structure Image*

- **Utilize Interfaces and Abstract Classes:** Define common interfaces or abstract classes that can be implemented or extended by platform-specific modules. This allows for polymorphism and promotes code reuse while maintaining flexibility.

  Example:

```
interface UserRepository {
   fun getUser(id: String): User
   fun saveUser(user: User)
}
```

- **Leverage Extension Functions:** Use Kotlin's extension functions to add functionality to existing classes without modifying their source code. This technique can enhance reusability by allowing you to extend the capabilities of classes in a modular way.

  Example:

```
fun String.isEmailValid(): Boolean {
   return this.contains("@") && this.contains(".")
}
```

- **Implement Common Libraries:** Develop common libraries that encapsulate frequently used functionalities (for example, logging, networking, data processing) and can be shared across different projects. This promotes consistency and reduces the need to rewrite similar code.

- **Use Dependency Injection:** Implement dependency injection to manage dependencies within your application. This approach allows for greater flexibility in swapping implementations and enhances the reusability of code components.

Best Practices for Code Reuse

Code reuse is a cornerstone of efficient software development, especially in Kotlin Multiplatform projects where maximizing shared logic is key. By reusing well-tested and well-documented components, developers can accelerate development, reduce bugs, and maintain consistency across platforms.

This section outlines proven strategies to make your codebase more reusable and maintainable. You will learn how to apply the DRY principle, manage shared code with version control, document functionality effectively, and ensure quality through testing and reviews. Whether you are building new shared modules or refactoring legacy code, these best practices will help you create a solid foundation for scalable, cross-platform development.

- **Follow the DRY Principle:** Adhere to the "*Don't Repeat Yourself*" (DRY) principle by avoiding code duplication. Centralize common functionalities in shared modules or libraries to ensure that changes are made in one place.
- **Document Shared Code:** Provide clear documentation for shared code, including usage examples and explanations of functionalities. Good documentation helps other developers understand how to use the code effectively and encourages its reuse.
- **Use Version Control for Shared Libraries:** If you create shared libraries, manage them using version control systems. This allows you to track changes, manage releases, and ensure that different projects can depend on stable versions of the libraries.
- **Test Shared Code Thoroughly:** Ensure that you have adequate tests covering the functionality provided by your dependencies. This practice helps identify issues that may arise from updates or changes to the libraries you rely on.
- **Encourage Code Reviews:** Foster a culture of code reviews, especially for shared modules and libraries. Peer reviews can help identify potential issues and improve the quality of reusable code.
- **Modularize Gradually:** If you are refactoring the existing code into reusable modules, do so gradually. Start by identifying the most commonly used functionalities, and refactor them into shared modules before addressing less frequently used code.

Thus, by employing these techniques and best practices for ensuring code reusability, Kotlin Multiplatform developers can create applications that are more maintainable, scalable, and efficient. This focus on reusability not only reduces duplication but also enhances collaboration among team members and improves overall code quality.

Security Best Practices

Security in **Kotlin Multiplatform (KMP)** applications requires a holistic approach. Unlike traditional backend development, where most vulnerabilities are server-side, KMP developers must ensure that both **shared Kotlin code** and **platform-specific implementations** are secure. Because a single shared codebase is deployed to Android, iOS, web, and desktop, insecure practices in one layer can compromise the entire ecosystem.

This section explores **best practices for writing secure KMP applications**, organized into two areas: **Ensuring Secure Code** and **Avoiding Common Pitfalls**.

Ensuring Secure Code

Writing secure code in a **Kotlin Multiplatform** project is not just about following general programming best practices–it is about recognizing the unique challenges of sharing logic across Android, iOS, web, and desktop targets. The same code that handles authentication, networking, or data storage will ultimately run on multiple platforms, and any weakness in the shared layer can potentially compromise security everywhere.

In this section, we will explore the most critical areas where multiplatform developers need to be especially vigilant:

- **Protecting sensitive data** such as tokens and credentials.
- **Securing network communication** in shared Ktor clients.
- **Validating input during serialization** to prevent crashes or data corruption.
- **Managing coroutines responsibly** to avoid data leaks and unintended background operations.
- Preventing sensitive information from leaking through logs by using log redaction and masking (**Secure Logging**).

Each topic is illustrated with *bad versus good* examples, showing common pitfalls and the recommended Kotlin Multiplatform approaches. By adopting these practices, you can ensure your shared code is robust, consistent, and secure across all platforms.

Protecting Sensitive Data

Never hardcode sensitive values (such as API keys, tokens, or credentials) in shared code, as compiled binaries can be reverse-engineered. Instead, delegate secure storage to platform APIs.

Bad Example (in shared code):

```
// ✖ Never store secrets in shared code
const val API_KEY = "my-super-secret-key"
```

Good Example (using expect/actual):

```
// commonMain
expect class SecureStorage {
   fun save(key: String, value: String)
   fun read(key: String): String?
}

// androidMain
actual class SecureStorage {
   private val prefs = EncryptedSharedPreferences.create(
        "secure_store",
        "master_key",
        context,
        MasterKey.Builder(context).setKeyScheme(MasterKey.
KeyScheme.AES256_GCM).build(),
        EncryptedSharedPreferences.PrefKeyEncryptionScheme.AES256_
SIV,
         EncryptedSharedPreferences.PrefValueEncryptionScheme.
AES256_GCM
   )

   override fun save(key: String, value: String) = prefs.edit().
putString(key, value).apply()

   override fun read(key: String) = prefs.getString(key, null)

}

// iosMain
actual class SecureStorage {
   override fun save(key: String, value: String) {
        val query = mapOf(
             kSecClass to kSecClassGenericPassword,
             kSecAttrAccount to key,
             kSecValueData to value.encodeToByteArray()
        ) SecItemAdd (query, null)
   }
```

```
    override fun read(key: String): String? {

        val query = mapOf(
            kSecClass to kSecClassGenericPassword,
            kSecAttrAccount to key,
            kSecReturnData to true
        )

        val result = memScoped {
            val data = alloc<CFTypeRefVar>()
            SecItemCopyMatching(query.toCFDictionary(), data.ptr)
            (data.value as? NSData)?.toByteArray()?.decodeTo-
String()
        }

        return result
    }
}
```

This pattern ensures secure storage across platforms without exposing keys in shared code.

Securing Network Communication with Ktor

Networking logic often resides in shared modules using **Ktor**. Always enforce HTTPS, validate hosts, and avoid logging sensitive data.

Bad Example:

```
val client = HttpClient()
suspend fun fetchData() = client.get("http://example.com/api") //
❌ No HTTPS
```

Good Example:

```
val client = HttpClient {
   install(HttpTimeout) {
       requestTimeoutMillis = 15_000
   } engine { // Platform-specific TLS validation
   }
}

suspend fun fetchData(): ApiResponse {
   return client.get("https://secure.example.com/api") {
       headers {
           append(
               "Authorization",
               "Bearer ${getAccessToken()}"
```

```
            )
        }
    }
}
```

Additionally, apply **certificate pinning** on Android/iOS engines where supported to prevent MITM attacks.

Safe Data Serialization

When using **kotlinx.serialization**, validate inputs to avoid crashes or injection attacks.

Bad Example:

```
@Serializable
data class User(val id: Int, val name: String)

val user = Json.decodeFromString(rawJson) // ✖ May throw on
malformed input
```

Good Example:

```
val safeUser = try {
   Json { ignoreUnknownKeys = true }.decodeFromString<User>
(rawJson)
} catch (e: SerializationException) {
   // Log or report the error for debugging/monitoring
   Log.e("UserParse", "Failed to deserialize user object", e)
   null // Return null if deserialization fails—handled gracefully
}
```

Coroutines and Sensitive Operations

Leaking coroutines (for example, continuing network requests after logout) can expose user data.

Bad Example:

```
fun fetchUserData() {
   GlobalScope.launch { api.getUserProfile() } // ✖ Leaks
coroutine lifecycle
}
```

Good Example:

```
class UserViewModel(private val scope: CoroutineScope) {
   fun fetchUserData() {
        scope.launch {
```

```
            val profile = api.getUserProfile() // Handle securely
        }
    }
}
```

Always tie coroutines to structured scopes (such as ViewModel or lifecycle owners).

Secure Logging (Log Redaction and Masking)

Because shared code runs across Android, iOS, Web, and Desktop, the same logging statement can end up in Logcat, iOS system logs, or browser consoles. A careless log statement such as **`println("User=$user")`** may expose PII or tokens everywhere.

Risks: (i) Logging raw PII/PHI (emails, phone numbers, medical data). (ii) Logging full tokens, cookies, or API keys. (iii) Logging unmasked financial identifiers.

Best Practices: Default to no sensitive data in logs.

- **Mask or redact** tokens, emails, phone numbers, and card numbers.
- **Environment-aware logging** allows verbose logs in debug, but strip sensitive logs in release.
- **Centralize logging utilities** in **`commonMain`** so masking happens before logs reach platform sinks.

Good Example (log masking utility):

```
object Redact {
   fun token(value: String?) = value?.take(4)?.plus("****") ?:
"null"
   fun email(value: String?) = value?.replace(Re-
gex("(^.).+(@.+$)"), "$1****$2") ?: "null"
}


fun logLogin(email: String?, token: String) {
   Napier.i("Login failed for email=${Redact.email(email)}
token=${Redact.token(token)}")
}
```

With this approach, logs remain useful for debugging while ensuring that sensitive information is never exposed.

Common Security Pitfalls

Even with the best intentions, developers can unintentionally introduce vulnerabilities when working on Kotlin Multiplatform projects. Because the same shared code is compiled for multiple targets, mistakes are amplified across platforms, putting sensitive data and application integrity at risk.

This section highlights some of the **most common pitfalls** that occur in KMP development. These include insecure practices such as storing sensitive information in shared modules, assuming code obfuscation is enough to prevent reverse-engineering, exposing too much detail in error messages, and neglecting to update third-party dependencies.

By recognizing these risks early, you can avoid them in your own projects and ensure that your multiplatform applications remain **secure, resilient, and maintainable** across Android, iOS, web, and beyond.

Storing Data in Shared Code

Developers sometimes implement their own storage in **`commonMain`**, for example, writing files directly. This can expose sensitive user data on disk.

Always use platform-provided secure storage APIs through **`expect/actual`**.

Example:

```
commonMain

// Expect declaration in shared code
expect fun saveTokenSecurely(token: String)

androidMain

import android.security.keystore.KeyGenParameterSpec
import android.security.keystore.KeyProperties
import javax.crypto.Cipher
import javax.crypto.KeyGenerator
import javax.crypto.SecretKey
import android.content.Context
import android.util.Base64

actual fun saveTokenSecurely(token: String) {
        // Use Android Keystore APIs or consider up-to-date
libraries like Tink.
        // Example with Keystore is non-trivial; latest libraries
abstract this step.
        // See Google's Jetpack Security/Crypto documentation for
current recommendations.
}
```

```
iosMain

import Security
actual fun saveTokenSecurely(token: String) {
        // Save to iOS Keychain using Security framework
        // Implementation can use a Kotlin/Native bridge or shared
Swift function
        // e.g., KeychainWrapper.standard.set(token, forKey:
"token")
}
```

Over-Reliance on Obfuscation

Kotlin/Native (iOS) and Kotlin/JS outputs can be reverse-engineered. Obfuscation is *not* security.

Instead, enforce:

- Server-side validation of requests.
- Expiry for tokens and sessions.
- Rate limiting to prevent brute-force attacks.

Verbose Error Messages

Returning raw stack traces or exception messages to the UI can leak internal implementation details.

Bad Example:

```
catch(e: Exception) {
   return "Error: ${e.stackTraceToString()}" // ❌ Leaks details
}
```

Good Example:

```
catch(e: Exception) {
   return "An unexpected error occurred. Please try again." // ✅
User-friendly
}
```

Centralizing error handling in shared code ensures consistency across platforms.

Dependency Risks

Outdated third-party libraries (for example, old **Ktor** or **SQLDelight** versions) may contain vulnerabilities.

Use **Dependabot** or Gradle Version Catalog to enforce regular updates across multiplatform modules.

Example Version Catalog (`libs.versions.toml`):

```
[versions]
ktor = "2.3.4"
serialization = "1.6.0"

[libraries]
ktor-client = { module = "io.ktor:ktor-client-core", version.ref
= "ktor" }
kotlinx-serialization = { module = "org.jetbrains.kotlinx:kotlinx
-serialization-json", version.ref = "serialization" }
```

Summary

By applying these practices:

- Keep **secrets in secure storage**, not shared code.
- Enforce **TLS, token validation, and input sanitization** in networking.
- Use **structured concurrency** to avoid leaks.
- Prevent pitfalls such as insecure shared storage, exposing stack traces, or outdated dependencies.

In KMP, security must be **both cross-platform and platform-specific**. Shared logic should never weaken the guarantees provided by Android or iOS native APIs.

Managing Dependencies Effectively

Effective dependency management is crucial for the success of Kotlin Multiplatform applications. Properly managing dependencies ensures that your application remains stable, secure, and maintainable. This section discusses tools for dependency management and outlines strategies for effectively managing dependencies in your projects.

Tools for Dependency Management

Efficient dependency management is vital to maintaining a stable, secure, and scalable Kotlin Multiplatform project. With shared and platform-specific code coexisting in the same project, managing dependencies across targets requires careful coordination and the right tooling.

This section introduces the key tools and techniques for handling dependencies in a multiplatform environment. You will learn how to leverage Gradle for defining and resolving dependencies per platform, handle version conflicts, and automate vulnerability monitoring using tools such as Dependabot and Snyk. We will also touch on Kotlin Multiplatform-friendly libraries that streamline dependency sharing across targets—helping you build reliable applications with minimal friction.

- **Gradle:** Gradle is the primary build tool used in Kotlin Multiplatform projects, providing robust dependency management capabilities. It allows you to declare dependencies for different platforms and manage versions easily.
    - Gradle's dependency management features include:
        - **Transitive Dependencies:** Automatically resolving dependencies required by your declared dependencies, which simplifies dependency management.
        - **Version Conflict Resolution:** Gradle helps manage conflicts when multiple dependencies require different versions of the same library.

    Example of declaring dependencies in a Gradle file:

```
kotlin {
    sourceSets {
        val commonMain by getting {
            dependencies {
                implementation("org.jetbrains.kotlin:kotlin-
stdlib-common")
                implementation("com.squareup.retrofit2:retrofit
:2.9.0")
            }
        }

        val androidMain by getting {
            dependencies {
                implementation("com.android.support:appcompat
-v7:1.0.0")
            }
        }

        val iosMain by getting {
            dependencies {
                implementation("org.jetbrains.kotlinx:kotlinx
-coroutines-core:1.3.9")
            }
        }
    }
}
```

- **Dependency Management Tools:** Tools such as **Dependabot** and **Snyk** can automate the process of monitoring dependencies for vulnerabilities and outdated versions. These tools can alert you when updates are available or when security issues are detected.

- **Kotlin Multiplatform Libraries:** Utilize libraries specifically designed for Kotlin Multiplatform that help manage dependencies across platforms. These libraries can simplify the process of sharing code and dependencies.

Strategies for Managing Dependencies

Managing dependencies effectively is crucial for building reliable and maintainable Kotlin Multiplatform applications. With multiple targets and shared code in play, poor dependency practices can lead to bloated builds, version conflicts, and security risks.

This section outlines practical strategies for maintaining a clean and efficient dependency setup. You will learn how to keep dependencies up to date, limit their scope, document their purpose, and use techniques such as version ranges and dependency injection to maintain flexibility and control. Regular audits and thorough testing of dependencies will further ensure your project remains secure, performant, and easy to evolve over time.

- **Keep Dependencies Updated:** Regularly check for updates to your dependencies and apply them promptly. This practice helps ensure that you benefit from the latest features, improvements, and security patches.
- **Limit Dependency Scope:** Only include dependencies that are necessary for your application. Avoid adding unnecessary libraries, as this can bloat your application and increase the risk of conflicts and security vulnerabilities.
- **Use Version Ranges:** When declaring dependencies, consider using version ranges to allow for flexibility in updates. This approach enables your application to benefit from minor updates while avoiding breaking changes.

  Example:

  ```
  implementation("com.squareup.retrofit2:retrofit:[2.9.0,3.0.0)")
  ```
- **Document Dependency Purpose:** Maintain documentation that explains the purpose of each dependency in your project. This helps team members understand why certain libraries are included and facilitates better decision-making when considering updates or replacements.
- **Regularly Audit Dependencies:** Periodically audit your dependencies to identify any that are no longer in use or that could be replaced with lighter alternatives. This helps to keep your project clean and maintainable.
- **Implement Dependency Injection:** Use dependency injection frameworks to manage dependencies within your application. This approach allows for better control over how components are instantiated and can facilitate easier testing and mocking.

- **Test Dependencies Thoroughly:** Ensure that you have adequate tests covering the functionality provided by your dependencies. This practice helps identify issues that may arise from updates or changes to the libraries you rely on.

Therefore, by effectively managing dependencies and utilizing the right tools, Kotlin Multiplatform developers can create stable, maintainable, and secure applications. This focus on dependency management not only enhances collaboration among team members but also contributes to the overall quality and reliability of the software.

Documentation and Code Comments

Effective documentation and code comments are vital components of software development, especially in Kotlin Multiplatform projects. They provide clarity and context, ensuring that the code is understandable and maintainable for current and future developers. This section discusses the importance of documentation and outlines best practices for writing effective code comments.

Importance of Documentation

In Kotlin Multiplatform projects, where teams may be distributed across different platforms and responsibilities, good documentation is more than a courtesy—it is a necessity. Clear and comprehensive documentation ensures that code is understandable, maintainable, and accessible to everyone involved.

This section highlights why documentation is critical at every stage of development. From improving code clarity and easing onboarding to enhancing collaboration and supporting long-term maintenance, we will explore how strong documentation practices contribute to higher code quality, faster troubleshooting, and more efficient teamwork.

- **Enhances Code Understandability:** Documentation serves as a guide for developers, making it easier to understand the purpose and functionality of the code. This is especially important in a multiplatform context where different teams may work on various parts of the application.
- **Facilitates Onboarding:** Well-documented code helps new team members quickly acclimate to the codebase. Clear explanations of modules, functions, and workflows reduce the learning curve and accelerate the onboarding process.
- **Improves Collaboration:** Documentation fosters better collaboration among team members by providing a shared understanding of the code. It helps align team efforts, ensuring that everyone is aware of the functionalities and dependencies within the project.

- **Supports Maintenance and Updates:** As applications evolve, documentation helps developers understand the rationale behind design decisions and the context of specific implementations. This understanding is crucial when making updates or refactoring code.
- **Aids in Debugging and Troubleshooting:** When issues arise, documentation can assist developers in tracing back to the original design and functionality. This context can be invaluable for identifying and resolving bugs effectively.
- **Promotes Code Quality:** Regular documentation encourages developers to write cleaner, more organized code. When developers know that their code will be reviewed and documented, they are more likely to adhere to best practices and coding standards.

Best Practices for Code Comments

In Kotlin Multiplatform projects, where code is often shared and maintained by multiple teams across platforms, effective commenting plays a crucial role in making the codebase approachable and maintainable. Good comments bridge the gap between what code does and why it does it, offering valuable insights that are not always apparent from the implementation alone.

This section outlines the best practices for writing meaningful and maintainable comments. You will learn how to be clear and concise, document the reasoning behind decisions, maintain a consistent style, and ensure public APIs are well-explained. With thoughtful commenting, developers can foster better collaboration, reduce onboarding time, and future-proof their code for ongoing updates and debugging.

- **Be Clear and Concise:** Write comments that are clear and to the point. Avoid overly verbose explanations; instead, focus on conveying essential information in a straightforward manner.

  Example:

  ```
  // Calculate the total price of items in the cart

  val totalPrice = items.sumOf { it.price }
  ```

- **Explain Why, Not Just What:** Focus on explaining the reasoning behind complex logic or decisions rather than simply stating what the code does. This context helps future developers understand the intent behind the implementation.

  Example:

  ```
  // Using a map for faster lookups instead of a list due to
  performance concerns

  val userMap = users.associateBy { it.id }
  ```

- **Use Consistent Commenting Style:** Maintain a consistent style for comments throughout the codebase. This includes using the same format for function documentation, inline comments, and block comments.
- **Document Public APIs:** Provide comprehensive documentation for public APIs, including parameters, return values, and exceptions. This is particularly important for shared modules that will be used across different platforms.

  Example:

```
/**
* Retrieves a user by their ID.
* @param id The unique identifier of the user.
* @return The user object if found, null otherwise.
*/

fun getUserById(id: String): User? {
    // Implementation here
}
```

- **Update Comments Regularly:** Ensure that comments are kept up to date with code changes. Outdated comments can create confusion and lead to misunderstandings about the code's functionality.
- **Avoid Obvious Comments:** Refrain from adding comments that state the obvious or repeat what the code already conveys. Focus on adding value through comments that provide additional context or clarification.

  Example:

```
// Bad comment
val count = items.size // Get the size of the items list

// Good comment
// Track the number of items for inventory management
val count = items.size
```

By prioritizing documentation and following best practices for code comments, Kotlin Multiplatform developers can create maintainable, scalable, and secure applications. Effective documentation not only enhances collaboration and understanding but also contributes to the overall quality and longevity of the codebase.

Practical Tips and Examples

In this section, we will provide practical tips and real-world examples to help you effectively implement best practices for Kotlin Multiplatform development. These insights will guide you in creating maintainable, scalable, and secure applications while leveraging the full potential of Kotlin Multiplatform.

Real-World Examples

Theory and best practices gain true value when applied in real-world scenarios. In Kotlin Multiplatform development, practical implementation of modularization, dependency management, and code organization strategies can significantly impact productivity, scalability, and code quality.

This section highlights two real-world case studies that demonstrate how development teams successfully applied modular architecture and robust dependency management in production environments. From a banking app that streamlined shared business logic to an e-commerce platform that optimized dependency control, these examples showcase the tangible benefits and outcomes of adopting structured, multiplatform development practices.

Example 1: Modularization in a Banking Application

A banking application developed for Android and iOS utilized modularization to enhance code organization and reusability. The development team created separate modules for core functionalities such as authentication, transaction processing, and user interface components.

- **Shared Module:** The core business logic, including user authentication and transaction management, was placed in a shared module. This allowed both Android and iOS applications to utilize the same codebase, ensuring consistency across platforms.
- **Platform-Specific Modules:** Android-specific and iOS-specific modules were created to handle platform-specific UI components and interactions. This modularization allowed the team to implement platform-specific features without duplicating the core business logic.
- **Results:** The modular approach led to a significant reduction in code duplication, improved collaboration among team members, and easier maintenance. The application was able to scale more efficiently as new features were added.

Example 2: Dependency Management in a Cross-Platform E-commerce App

In a cross-platform e-commerce application, the development team faced challenges with managing dependencies across different platforms. To address this, they implemented the following strategies:

- **Centralized Dependency Management:** The team utilized Gradle to manage dependencies across all modules, ensuring that versions were consistent and conflicts were minimized. They defined dependencies in a centralized manner, allowing for easier updates and maintenance.

- **Regular Dependency Audits:** The team scheduled regular audits of their dependencies to identify outdated or vulnerable libraries. They used tools such as Dependabot to automate this process and receive alerts for necessary updates.
- **Results:** By effectively managing dependencies, the team reduced the risk of security vulnerabilities and improved application stability. The streamlined process allowed for faster development cycles and reduced overhead when updating libraries.

Tips for Effective Multiplatform Development

Developing multiplatform applications requires a blend of strategy, consistency, and continuous improvement. With shared codebases and diverse platform requirements, it is essential to adopt practices that not only ensure efficient code reuse but also maintain high-quality, robust applications.

In this section, you will find practical tips to streamline your multiplatform development process–from prioritizing code reuse and adopting a consistent coding style to leveraging Kotlin's unique language features and implementing automated CI/CD pipelines. We will also emphasize the importance of thorough documentation, regular code reviews, and staying updated with industry best practices. These tips will help you build scalable, maintainable, and high-performing applications across Android, iOS, Web, and beyond.

- **Prioritize Code Reusability:** Always look for opportunities to reuse code across platforms. Create shared modules for common functionalities and avoid duplicating code whenever possible.
- **Adopt a Consistent Coding Style:** Use consistent coding conventions and styles across all platforms to improve readability and maintainability. This consistency helps team members quickly understand each other's code.
- **Leverage Kotlin Features:** Take advantage of Kotlin's language features, such as extension functions and higher-order functions, to write cleaner and more expressive code. These features can enhance code reusability and reduce boilerplate.
- **Implement Continuous Integration:** Set up a CI/CD pipeline to automate testing and deployment processes. This practice helps catch issues early in the development cycle and ensures that all platforms are consistently built and tested.
- **Document Your Code:** Maintain thorough documentation for shared modules and public APIs. Clear documentation helps team members understand how to use the code effectively and facilitates better collaboration.

- **Regularly Review and Refactor:** Schedule regular code reviews and refactoring sessions to improve code quality. This practice helps identify areas for improvement and ensures that the codebase remains clean and maintainable.
- **Stay Updated on Best Practices:** Keep abreast of the latest best practices and trends in Kotlin Multiplatform development. Engaging with the community through forums, conferences, and workshops can provide valuable insights and inspiration.

Thus, by applying these practical tips and learning from real-world examples, developers can enhance their Kotlin Multiplatform projects. Implementing best practices not only leads to better code quality but also fosters a collaborative and efficient development environment, ultimately resulting in successful and maintainable applications.

Conclusion

This chapter provided a comprehensive overview of best practices for Kotlin Multiplatform development, covering essential topics such as code organization, modularization, reusability, security, dependency management, and effective documentation. By applying these strategies, developers can build maintainable, scalable, and secure applications that are easier to collaborate on and evolve over time.

As we wrap up this chapter, we transition from best practices to real-world applications. In the final chapter, we will explore case studies from successful Kotlin Multiplatform projects and examine emerging trends shaping the future of cross-platform development. These insights will not only reinforce the techniques you have learned so far but also prepare you to stay ahead in an ever-evolving development landscape.

CHAPTER 14
Case Studies and Future Trends

Introduction

This chapter delves into real-world case studies showcasing successful Kotlin Multiplatform projects, emphasizing practical applications and lessons learned. By examining these examples, developers gain valuable insights into best practices, architectural choices, and integration strategies that lead to maintainable, scalable multiplatform applications. Additionally, the chapter explores emerging trends, technologies, and tools that are shaping the future of multiplatform development, preparing developers to adapt to evolving industry demands. Understanding these concepts will empower you to build robust applications with Kotlin Multiplatform, achieving efficiency and consistency across diverse platforms.

Structure

In this chapter, we will cover the following topics:

- Case Studies of Successful Multiplatform Projects
- Lessons Learned and Best Practices
- Future Trends in Multiplatform Development
- Emerging Technologies and Tools
- Predictions for Kotlin Multiplatform
- Practical Insights and Recommendations

Case Studies of Successful Multiplatform Projects

Exploring real-world case studies provides valuable insights into how Kotlin Multiplatform can be effectively utilized to build robust and scalable applications. This section presents an overview of successful multiplatform projects and highlights key takeaways that can guide your own development efforts.

Overview of Case Studies

To showcase the real-world impact and versatility of Kotlin Multiplatform, this section presents a series of case studies demonstrating its application across diverse domains. From banking and e-commerce to health tracking and real-time communication, these examples highlight how development teams have leveraged Kotlin Multiplatform to streamline code sharing, accelerate delivery, and maintain cross-platform consistency. Each case study outlines key features, architectural decisions, and outcomes, providing practical insights into building scalable and maintainable multiplatform applications.

Case Study 1: A Cross-Platform Banking Application

- This project involved developing a banking application targeting Android, iOS, and web platforms. The team leveraged Kotlin Multiplatform to share business logic, data models, and network communication code across platforms while implementing platform-specific user interfaces.
- Key features included secure transaction processing, real-time notifications, and multi-factor authentication.
- The shared codebase reduced development time significantly and ensured consistency across platforms.

Case Study 2: A Multiplatform E-commerce Platform

- An e-commerce company utilized Kotlin Multiplatform to build a shopping app available on Android, iOS, and desktop environments.
- The project focused on sharing core logic such as product catalog management, shopping cart functionality, and payment processing.
- Platform-specific modules handled UI rendering and device-specific features.
- The modular architecture facilitated easy maintenance and quick rollout of new features.

Case Study 3: A Health and Fitness Tracker

- This application provided health tracking features across mobile and web platforms.
- The development team used Kotlin Multiplatform to share data synchronization logic, activity tracking algorithms, and user profile management.

- The approach improved code quality and reduced bugs by centralizing core functionalities.

Case Study 4: A Real-Time Messaging Application

- A messaging app implemented Kotlin Multiplatform to unify business logic such as message encryption, synchronization, and notification handling.
- The project achieved a seamless user experience across Android and iOS with minimal platform-specific code.
- Continuous integration and deployment pipelines were set up to streamline development and release cycles.

Key Takeaways from Successful Projects

The success of Kotlin Multiplatform in production environments hinges on strategic architectural choices and disciplined development practices. This section distills the most impactful lessons drawn from real-world implementations, highlighting what works when building and scaling multiplatform applications. From maximizing code reuse to investing in robust testing and CI/CD pipelines, these key takeaways provide a roadmap for teams aiming to deliver high-quality, maintainable apps across Android, iOS, and beyond.

- **Maximize Shared Code for Business Logic:** Successful projects emphasized sharing as much business logic as possible across platforms. This approach reduces duplication, ensures consistency, and accelerates development.
- **Maintain Clear Separation of Concerns:** Keeping platform-specific code separate from shared code allows teams to leverage native capabilities without compromising the benefits of code sharing.
- **Adopt Modular Architecture:** Modularizing the codebase into well-defined components improves maintainability and facilitates parallel development among teams.
- **Invest in Testing and Continuous Integration:** Comprehensive testing across all platforms and automated CI/CD pipelines are critical for maintaining code quality and ensuring reliable releases.
- **Focus on Performance Optimization:** Addressing performance considerations early, such as optimizing shared code and platform-specific implementations, leads to smoother user experiences.
- **Leverage Kotlin Multiplatform Ecosystem:** Utilizing libraries, tools, and community resources tailored for Kotlin Multiplatform enhances productivity and accelerates development.

- **Plan for Scalability and Future Growth:** Designing applications with scalability in mind ensures that they can evolve and adapt to new requirements and platforms over time.

By learning from these case studies and key takeaways, developers can better understand how to harness Kotlin Multiplatform effectively. Applying these insights will help you build maintainable, scalable, and high-quality multiplatform applications that meet the demands of modern users.

Lessons Learned and Best Practices

Drawing from real-world Kotlin Multiplatform projects, this section highlights valuable lessons learned and best practices that can guide developers in creating effective and maintainable multiplatform applications. Understanding these insights will help you avoid common pitfalls and adopt strategies that lead to successful project outcomes.

Lessons from Real-World Projects

Building Kotlin Multiplatform applications at scale brings unique challenges and opportunities. This section captures practical lessons learned from teams that have successfully navigated the journey—from defining architecture and managing platform nuances to optimizing performance and fostering team collaboration. These insights serve as a guide for making informed decisions, avoiding common pitfalls, and maximizing the effectiveness of your multiplatform strategy.

- **Start with a Clear Architecture:** Successful projects emphasize the importance of defining a clear and scalable architecture from the outset. This includes deciding which parts of the codebase will be shared and which will be platform-specific, ensuring a clean separation of concerns.
- **Incremental Adoption:** Gradually introducing Kotlin Multiplatform into existing projects rather than rewriting everything at once reduces risk. Incremental adoption allows teams to validate benefits and address challenges progressively.
- **Effective Communication Between Teams:** Cross-platform development often involves multiple teams working on different platforms. Maintaining clear communication channels and shared documentation is crucial to align efforts and avoid duplication.
- **Invest in Automated Testing:** Comprehensive automated testing across shared and platform-specific codebases is vital for maintaining code quality and catching platform-specific issues early.

- **Manage Platform Differences Thoughtfully:** Recognize and plan for platform-specific constraints and capabilities. Abstracting platform differences carefully prevents code duplication and maintains a clean shared codebase.
- **Performance Considerations Are Key:** Early attention to performance optimization, including profiling and platform-specific tuning, helps prevent bottlenecks and ensures smooth user experiences.
- **Leverage Community and Ecosystem:** Engaging with the Kotlin Multiplatform community and utilizing existing libraries and tools accelerates development and helps solve common challenges.

Best Practices for Multiplatform Development

To succeed with Kotlin Multiplatform, it is essential to go beyond just writing shared code–you need a strategic approach to architecture, tooling, and team collaboration. This section outlines best practices adopted by experienced teams to build robust, maintainable, and secure multiplatform applications. From modularization and dependency management to automation and performance monitoring, these guidelines help ensure your codebase scales effectively while delivering a consistent user experience across platforms.

- **Modularize Your Codebase:** Break your project into well-defined modules to improve maintainability, enable parallel development, and facilitate code reuse.
- **Maximize Shared Code:** Share as much business logic and core functionality as possible to reduce duplication and ensure consistency across platforms.
- **Use Platform-Specific Code Sparingly:** Limit platform-specific implementations to areas where native capabilities are necessary, keeping the shared codebase clean and portable.
- **Maintain Consistent Coding Standards:** Adopt consistent coding conventions and styles across all platforms to enhance readability and ease collaboration.
- **Implement Robust Dependency Management:** Use tools such as Gradle effectively to manage dependencies, ensuring compatibility and minimizing conflicts.
- **Prioritize Security:** Incorporate security best practices throughout the development lifecycle, including secure coding, dependency management, and regular security audits.
- **Document Thoroughly:** Maintain clear and comprehensive documentation for shared modules and APIs to facilitate onboarding and collaboration.

- **Automate Builds and Testing:** Set up continuous integration and continuous deployment (CI/CD) pipelines to automate building, testing, and releasing your multiplatform applications.
- **Monitor and Profile Regularly:** Continuously monitor application performance and profile both shared and platform-specific code to identify and resolve issues proactively.
- **Stay Informed and Adapt:** Keep up with the latest developments in Kotlin Multiplatform and related technologies to leverage new features and best practices.

Hence, by applying these lessons and best practices, developers can navigate the complexities of Kotlin Multiplatform development more effectively. This approach leads to building scalable, maintainable, and high-quality applications that deliver consistent experiences across multiple platforms.

Future Trends in Multiplatform Development

As the landscape of software development continues to evolve, Kotlin Multiplatform is poised to play a significant role in shaping the future of cross-platform application development. This section explores emerging trends and technologies that are influencing multiplatform development and offers predictions for its future trajectory.

Emerging Trends and Technologies

As Kotlin Multiplatform continues to mature, it is rapidly evolving to meet the demands of modern application development. This section explores the emerging trends and technological advancements that are driving its growth—from increased industry adoption and improved tooling to the rise of Compose Multiplatform and cloud-native integration. Understanding these trends helps developers stay ahead of the curve, make informed architectural decisions, and unlock new possibilities in building cross-platform solutions.

- **Increased Adoption of Kotlin Multiplatform:** More organizations are recognizing the benefits of Kotlin Multiplatform for sharing code across platforms, leading to broader adoption in various industries, including finance, healthcare, and e-commerce.
- **Enhanced Tooling and IDE Support:** Continuous improvements in tooling, such as better integration with IntelliJ IDEA and Android Studio, enhanced debugging capabilities, and streamlined build processes, are making multiplatform development more accessible and efficient.

- **Integration with Compose Multiplatform:** Jetpack Compose for Desktop and Web, alongside Android Compose, is gaining traction as a unified UI toolkit. This integration allows developers to build declarative UIs across platforms using shared Kotlin code, simplifying UI development.
- **Growth of Multiplatform Libraries:** The ecosystem of multiplatform libraries is expanding, providing ready-to-use solutions for networking, serialization, database access, and more. This growth reduces the need for platform-specific implementations and accelerates development.
- **Focus on Performance Optimization:** Emerging techniques and tools for profiling and optimizing multiplatform applications are becoming more sophisticated, enabling developers to deliver high-performance apps that meet user expectations across devices.
- **Cloud-Native and Server-Side Multiplatform:** Kotlin Multiplatform is extending its reach into server-side and cloud-native development, allowing shared codebases between client applications and backend services, fostering consistency and reducing duplication.
- **Increased Emphasis on Security:** With the rise of multiplatform applications, security frameworks and best practices tailored for multiplatform contexts are evolving to address unique challenges posed by shared codebases.
- **AI and Machine Learning Integration:** Integration of AI and machine learning capabilities into multiplatform projects is becoming more feasible, with libraries and frameworks emerging to support these features across platforms.

Predictions for the Future of Multiplatform Development

The future of Kotlin Multiplatform is poised for transformative growth as it edges closer to becoming a standard in cross-platform development. This section presents forward-looking predictions that highlight where the technology is headed–from broader adoption and unified tooling to new domains such as IoT and embedded systems. As UI frameworks evolve and community support strengthens, Kotlin Multiplatform is set to empower developers with greater flexibility, performance, and productivity in building applications that span an increasingly diverse range of platforms.

- **Mainstream Cross-Platform Development:** Kotlin Multiplatform is expected to become a mainstream choice for cross-platform development, rivaling other frameworks by offering native performance and shared business logic.
- **Unified Development Experience:** Developers will benefit from increasingly unified development experiences, with tools and frameworks that seamlessly support multiplatform projects from coding to testing and deployment.

- **Expansion Beyond Mobile and Web:** The scope of multiplatform development will extend further into areas such as embedded systems, IoT devices, and desktop applications, broadening the applicability of shared Kotlin code.
- **Improved Interoperability:** Advances in interoperability between Kotlin and other languages/platforms will facilitate easier integration of multiplatform modules into existing projects, promoting gradual adoption.
- **Community and Ecosystem Growth:** The Kotlin Multiplatform community will continue to grow, contributing to a richer ecosystem of libraries, tools, and best practices, fostering innovation and collaboration.
- **Greater Focus on Developer Productivity:** Future developments will emphasize enhancing developer productivity through better abstractions, automation, and intelligent tooling, reducing the complexity of managing multiplatform projects.
- **Evolution of Multiplatform UI Frameworks:** UI frameworks such as Compose Multiplatform will mature, offering more robust and feature-rich solutions for building consistent user interfaces across diverse platforms.

By staying informed about these emerging trends and preparing for future developments, Kotlin Multiplatform developers can position themselves to leverage the full potential of this technology. Embracing these advancements will enable the creation of versatile, high-quality applications that meet the evolving demands of users and businesses alike.

Emerging Technologies and Tools

The landscape of Kotlin Multiplatform development is rapidly evolving with the introduction of new tools and technologies designed to streamline development, improve performance, and expand capabilities. This section explores some of the latest tools and technologies that are shaping the future of multiplatform development.

New Tools for Multiplatform Development

As Kotlin Multiplatform evolves, a new generation of tools and frameworks is emerging to enhance the developer experience and streamline cross-platform workflows. This section introduces cutting-edge innovations–from UI frameworks such as Compose Multiplatform to powerful build and debugging enhancements. Together, these tools reduce complexity, accelerate development, and expand what is possible in building high-quality applications with shared Kotlin code.

- **Compose Multiplatform:** Jetpack Compose has extended beyond Android to support desktop and web platforms, enabling developers to create declarative

UIs with shared Kotlin code. Compose Multiplatform simplifies UI development by providing a consistent framework across platforms.

- **Kotlin Native Debugger Enhancements:** Improvements in Kotlin Native debugging tools enhance the developer experience by providing better support for debugging native code on iOS, macOS, Linux, and Windows platforms.
- **Kotlin Multiplatform Mobile (KMM) Plugin:** The KMM plugin for Android Studio simplifies the setup and management of multiplatform projects targeting mobile platforms. It integrates build tools, dependencies, and project configuration, streamlining the development workflow.
- **Kotlin Symbol Processing (KSP):** KSP is a new tool for processing Kotlin code annotations, offering faster and more efficient code generation compared to previous tools such as KAPT. It supports multiplatform projects and enhances compile-time processing capabilities.
- **Gradle Version Catalogs:** Gradle's version catalogs feature helps manage dependencies more effectively by centralizing version declarations. This improves consistency and simplifies dependency updates across multiplatform projects.
- **Multiplatform Libraries and Frameworks:** The ecosystem of multiplatform libraries continues to grow, with libraries such as Ktor for networking, SQLDelight for database access, and `kotlinx.serialization` for JSON parsing, all supporting multiplatform targets.

Technologies Shaping the Future

Kotlin Multiplatform is evolving in step with powerful trends reshaping the software development landscape. From declarative UI frameworks and backend code sharing to cloud-native architectures and AI integration, this section explores the technologies that are redefining what is possible in cross-platform development. As tooling and platform support continue to advance, these innovations are setting the stage for more unified, intelligent, and scalable application experiences across devices and environments.

- **Declarative UI Frameworks:** The rise of declarative UI frameworks such as Compose Multiplatform is transforming how developers build user interfaces, promoting code reuse and consistency across platforms.
- **Cross-Platform Backend Integration:** Technologies enabling shared code between frontend and backend (for example, Kotlin for server-side development) are fostering unified development experiences and reducing duplication.

- **Cloud-Native Development:** The integration of multiplatform applications with cloud-native architectures, including microservices and serverless computing, is enabling scalable and resilient application designs.
- **AI and Machine Learning Integration:** Emerging tools and frameworks are making it easier to incorporate AI and machine learning capabilities into multiplatform applications, expanding the scope of features and user experiences.
- **Improved Tooling for Native Platforms:** Continued enhancements in tooling for native platforms (iOS, macOS, Windows, Linux) are improving support for multiplatform projects, including better debugging, profiling, and build performance.
- **WebAssembly (Wasm):** WebAssembly is gaining traction as a target for Kotlin Multiplatform, enabling high-performance web applications that can leverage shared code with native platforms.
- **Enhanced Security Frameworks:** New security frameworks tailored for multiplatform development are emerging, addressing the unique challenges of securing shared codebases and cross-platform data management.

Thus, by embracing these new tools and technologies, Kotlin Multiplatform developers can build more efficient, scalable, and feature-rich applications. Staying abreast of these advancements is essential for leveraging the full potential of multiplatform development, and delivering cutting-edge solutions in an ever-evolving technological landscape.

Predictions for Kotlin Multiplatform

Kotlin Multiplatform is rapidly evolving and gaining traction as a powerful solution for cross-platform development. This section explores the future directions for Kotlin Multiplatform and presents industry predictions that highlight its potential impact on software development.

Future Directions for Kotlin Multiplatform

Kotlin Multiplatform is on a trajectory of rapid innovation, with its roadmap pointing toward broader platform support, tighter UI integration, and a vastly improved developer experience. This section outlines the anticipated directions in which Kotlin Multiplatform is heading–from enhanced tooling and performance to deeper Compose integration and expanded ecosystem support. These advancements promise to make cross-platform development more seamless, powerful, and accessible than ever before.

- **Expanded Platform Support:** Kotlin Multiplatform is expected to broaden its platform support beyond mobile and web to include desktop environments, embedded systems, and IoT devices. This expansion will enable developers to use a single codebase across an even wider range of platforms.

- **Improved Tooling and Developer Experience:** Future updates will focus on enhancing tooling support, including better IDE integration, faster build times, and more intuitive debugging capabilities. These improvements will streamline development workflows and reduce friction for developers.
- **Deeper Integration with Compose Multiplatform:** The integration between Kotlin Multiplatform and Compose Multiplatform will deepen, providing a unified declarative UI framework that works seamlessly across Android, iOS, desktop, and web platforms.
- **Stronger Emphasis on Performance Optimization:** Continued efforts will be made to optimize the performance of shared code and platform-specific implementations, ensuring that multiplatform applications deliver native-like responsiveness and efficiency.
- **Enhanced Security Features:** Security frameworks and best practices tailored for multiplatform environments will evolve, addressing the unique challenges of shared codebases and cross-platform data protection.
- **Growing Ecosystem and Community:** The ecosystem around Kotlin Multiplatform will continue to grow, with more libraries, tools, and community-driven resources becoming available to support developers.

Industry Predictions

As cross-platform demands grow, Kotlin Multiplatform is poised to become a key player in shaping the future of software development. This section explores expert predictions about the industry's direction–from the rise of unified codebases and multiplatform UI frameworks to deeper integration with emerging technologies such as AI and cloud-native systems. These insights offer a strategic outlook on how Kotlin Multiplatform will evolve and how developers and organizations can align with the momentum to stay ahead of the curve.

- **Mainstream Adoption of Kotlin Multiplatform:** Industry experts predict that Kotlin Multiplatform will become a mainstream choice for cross-platform development, favored for its ability to share business logic while maintaining native performance and user experience.
- **Shift toward Unified Codebases:** Organizations will increasingly adopt unified codebases to reduce development costs and improve consistency across platforms, with Kotlin Multiplatform playing a central role in this shift.
- **Increased Investment in Multiplatform Tooling:** Major IDEs and tool vendors are expected to invest heavily in multiplatform support, enhancing developer productivity and making multiplatform development more accessible.

- **Rise of Multiplatform UI Frameworks:** The popularity of multiplatform UI frameworks such as Compose Multiplatform will grow, simplifying UI development and fostering more consistent user interfaces across platforms.
- **Integration with Emerging Technologies:** Kotlin Multiplatform will increasingly integrate with emerging technologies such as AI, machine learning, and cloud-native architectures, enabling developers to build sophisticated, scalable applications.
- **Community-Driven Innovation:** The Kotlin community will continue to drive innovation by contributing libraries, tools, and best practices, accelerating the evolution of multiplatform development.

By understanding these future directions and industry predictions, developers and organizations can better prepare for the evolving landscape of Kotlin Multiplatform development. Embracing these trends will position them to leverage the full potential of multiplatform technologies and deliver innovative, high-quality applications.

Practical Insights and Recommendations

Gaining practical insights from experts and industry leaders can provide valuable guidance for Kotlin Multiplatform developers. This section shares expert insights and offers actionable recommendations to help developers navigate the complexities of multiplatform development and achieve successful project outcomes.

Insights from Experts

Drawing from hands-on experience and industry leadership, seasoned Kotlin Multiplatform experts offer valuable advice for navigating the complexities of cross-platform development. This section distills their insights into actionable recommendations–ranging from incremental adoption strategies to best practices in performance, security, tooling, and community engagement. These expert-backed principles help development teams build scalable, maintainable, and high-quality multiplatform applications with confidence.

- **Embrace Incremental Adoption:** Experts recommend adopting Kotlin Multiplatform incrementally, integrating it into existing projects gradually. This approach reduces risk and allows teams to gain experience and confidence with the technology over time.
- **Focus on Shared Business Logic:** Prioritize sharing business logic and core functionalities across platforms while keeping UI and platform-specific features separate. This balance maximizes code reuse without compromising native user experience.

- **Invest in Tooling and Automation:** Leveraging modern tooling, including CI/CD pipelines and automated testing frameworks, is essential for maintaining code quality and streamlining multiplatform development workflows.
- **Prioritize Performance and Security:** Experts emphasize the importance of addressing performance optimization and security considerations early in the development process to avoid costly issues later.
- **Engage with the Community:** Active participation in the Kotlin Multiplatform community provides access to shared knowledge, best practices, and support, accelerating learning and problem-solving.
- **Maintain Clear Documentation:** Comprehensive documentation is vital for collaboration, onboarding new team members, and ensuring long-term maintainability of multiplatform projects.

Recommendations for Developers

Whether you are new to Kotlin Multiplatform or looking to refine your approach, applying proven strategies can significantly boost your project's success. This section offers actionable recommendations tailored for developers–covering everything from modular architecture and platform-agnostic coding to automated testing and performance monitoring. These best practices help teams build reliable, scalable, and maintainable applications while staying aligned with the latest trends in the Kotlin ecosystem.

- **Start Small and Iterate:** Begin with small, well-defined modules for sharing code and gradually expand as you gain proficiency. Iterative development helps manage complexity and mitigates risks.
- **Adopt Modular Architecture:** Design your application with modularity in mind, enabling independent development, testing, and deployment of components.
- **Write Platform-Agnostic Code:** Aim to write code that is as platform-agnostic as possible in shared modules, using expect/actual declarations to handle platform-specific differences cleanly.
- **Use Automated Testing Extensively:** Implement comprehensive automated tests for both shared and platform-specific code to ensure reliability and facilitate refactoring.
- **Leverage Existing Libraries:** Utilize established multiplatform libraries and frameworks to avoid reinventing the wheel and accelerate development.
- **Monitor and Profile Regularly:** Continuously monitor application performance and profile both shared and platform-specific code to identify and address bottlenecks proactively.

- **Stay Updated with Kotlin Ecosystem:** Keep abreast of the latest developments in Kotlin Multiplatform and related tools to leverage new features and improvements.
- **Collaborate and Communicate:** Foster strong collaboration and communication within your development team to align efforts, share knowledge, and resolve challenges effectively.

By incorporating these insights and recommendations into your development practices, you can enhance the quality, maintainability, and success of your Kotlin Multiplatform projects. Staying informed and adopting proven strategies will enable you to navigate the evolving multiplatform landscape with confidence and agility.

Conclusion

In this final chapter, we explored a comprehensive range of real-world case studies that demonstrated the practical power of Kotlin Multiplatform. From foundational lessons to strategic best practices, we highlighted how successful teams structure, optimize, and scale their cross-platform applications. Alongside these insights, we examined emerging tools, technologies, and trends that are shaping the future of the multiplatform ecosystem.

Whether it is adopting modular architectures, leveraging shared business logic, or preparing for new innovations such as Compose Multiplatform and cloud-native integration, this chapter has provided you with the practical knowledge needed to thrive in modern multiplatform development.

As you move forward, continue applying these principles, exploring new possibilities, and refining your skills. The Kotlin Multiplatform journey is rich with opportunity—and with the right mindset and tools, you are well-equipped to lead in this evolving space.

Thank you for joining this journey. Wishing you continued success in building scalable, maintainable, and innovative multiplatform applications. Happy coding!

Index

D

E

F

R

S